STUDIES

IN

CONTEMPORARY BIOGRAPHY

STUDIES

IN

CONTEMPORARY

BIOGRAPHY

BY

JAMES BRYCE

Essay Index Reprint Series

BOOKS FOR LIBRARIES PRESS
FREEPORT, NEW YORK

First Published 1903
Reprinted 1971

INTERNATIONAL STANDARD BOOK NUMBER:
0-8369-2271-9

LIBRARY OF CONGRESS CATALOG CARD NUMBER:
77-156619

PRINTED IN THE UNITED STATES OF AMERICA

TO

CHARLES WILLIAM ELIOT
PRESIDENT OF HARVARD UNIVERSITY

IN COMMEMORATION OF A LONG AND

VALUED FRIENDSHIP

PREFACE

THE first and the last of these Studies relate to
persons whose fame has gone out into all lands,
and about whom so much remains to be said
that one who has reflected on their careers need
not offer an apology for saying something. Of
the other eighteen sketches, some deal with eminent men whose names are still familiar, but
whose personalities have begun to fade from the
minds of the present generation. The rest treat
of persons who came less before the public, but
whose brilliant gifts and solid services to the
world make them equally deserve to be remembered with honour. Having been privileged to
enjoy their friendship, I have felt it a duty to do
what a friend can to present a faithful record
of their excellence which may help to keep their
memory fresh and green.

These Studies are, however, not to be re-

garded as biographies, even in miniature.   My
aim has rather been to analyse the character and
powers of each of the persons described, and, as
far as possible, to convey the impression which
each made in the daily converse of life.   All of
them, except Lord Beaconsfield, were personally,
and most of them intimately, known to me.

In the six Studies which treat of politicians I
have sought to set aside political predilections,
and have refrained from expressing political
opinions, though it has now and then been
necessary to point out instances in which the
subsequent course of events has shown the
action of Lord Beaconsfield, Mr. Lowe, and
Mr. Gladstone to have been right or wrong (as
the case may be) in the action they respectively
took.

The sketches of T. H. Green, E. A. Freeman,
and J. R. Green were originally written for English magazines, and most of the other Studies
have been published in the United States.   All
of those that had already appeared in print have
been enlarged and revised, some indeed virtually
rewritten.

MARCH 6, 1903.

CONTENTS

ix

BENJAMIN DISRAELI, EARL OF BEACONSFIELD[1]

WHEN Lord Beaconsfield died in 1881 we all wondered what people would think of him fifty years thereafter. Divided as our own judgments were, we asked whether he would still seem a problem. Would opposite views regarding his aims, his ideas, the sources of his power, still divide the learned, and perplex the ordinary reader? Would men complain that history cannot be good for much when, with the abundant materials at her disposal, she had not framed a consistent theory of one who played so great a part in so ample a theatre? People called him a riddle; and he certainly affected a sphinx-like attitude. Would the riddle be easier then than it was for us, from among whom the man had even now departed?

When he died, there were many in England who revered him as a profound thinker and a lofty character, animated by sincere patriotism.

---

[1] No "authorised" life of Lord Beaconsfield, nor indeed any life commensurate with the part he played in English politics, has yet appeared.

Others, probably as numerous, held him for no better than a cynical charlatan, bent through life on his own advancement, who permitted no sense of public duty, and very little human compassion, to stand in the way of his insatiate ambition. The rest did not know what to think. They felt in him the presence of power; they felt also something repellent. They could not understand how a man who seemed hard and unscrupulous could win so much attachment and command so much obedience.

Since Disraeli departed, nearly one-half of those fifty years has passed away. Few are living who can claim to have been his personal friends, none who were personal enemies. No living statesman professes to be his political disciple. The time has come when one may discuss his character and estimate his career without being suspected of doing so with a party bias or from a party motive. Doubtless those who condemn and those who defend or excuse some momentous parts of his conduct, such as, for instance, his policy in the East and in Afghanistan from 1876 to 1879, will differ in their judgment of his wisdom and foresight. If this be a difficulty, it is an unavoidable one, and may never quite disappear. There were in the days of Augustus some who blamed that sagacious ruler for seeking to check the expansion of the Roman Empire. There were in the days of King

Henry the Second some who censured and others who praised him for issuing the Constitutions of Clarendon. Both questions still remain open to argument; and the conclusion any one forms must affect in some measure his judgment of each monarch's statesmanship. So differences of opinion about particular parts of Disraeli's long career need not prevent us from dispassionately inquiring what were the causes that enabled him to attain so striking a success, and what is the place which posterity is likely to assign to him among the rulers of England.

First, a few words about the salient events of his life, not by way of writing a biography, but to explain what follows.

He was born in London, in 1804. His father, Isaac Disraeli, was a literary man of cultivated taste and independent means, who wrote a good many books, the best known of which is his *Curiosities of Literature*, a rambling work, full of entertaining matter. He belonged to that division of the Jewish race which is called the Sephardim, and traces itself to Spain and Portugal;[1] but he had ceased to frequent the synagogue — had, in fact, broken with his co-religionists. Isaac had access to good society, so that the boy saw eminent and polished men from his early years, and, before he had reached man-

[1] Disraeli's family claimed to be of Spanish origin, but had come from Italy to England shortly before 1748.

hood, began to make his way in drawing-rooms where he met the wittiest and best-known people of the day. He was articled to a firm of attorneys in London in 1821, but after two or three years quitted a sphere for which his peculiar gifts were ill suited.[1] Samuel Rogers, the poet, took a fancy to him, and had him baptised at the age of thirteen. As he grew up, he was often to be seen with Count d'Orsay and Lady Blessington, well-known figures who fluttered on the confines of fashion and Bohemia. It is worth remarking that he never went either to a public school or to a university. In England it has become the fashion to assume that nearly all the persons who have shone in public life have been educated in one of the great public schools, and that they owe to its training their power of dealing with men and assemblies. Such a superstition is sufficiently refuted by the examples of men like Pitt, Macaulay, Bishop Wilberforce, Disraeli, Cobden, Bright, and Cecil Rhodes, not to add instances drawn from Ireland and Scotland, where till very recently there have been no public schools in the current English sense.

Disraeli first appeared before the public in 1826, when he published *Vivian Grey*, an amazing

---

[1] There are few legal allusions in his novels, fewer in proportion than in Shakespeare's plays, but an ingenious travesty of the English use of legal fictions may be found in the *Voyage of Captain Popanilla*, a satire on the English constitution and government. Popanilla, who is to be tried for treason, is, to his astonishment, indicted for killing a camelopard.

book to be the production of a youth of twenty-
two.   Other novels — *The Young Duke, Venetia,
Contarini Fleming, Henrietta Temple* — maintained without greatly increasing his reputation
between 1831 and 1837.   Then came two political stories, *Coningsby* and *Sybil,* in 1844 and 1845,
followed by *Tancred* in 1847 and *The Life of
Lord George Bentinck* in 1852; with a long interval of silence, till, in 1870, he produced *Lothair,*
in 1880 *Endymion.*   Besides these he published
in 1839 the tragedy of *Alarcos,* and in 1835 the
more ambitious *Revolutionary Epick,* neither of
which had much success.   In 1828-31 he took a
journey through the East, visiting Constantinople,
Syria, and Egypt, and it was then, no doubt, in
lands peculiarly interesting to a man of his race,
that he conceived those ideas about the East and
its mysterious influences which figure largely in
some of his stories, notably in *Tancred,* and which
in 1878 had no small share in shaping his policy
and that of England.   Meanwhile, he had not forgotten the political aspirations which we see in
Vivian Grey.   In 1832, just before the passing of
the Reform Bill, he appeared as candidate for the
petty borough of High Wycombe in Buckinghamshire, and was defeated by a majority of twenty-
three to twelve, so few were the voters in many
boroughs of those days.   After the Bill had enlarged the constituency, he tried his luck twice
again, in 1833 and 1835, both times unsuccess-

fully, and came before two other boroughs also, Taunton and Marylebone, though in the latter case no contest took place. Such activity in a youth with little backing from friends and comparatively slender means marked him already as a man of spirit and ambition. His next attempt was more lucky. At the general election of 1837 he was returned for Maidstone.

His political professions during this period have been keenly canvassed; nor is it easy to form a fair judgment on them. In 1832 he had sought and obtained recommendations from Joseph Hume and Daniel O'Connell, and people had therefore set him down as a Radical. Although, however, his professions of political faith included dogmas which, like triennial parliaments, the ballot, and the imposition of a new land-tax, were part of the so-called " Radical " platform, still there was a vague and fanciful note in his utterances, and an aversion to the conventional Whig way of putting things, which showed that he was not a thorough-going adherent of any of the then existing political parties, but was trying to strike out a new line and attract men by the promise of something fresher and bolder than the recognised schools offered. In 1834 his hostility to Whiggism was becoming more pronounced, and a tenderness for some Tory doctrines more discernible. Finally, in 1835, he appeared as an avowed

Tory, accepting the regular creed of the party, and declaring himself a follower of Sir Robert Peel, but still putting forward a number of views peculiar to himself, which he thereafter developed not only in his speeches but in his novels. *Coningsby* and *Sybil* were meant to be a kind of manifesto of the " Young England " party — a party which can hardly be said to have existed outside his own mind, though a small knot of aristocratic youths who caught up and repeated his phrases seemed to form a nucleus for it.

The fair conclusion from his deliverances during these early years is that he was at first much more of a Liberal than a Tory, yet with ideas distinctively his own which made him appear in a manner independent of both parties. The old party lines might seem to have been almost effaced by the struggle over the Reform Bill; and it was natural for a bold and inventive mind to imagine a new departure, and put forward a programme in which a sort of Radicalism was mingled with doctrines of a different type. But when it became clear after a time that the old political divisions still subsisted, and that such a distinctive position as he had conceived could not be maintained, he then, having to choose between one or other of the two recognised parties, chose the Tories, dropping some tenets he had previously advocated which were inconsistent with their

creed, but retaining much of his peculiar way
of looking at political questions. How far the
change which passed over him was a natural
development, how far due to mere calculations of
interest, there is little use discussing: perhaps he
did not quite know himself. Looking back, we of
to-day might be inclined to think that he received
more blame for it than he deserved, but contemporary observers generally set it down to a want
of principle. In one thing, however, he was consistent then, and remained consistent ever after —
his hearty hatred of the Whigs. There was something in the dryness and coldness of the great
Whig families, their stiff constitutionalism, their
belief in political economy, perhaps also their
occasional toyings with the Nonconformists
(always an object of dislike to Disraeli), which
roused all the antagonisms of his nature, personal
and Oriental.

When he entered the House of Commons he
was already well known to fashionable London,
partly by his striking face and his powers of conversation, partly by the eccentricities of his dress,
— he loved bright-coloured waistcoats, and decked
himself with rings, — partly by his novels, whose
satirical pungency had made a noise in society.
He had also become, owing to his apparent change
of front, the object of angry criticism. A quarrel
with Daniel O'Connell, in the course of which he
challenged the great Irishman to fight a duel, each

party having described the other with a freedom of language bordering on scurrility, made him, for a time, the talk of the political world. Thus there was more curiosity evoked by his first speech than usually awaits a new member. It was unsuccessful, not from want of ability, but because its tone did not suit the temper of the House of Commons, and because a hostile section of the audience sought to disconcert him by their laughter. Undeterred by this ridicule, he continued to speak, though in a less ambitious and less artificial vein, till after a few years he had become one of the most conspicuous unofficial members. At first no one had eulogised Peel more warmly, but after a time he edged away from the minister, whether repelled by his coldness, which showed that in that quarter no promotion was to be expected, or shrewdly perceiving that Peel was taking a line which would ultimately separate him from the bulk of the Conservative party. This happened in 1846, when Peel, convinced that the import duties on corn were economically unsound, proposed their abolition. Disraeli, who, since 1843, had taken repeated opportunities of firing stray shots at the powerful Prime Minister, now bore a foremost part not only in attacking him, but in organising the Protectionist party, and prompting its leader, Lord George Bentinck. In embracing free trade, Peel carried with him his own personal

friends and disciples, men like Gladstone, Sidney
Herbert, Lord Lincoln, Sir James Graham, Card-
well, and a good many others, the intellectual *élite*
of the Tory party. The more numerous section
who clung to Protection had numbers, wealth,
respectability, cohesion, but brains and tongues
were scarce. An adroit tactician and incisive
speaker was of priceless value to them. Such
a man they found in Disraeli, while he gained,
sooner than he had expected, an opportunity of
playing a leading part in the eyes of Parliament
and the country. In the end of 1848, Lord
George Bentinck, who, though a man of natural
force and capable of industry when he pleased,
had been to some extent Disraeli's mouthpiece,
died, leaving his prompter indisputably the keenest
intellect in the Tory-Protectionist party. In 1850,
Peel, who might possibly have in time brought
the bulk of that party back to its allegiance
to him, was killed by a fall from his horse.
The Peelites drifted more and more towards
Liberalism, so that when Lord Derby, who, in
1851, had been commissioned as head of the
Tory party to form a ministry, invited them to
join him, they refused to do so, imagining him
to be still in favour of the corn duties, and
resenting the behaviour of the Protectionist
section to their own master. Being thus unable to find one of them to lead his followers in
the House of Commons, Lord Derby turned in

1852 to Disraeli, giving him, with the leadership, the office of Chancellor of the Exchequer. The appointment was thought a strange one, because Disraeli brought to it absolutely no knowledge of finance and no official experience. He had never been so much as an Under-Secretary. The Tories themselves murmured that one whom they regarded as an adventurer should be raised to so high a place. After a few months Lord Derby's ministry fell, defeated on the Chancellor of the Exchequer's Budget, which had been vehemently attacked by Mr. Gladstone. This was the beginning of that protracted duel between him and Mr. Disraeli which lasted down till the end of the latter's life.

For the following fourteen years Disraeli's occupation was that of a leader of opposition, varied by one brief interval of office in 1858-59. His party was in a permanent minority, so that nothing was left for its chief but to fight with skill, courage, and resolution a series of losing battles. This he did with admirable tenacity of purpose. Once or twice in every session he used to rally his forces for a general engagement, and though always defeated, he never suffered himself to be dispirited by defeat. During the rest of the time he was keenly watchful, exposing all the mistakes in domestic affairs of the successive Liberal Governments, and when complications arose in foreign politics, always professing, and generally

manifesting, a patriotic desire not to embarrass
the Executive, lest national interests should suffer.
Through all these years he had to struggle, not
only with a hostile majority in office, but also
with disaffection among his own followers. Many
of the landed aristocracy could not bring themselves to acquiesce in the leadership of a new
man, of foreign origin, whose career had been
erratic, and whose ideas they found it hard to
assimilate. Ascribing their long exclusion from
power to his presence, they more than once
conspired to dethrone him. In 1861 these plots
were thickest, and Disraeli was for a time left
almost alone. But as it happened, there never
arose in the House of Commons any one on the
Conservative side possessing gifts of speech and
of strategy comparable to those which in him
had been matured and polished by long experience, while he had the address to acquire
an ascendency over the mind of Lord Derby,
still the titular head of the party, who, being
a man of straightforward character, high social
position, and brilliant oratorical talent, was there-
withal somewhat lazy and superficial, and therefore disposed to lean on his lieutenant in the
Lower House, and to borrow from him those
astute schemes of policy which Disraeli was fertile
in devising. Thus, through Lord Derby's support,
and by his own imperturbable confidence, he frus-
trated all the plots of the malcontent Tories.

New men came up who had not witnessed his
earlier escapades, but knew him only as the bold
and skilful leader of their party in the House of
Commons. He made himself personally agreeable to them, encouraged them in their first
efforts, diffused his ideas among them, stimulated
the local organisation of the party, and held out
hopes of great things to be done when fortune
should at last revisit the Tory banner.

While Lord Palmerston lived, these exertions
seemed to bear little fruit. That minister had, in
his later years, settled down into a sort of practical
Toryism, and both parties acquiesced in his rule.
But, on his death, the scene changed. Lord Russell and Mr. Gladstone brought forward a Reform
Bill strong enough to evoke the latent Conservative feeling of a House of Commons which,
though showing a nominally Liberal majority,
had been chosen under Palmerstonian auspices.
The defeat of the Bill, due to the defection of
the more timorous Whigs, was followed by the
resignation of Lord Russell's Ministry. Lord
Derby and Mr. Disraeli came into power, and,
next year, carried a Reform Bill which, as it was
finally shaped in its passage through the House,
really went further than Lord Russell's had done,
enfranchising a much larger number of the working classes in boroughs. To have carried this Bill
remains the greatest of Disraeli's triumphs. He
had to push it gently through a hostile House of

Commons by wheedling a section of the Liberal majority, against the appeals of their legitimate leader. He had also to persuade his own followers to support a measure which they had all their lives been condemning, and which was, or in their view ought to have been, more dangerous to the Constitution than the one which they and the recalcitrant Whigs had thrown out in the preceding year. He had, as he happily and audaciously expressed it, to educate his party into doing the very thing which they (though certainly not he himself) had cordially and consistently denounced.

The process was scarcely complete when the retirement of Lord Derby, whose health had given way, opened Disraeli's path to the post of first Minister of the Crown. He dissolved Parliament, expecting to receive a majority from the gratitude of the working class whom his Act had admitted to the suffrage. To his own surprise, and to the boundless disgust of the Tories, a Liberal House of Commons was again returned, which drove him and his friends once more into the cold shade of opposition. He was now sixty-four years of age, had suffered an unexpected and mortifying discomfiture, and had no longer the great name of Lord Derby to cover him. Disaffected voices were again heard among his own party, while the Liberals, reinstalled in power, were led by the rival whose unequalled popularity in the country made him for the time omnipotent. Still Mr.

Disraeli was not disheartened. He fought the battle of apparently hopeless resistance with his old tact, wariness, and tenacity, losing no occasion for any criticism that could damage the measures — strong and large measures — which Mr. Gladstone's government brought forward.

Before long the tide turned. The Dissenters resented the Education Act of 1870. A reaction in favour of Conservatism set in, which grew so fast that, in 1874, the general election gave, for the first time since 1846, a decided Conservative majority. Mr. Disraeli became again Prime Minister, and now a Prime Minister no longer on sufferance, but with the absolute command of a dominant party, rising so much above the rest of the Cabinet as to appear the sole author of its policy. In 1876, feeling the weight of age, he transferred himself to the House of Lords as Earl of Beaconsfield. The policy he followed (from 1876 till 1880) in the troubles which arose in the Turkish East out of the insurrection in Herzegovina and the massacres in Bulgaria, as well as that subsequently pursued in Afghanistan and in South Africa, while it received the enthusiastic approval of the soldiers, the stockbrokers, and the richer classes generally, raised no less vehement opposition in other sections of the nation, and especially in those two which, when heartily united and excited, have usually been masters of England — the Protestant Nonconformists and the upper part of the working class. An election fought with unusual heat left him in so decided a minority that he resigned office in April 1880, without waiting for an adverse vote in Parliament. When the result had become clear he observed, " They," meaning his friends, "will come in again, but I shall not." A year later he died.

Here is a wonderful career, not less wonderful to those who live in the midst of English politics and society than it appears to observers in other countries. A man with few external advantages, not even that of education at a university, where useful friendships are formed, with grave positive disadvantages in his Jewish extraction and the vagaries of his first years of public life, presses forward, step by step, through slights and disappointments which retard but never dishearten him, assumes as of right the leadership of a party, — the aristocratic party, the party in those days peculiarly suspicious of new men and poor men, — wins a reputation for sagacity which makes his early errors forgotten, becomes in old age the favourite of a court, the master of a great country, one of the three or four arbiters of Europe. There is here more than one problem to solve, or, at least, a problem with more than one aspect. What was the true character of the man who had sustained such a part? Did he hold any principles, or was he merely playing with them as counters?

By what gifts or arts did he win such a success?
Was there really a mystery beneath the wizard's
robe which he delighted to wrap around him?
And how, being so unlike the Englishmen among
whom his lot was cast, did he so fascinate and
rule them?

Imagine a man of strong will and brilliant
intellectual powers, belonging to an ancient and
persecuted race, who finds himself born in a
foreign country, amid a people for whose ideas
and habits he has no sympathy and scant
respect. Suppose him proud, ambitious, self-
confident — too ambitious to rest content in a
private station, so self-confident as to believe that
he can win whatever he aspires to. To achieve
success, he must bend his pride, must use the
language and humour the prejudices of those he
has to deal with; while his pride avenges itself by
silent scorn or thinly disguised irony. Accustomed to observe things from without, he discerns
the weak points of all political parties, the hollowness of institutions and watchwords, the instability
of popular passion. If his imagination be more
susceptible than his emotions, his intellect more
active than his conscience, the isolation in which
he stands and the superior insight it affords him
may render him cold, calculating, self-centred.
The sentiment of personal honour may remain,
because his pride will support it; and he will be
tenacious of the ideas which he has struck out,

c

because they are his own. But for ordinary principles of conduct he may have small regard, because he has not grown up under the conventional morality of the time and nation, but has looked on it merely as a phenomenon to be recognised and reckoned with, because he has noted how much there is in it of unreality or pharisaism — how far it sometimes is from representing or expressing either the higher judgments of philosophy or the higher precepts of religion. Realising and perhaps exaggerating the power of his own intelligence, he will secretly revolve schemes of ambition wherein genius, uncontrolled by fears or by conscience, makes all things bend to its purposes, till the scruples and hesitations of common humanity seem to him only parts of men's cowardice or stupidity. What success he will win when he comes to carry out such schemes in practice will largely depend on the circumstances in which he finds himself, as well as on his gift for judging of them. He may become a Napoleon. He may fall in a premature collision with forces which want of sympathy has prevented him from estimating.

In some of his novels, and most fully in the first of them, Mr. Disraeli sketched a character and foreshadowed a career not altogether unlike that which has just been indicated. It would be unfair to treat as autobiographical, though some of his critics have done so, the picture of Vivian

Grey. What that singular book shows is that, at an age when his contemporaries were lads at college, absorbed in cricket matches or Latin verse-making, Disraeli had already meditated profoundly on the conditions and methods of worldly success, had rejected the allurements of pleasure and the attractions of literature, as well as the ideal life of philosophy, had conceived of a character isolated, ambitious, intense, resolute, untrammelled by scruples, who moulds men to his purposes by the sheer force of his intellect, humouring their foibles, using their weaknesses, and luring them into his chosen path by the bait of self-interest.

To lay stress on the fact that Mr. Disraeli was of Hebrew birth is not, though some of his political antagonists stooped so to use it, to cast any reproach upon him: it is only to note a fact of the utmost importance for a proper comprehension of his position. The Jews were at the beginning of the nineteenth century still foreigners in England, not only on account of their religion, with its mass of ancient rites and usages, but also because they were filled with the memory of centuries of persecution, and perceived that in some parts of Europe the old spirit of hatred had not died out. The antiquity of their race, their sense of its long-suffering and isolation, their pride in the intellectual achievements of those ancestors whose blood, not largely mixed with that of any other race, flows in their veins, leads the stronger or more reflective spirits to revenge themselves by a kind of scorn upon the upstart Western peoples among whom their lot is cast. The mockery one finds in Heinrich Heine could not have come from a Teuton. Even while imitating, as the wealthier of them have latterly begun to imitate, the manners and luxury of those nominal Christians among whom they live, they retain their feeling of detachment, and are apt to regard with a coldly observant curiosity the beliefs, prejudices, enthusiasms of the nations of Europe. The same passionate intensity which makes the grandeur of the ancient Hebrew literature still lives among them, though often narrowed by ages of oppression, and gives them the peculiar effectiveness that comes from turning all the powers of the mind, imaginative as well as reasoning, into a single channel, be that channel what it may. They produce, in proportion to their numbers, an unusually large number of able and successful men, as any one may prove by recounting the eminent Jews of the last seventy years. This success has most often been won in practical life, in commerce, or at the bar, or in the press (which over the European continent they so largely control); yet often also in the higher walks of literature or science, less frequently in art, most frequently in music.

Mr. Disraeli had three of these characteristics

of his race in full measure —detachment, intensity,
the passion for material success. Nature gave
him a resolute will, a keen and precociously active
intellect, a vehement individuality, that is to
say, a consciousness of his own powers, and a
determination to make them recognised by his
fellows. In some men, the passion to succeed is
clogged by the fear of failure; in others, the
sense of their greatness is self-sufficing and in-
disposes them to effort. But with him ambition spurred self-confidence, and self-confidence
justified ambition. He grew up in a cultivated
home, familiar not only with books but with the
brightest and most polished men and women of
the day, whose conversation sharpened his wits
almost from childhood. No religious influences
worked upon him, for his father had ceased to
be a Jew in faith without becoming even nominally a Christian, and there is little in his writings to show that he had ever felt anything more
than an imaginative, or what may be called an
historical, interest in religion.[1] Thus his development was purely intellectual. The society he
moved in was a society of men and women of the
world — witty, superficial in its interests, without

[1] That historical interest he did feel deeply. One might almost say
of him that he was a Christian because he was a Jew, for Christianity was
to him the proper development of the ancient religion of Israel. "The
Jews," he observes in the *Life of Lord George Bentinck*, " represent the
Semitic principle, all that is most spiritual in our nature. . . . It is deplo-
rable that several millions of Jews still persist in believing only a part of
their religion."

seriousness or reverence. He felt himself no Englishman, and watched English life and politics as a
student of natural history might watch the habits
of bees or ants.   English society was then, and
perhaps is still, more complex, more full of in-
consistencies, of contrasts between theory and
practice, between appearances and realities, than
that of any other country.   Nowhere so much
limitation of view among the fashionable, so much
pharisaism among the respectable, so much vulgarity among the rich, mixed with so much real
earnestness, benevolence, and good sense; nowhere, therefore, so much to seem merely ridicu-
lous to one who looked at it from without, wanting
the sympathy which comes from the love of mankind, or even from the love of one's country.   It
was natural for a young man with Disraeli's gifts
to mock at what he saw.   But he would not sit
still in mere contempt.   The thirst for power
and fame gave him no rest.   He must gain what
he saw every one around him struggling for.
He must triumph over these people whose follies
amused him; and the sense that he perceived
and could use their follies would add zest to
his triumph.   He might have been a great
satirist; he resolved to become a great statesman.
For such a career, his Hebrew detachment gave
him some eminent advantages.   It enabled him
to take a cooler and more scientific view of the
social and political phenomena he had to deal

with. He was not led astray by party cries.
He did not share vulgar prejudices. He calculated the forces at work as an engineer calculates
the strength of his materials, the strain they have
to bear from the wind, and the weights they
must support. And what he had to plan was
not the success of a cause, which might depend
on a thousand things out of his ken, but his own
success, a simpler matter.

A still greater source of strength lay in his
Hebrew intensity. It would have pleased him,
so full of pride in the pure blood of his race,[1]
to attribute to that purity the singular power
of concentration which the Jews undoubtedly
possess. They have the faculty of throwing the
whole stress of their natures into the pursuit of
one object, fixing their eyes on it alone, sacri-
ficing to it other desires, clinging to it even when
it seems unattainable. Disraeli was only twenty-
eight when he made his first attempt to enter
the House of Commons. Four repulses did
not discourage him, though his means were but
scanty to support such contests; and the fifth

[1] Though it has been maintained that in the Dark and Middle Ages a
considerable number of Gentiles found their way into Jewish communities
and became Judaised.

The high average of intellectual power among the Jews need not be
attributed to purity of race; it is sufficiently explained by their history.
Nor is it clear that where two of the more advanced races are mixed by
intermarriage, the product is inferior to either of the parent stocks. On
the contrary, such a mixture, *e.g.* of Teutonic and Slavonic blood, or of
Celtic and Teutonic, gives a result at least equal in capacity to either of
the pure-blooded races which have been so commingled.

time he succeeded. When his first speech in
Parliament had been received with laughter, and
politicians were congratulating themselves that
this adventurer had found his level, he calmly
told them that he had always ended by succeeding in whatever he attempted, and that he
would succeed in this too. He received no help
from his own side, who regarded him with
suspicion, but forced himself into prominence,
and at last to leadership, by his complete superiority to rebuffs. Through the long years in
which he had to make head against a majority
in the House of Commons, he never seemed
disheartened by his repeated defeats, never relaxed the vigilance with which he watched his
adversaries, never indulged himself (though he
was physically indolent and often in poor health)
by staying away from Parliament, even when
business was slack; never missed an opportunity
for exposing a blunder of his adversaries, or
commending the good service of one of his
own followers. The same curious tenacity was
apparent in his ideas. Before he was twenty-
two years of age he had, under the inspiration
of Bolingbroke, excogitated a theory of the
Constitution of England, of the way England
should be governed at home and her policy
directed abroad, from which he hardly swerved
through all his later life. Often as he was
accused of inconsistency he probably believed

himself to be, and in a sense he was, substantially faithful, I will not say to the same
doctrines, but to the same notions or tendencies;
and one could discover from the phrases he employed how he fancied himself to be really following out these old notions, even when his conduct
seemed opposed to the traditions of his party.[1]
The weakness of intense minds is their tendency
to narrowness, and this weakness was in so far
his that, while always ready for new expedients,
he was not accessible to new ideas. Indeed,
the old ideas were too much a part of himself,
stamped with his own individuality, to be for-
saken or even varied. He did not love knowledge, nor enjoy speculation for its own sake; he
valued views as they pleased his imagination or
as they carried practical results with them; and
having framed his theory once for all and worked
steadily upon its lines, he was not the man to
admit that it had been defective, and to set himself in later life to repair it. His pride was involved in proving it correct by applying it.

With this resolute concentration of purpose
there went an undaunted courage — a quality less
rare among English statesmen, but eminently

[1] He had an intellectual arrogance, which made him dislike what
may be called the Radical conception of human equality. In the *Life
of Lord George Bentinck* he remarks, " The Jews are a living and the
most striking evidence of the falsity of that pernicious doctrine of modern
times, the natural equality of man. . . . All the tendencies of the Jewish
race are conservative. Their bias is to religion, property, and natural
aristocracy."

laudable in him, because for a great part of his career he had no family or party connections to back him up, but was obliged to face the world with nothing but his own self-confidence. So far from seeking to conceal his Jewish origin, he displayed his pride in it, and refused all support to the efforts which the Tory party made to maintain the exclusion of Jews from Parliament. Nobody showed more self-possession and (except on two or three occasions) more perfect self-command in the hot strife of Parliament than this suspected stranger. His opponents learnt to fear one who never feared for himself; his followers knew that their chief would not fail them in the hour of danger. His very face and bearing had in them an impassive calmness which magnetised those who watched him. He liked to surround himself with mystery, to pose as remote, majestic, self-centred, to appear above the need of a confidant. He would sit for hours on his bench in the House of Commons, listening with eyes half-shut to furious assaults on himself and his policy, not showing by the movement of a muscle that he had felt a wound; and when he rose to reply would discharge his sarcasms with an air of easy coolness. That this indifference was sometimes simulated appeared by the resentment he showed afterwards.

Ambition such as his could not afford to be scrupulous, nor have his admirers ever claimed conscientiousness as one of his merits. One who

sets power and fame before him as the main
ends to be pursued may no doubt be restrained
by pride from the use of such means as are
obviously low and dishonourable. Other questionable means he may reject because he knows
that the opinion of those whose good-will and
good word he must secure would condemn them.
But he will not be likely to allow kindliness or
compassion to stand in his way; nor will he be
very regardful of truth. To a statesman, who
must necessarily have many facts in his knowledge, or many plans in his mind, which the
interests of his colleagues, or of his party, or of
the nation, forbid him to reveal, the temptation to
put questioners on a false scent, and to seem to
agree where he really dissents, is at all times a
strong one. An honest man may sometimes be
betrayed into yielding to it; and those who know
how difficult are the cases of conscience that arise
will not deal harshly with a possibly misleading
silence, or even with the evasion of an embar-
rassing inquiry, where a real public interest
can be pleaded, for the existence of such a public
interest, if it does not justify, may palliate omis-
sions to make a full disclosure of the facts. All
things considered, the standard of truthfulness
among English public men has (of course with
some conspicuous exceptions) been a high one.
Of that standard Disraeli fell short. People did
not take his word for a thing as they would have

taken the word of the Duke of Wellington, or Lord Althorp, or Lord Derby, or Lord Russell, or even of that not very rigid moralist, Lord Palmerston. Instances of his lapses were not wanting as late as 1877. His behaviour toward Sir Robert Peel, whom he plied with every dart of sarcasm, after having shortly before lavished praises on him, and sought office under him, has often been commented on.[1] Disraeli was himself (as those who knew him have often stated) accustomed to justify it by observing that he was then an insignificant personage, to whom it was supremely important to attract public notice and make a political position; that the opportunity of attacking the powerful Prime Minister, at a moment when their altered attitude toward the Corn Laws had exposed the Ministry to the suspicions of their own party, was too good to be lost; and that he was therefore obliged to assail Peel, though he had himself no particular attachment to the Corn Laws, and believed Peel to have been a *bona fide* convert. It was therefore no personal resentment against one who had slighted him, but merely the exigencies of his own career, that drove him to this course, whose fortunate result proved the soundness of his calculations.

---

[1] On one occasion he went so far as to deny that he had asked Peel for office, relying on the fact that the letter which contained the request was marked "private," so that Peel could not use it to disprove his statement (*Letters of Sir Robert Peel*, by C. S. Parker, vol. ii. p. 486 ; vol. iii. pp. 347, 348).

This defence will not surprise any one who is familiar with Disraeli's earlier novels. These stories are as far as possible from being immoral; that is to say, there is nothing in them unbecoming or corrupting. Friendship, patriotism, love, are all recognised as powerful and worthy motives of conduct. That which is wanting is the sense of right and wrong. His personages have for certain purposes the conventional sense of honour, though seldom a fine sense, but they do not ask whether such and such a course is conformable to principle. They move in a world which is polished, agreeable, dignified, averse to baseness and vulgarity, but in which conscience and religion scarcely seem to exist. The men live for pleasure or fame, the women for pleasure or love.

Some allowance must, of course, be made for the circumstances of Disraeli's position and early training. He was brought up neither a Jew nor a Christian. The elder people who took him by the hand when he entered life, people like Samuel Rogers and Lady Blessington, were not the people to give lessons in morality. Lord Lyndhurst, the first of his powerful political friends, and the man whose example most affected him, was, with all his splendid gifts, conspicuously wanting in political principle. Add to this the isolation in which the young man found himself, standing outside the common stream of English life, not sharing its sentiments, perceiving the hollowness of much that passed for virtue and patriotism, and it is easy to understand how he should have been as perfect a cynic at twenty-five as their experience of the world makes many at sixty. If he had loved truth or mankind, he might have quickly worked through his youthful cynicism. But pride and ambition, the pride of race and the pride of genius, left no room for these sentiments. Nor was his cynicism the fruit merely of a keen and sceptical intelligence. It came from a cold heart.

The pursuit of fame and power, to which he gave all his efforts, is presented in his writings as the only alternative ideal to a life of pleasure; and he probably regarded those who pursued some other as either fools or weaklings. Early in his political life he said one night to Mr. Bright (from whom I heard the anecdote), as they took their umbrellas in the cloak-room of the House of Commons: "After all, what is it that brings you and me here? Fame! This is the true arena. I might have occupied a literary throne; but I have renounced it for this career." The external pomps and trappings of life, titles, stately houses and far-spreading parks, all those gauds and vanities with which sumptuous wealth surrounds itself, had throughout his life a singular fascination for him. He liked to mock at them in his novels, but they fascinated him none the less. One can understand how they might fire the imagination

of an ambitious youth who saw them from a
distance — might even retain their charm for one
who was just struggling into the society which
possessed them, and who desired to feel himself
the equal of the possessors. It is stranger that,
when he had harnessed the English aristocracy
to his chariot, and was driving them where he
pleased, he should have continued to admire such
things. So, however, it was. There was even
in him a vein of inordinate deference to rank
and wealth which would in a less eminent person
have been called snobbishness. In his will he
directs that his estate of Hughenden Manor, in
Buckinghamshire, shall pass under an entail as
strict as he could devise, that the person who
succeeds to it shall always bear the name of
Disraeli. His ambition is the common, not to
say vulgar, ambition of the English *parvenu*, to
found a "county family." In his story of
Endymion, published a few months before his
death, the hero, starting from small beginnings,
ends by becoming prime minister: this is the
crown of his career, the noblest triumph an
Englishman can achieve. It might have been
thought that one who had been through it all,
who had realised the dreams of his boyhood, who
had every opportunity of learning what power
and fame come to, would have liked to set forth
some other conception of the end of human life,
or would not have told the world so naively of his

self-content at having attained the aim he had
worked for.   With most men the flower they have
plucked withers.   It might have been expected
that one who was in other things an ironical cynic
would at least have sought to seem disillusionised.

To say that Disraeli's heart was somewhat
cold is by no means to say that he was heartless.
He was one of those strong natures who permit
neither persons nor principles to stand in their
way.   His doctrine was that politics had nothing
to do with sentiment; so those who appealed to
him on grounds of humanity appealed in vain.
No act of his life ever so much offended English
opinion as the airy fashion in which he tossed aside
the news of the Bulgarian massacre of 1876.   It
incensed sections who were strong enough, when
thoroughly roused, to bring about his fall.   But
he was far from being unkindly.   He knew how
to attach men to him by friendly deeds as well as
friendly words.   He seldom missed an opportunity of saying something pleasant and cheering
to a *débutant* in Parliament, whether of his own
party or the opposite.   He was not selfish in
little things; was always ready to consider the
comfort and convenience of those who surrounded
him.   Age and success, so far from making him
morose or supercilious, softened the asperities of
his character and developed the affectionate side
of it.   His last novel, published a few months
before his death, contains more human kindliness,

a fuller recognition of the worth of friendship and
the beauty of sisterly and conjugal love, than do
the writings of his earlier manhood.   What it
wants in intellectual power it makes up for in a
mellower and more tender tone.   Of loyalty to
his political friends he was a model, and nothing
did more to secure his command of the party
than its sense that his professional honour, so to
speak, could be implicitly relied upon.   To his
wife, a warm-hearted woman older than himself,
and inferior to him in education, he was uniformly affectionate and indeed devoted.   The
first use he made of his power as Prime Minister
was to procure for her the title of viscountess.
Being once asked point blank by a lady what
he thought of his life-long opponent, Mr. Gladstone answered that two things had always struck
him as very admirable in Lord Beaconsfield's
character — his perfect loyalty to his wife, and
his perfect loyalty to his own race.   A story
used to be told how, in Disraeli's earlier days,
when his political position was still far from
assured, he and his wife happened to be the
guests of the chief of the party, and that chief so
far forgot good manners as to quiz Mrs. Disraeli
at the dinner-table.   Next morning Disraeli,
whose visit was to have lasted for some days
longer, announced that he must leave immediately.
The host besought him to stay, and made all
possible apologies.   But Disraeli was inexorable,

D

and carried his wife off forthwith. To literary men, whatever their opinions, he was ready to give a helping hand, representing himself as one of their profession. In paying compliments he was singularly expert, and few used the art so well to win friends and disarm enemies. He knew how to please Englishmen, and especially the young, by showing interest in their tastes and pleasures, and, without being what would be called genial, was never wanting in *bonhomie*. In society he was a perfect man of the world — told his anecdote apropos, wound up a discussion by some epigrammatic phrase, talked to the guest next him, if he thought that guest's position made him worth talking to, as he would to an old acquaintance. But he had few intimates; nor did his apparent frankness unveil his real thoughts.

He was not of those who complicate political opposition with private hatreds. Looking on politics as a game, he liked, when he took off his armour, to feel himself on friendly terms with his antagonists, and often seemed surprised to find that they remembered as personal affronts the blows which he had dealt in the tournament. Two or three years before his death, a friend asked him whether there was in London any one with whom he would not shake hands. Reflecting for a moment, he answered, " Only one," and named Robert Lowe, who had said hard things of him, and to whom, when Lowe was on one occasion in his power, he had behaved with cruelty. Yet his resentments could smoulder long. In *Lothair* he attacked, under a thin disguise, a distinguished man of letters who had criticised his conduct years before. In *Endymion* he gratified what was evidently an ancient grudge by a spiteful presentation of Thackeray, as he had indulged his more bitter dislike of John Wilson Croker by portraying that politician in *Coningsby* under the name of Nicholas Rigby. For the greatest of his adversaries he felt, there is reason to believe, genuine admiration, mingled with inability to comprehend a nature so unlike his own. No passage in the striking speech which that adversary pronounced, one might almost say, over Lord Beaconsfield's grave — a speech which may possibly go down to posterity with its subject — was more impressive than the sentence in which he declared that he had the best reason to believe that, in their constant warfare, Lord Beaconsfield had not been actuated by any personal hostility. Brave men, if they can respect, seldom dislike, a formidable antagonist.

His mental powers were singularly well suited to the rest of his character — were, so to speak, all of a piece with it. One sometimes sees intellects which are out of keeping with the active or emotional parts of the man. One sees persons whose thought is vigorous, clear, comprehensive, while their conduct is timid; or a comparatively narrow intelligence joined to an enterprising spirit ; or a sober, reflective, sceptical turn of mind yoked to an ardent and impulsive temperament. What we call the follies of the wise often spring from some such source. Not so with him. His intelligence had the same boldness, intensity, concentration, directness, which we discover in the rest of the man. It was just the right instrument, not perhaps for the normal career of a normal Englishman seeking political success, but for the particular kind of work Disraeli had planned to do; and this inner harmony was one of the chief causes of his success, as the want of it has caused the failure of so many gifted natures.

The range of his mind was not wide. All its products were like one another. No one of them gives the impression that Disraeli could, had he so wished, have succeeded in a wholly diverse line. It was a peculiar mind : there is even more variety in minds than in faces. It was not logical or discursive, liking to mass and arrange stores of knowledge, and draw inferences from them, nor was it judicial, with a turn for weighing reasons and reaching a decision which recognises all the facts and is not confused by their seeming contradictions. Neither was it analytically subtle. It reached its conclusions by a process of intuition or divination in which there was an imaginative as well as a reflective element. It might almost have been called an artist's mind, capable of deep meditation, but meditating in an imaginative way, not so much on facts as on its own views of facts, on the pictures which its own creative faculty had called up. The meditation became dreamy, but the dreaminess was corrected by an exceedingly keen and quick power of observation, not the scientific observation of the philosopher, but rather the enjoying observation of the artist who sees how he can use the characteristic details which he notes, or the observation of the forensic advocate (an artist, too, in his way) who perceives how they can be fitted into the presentation of his case. There are, of course, other qualities in Disraeli's work. As a statesman he was obliged to learn how to state facts, to argue, to dissect an opponent's arguments. But the characteristic note, both of his speeches and of his writings, is the combination of a few large ideas, clear, perhaps, to himself, but generally expressed with grandiose vagueness, and often quite out of relation to the facts as other people saw them, with a turn for acutely fastening upon small incidents or personal traits. In his speeches he used his command of sonorous phrases and lively illustrations, sometimes to support the views he was advancing, but more frequently to conceal the weakness of those views, that is, to make up for the absence of such solid arguments as were likely to move his hearers. Everybody is now and then conscious of holding with assured conviction theories which he would find it hard to prove to a given audience, partly because it is too much trouble to trace out the process by which they were reached, partly because uninstructed listeners could not be made to feel the full cogency of the considerations on which his own mind relies.   Disraeli was usually in this condition with regard to his political and social doctrines. He believed them, but as he had not reached them by logic, he was not prepared to use logic to establish them; so he picked up some plausible illustration, or attacked the opposite doctrine and its supporters with a fire of raillery or invective.   This non-ratiocinative quality of his thinking was a source both of strength and of weakness — of weakness, because he could not prove his propositions; of strength, because, stated as he stated them, it was not less hard to disprove them.   That mark of a superior mind, that it must have a theory, was never wanting.   Some one said of him that he was "the ruins of a thinker."   He could not rest content, like many among his followers, with a prejudice, a dogma delivered by tradition, a stolid suspicion unamenable to argument.   He would not acquiesce in negation.   He must have a theory, a positive theory, to show not only that his antagonist's view was erroneous, but that he had himself a more excellent way.   These theories

generally had in them a measure of truth and
value for any one who could analyse them; but
as this was exactly what the rank and file of the
party could not do, they got into sad confusion
when they tried to talk his language.

He could hardly be called a well-read man,
nor were his intellectual interests numerous. His
education had consisted mainly in promiscuous
reading during boyhood and early youth. There
are worse kinds of education for an active intelligence than to let it have the run of a large
library. The wild browsings of youth, when
curiosity is strong as hunger, stir the mind and
give the memory some of the best food it ever
gets. The weak point of such a method is that it
does not teach accuracy nor the art of systematic
study. In middle life natural indolence and his
political occupations had kept Disraeli from filling
up the gaps in his knowledge, while, in conversation, what he liked best was persiflage. He
was, however, tolerably familiar with the ancient
classics, and with modern English and French
literature; enjoyed Quintilian and Lucian, preferred
Sophocles to Æschylus and (apparently) Horace
to Virgil, despised Browning, considered Tennyson the best of contemporary poets, but "not a
poet of a high order."[1] Physical science seems
never to have attracted him. Political economy

[1] See Sir S. Northcote's report of a conversation with Disraeli in his
last years (*Life of Sir Stafford Northcote*, vol. ii.).

he hated and mocked at almost as heartily as did Carlyle. People have measured his knowledge of history and geography by observing that he placed the Crucifixion in the lifetime of Augustus, and thought, down till 1878, when he had to make a speech about Afghanistan, that the Andes were the highest mountains in the world. But geography is a subject which a man of affairs does not think of reading up in later life: he is content if he can get information when he needs it. There are some bits of metaphysics and some historical allusions scattered over his novels, but these are mostly slight or superficial. He amused himself and the public by now and then propounding doctrines on agricultural matters, but would not appear to have mastered either husbandry or any other economical or commercial subject. Such things were not in his way. He had been so little in office as not to have been forced to apply himself to them, while the tide of pure intellectual curiosity had long since ebbed.

For so-called "sports" he had little taste. He liked to go mooning in a meditative way round his fields and copses, and he certainly enjoyed nature; but there seems to be no solid evidence that the primrose was his favourite flower. In his fondness for particular words and phrases there was a touch of his artistic quality, and a touch also of the cynical view that words are the counters with which the wise play their game. There is a passage in *Contarini Fleming* (a story into which he has put a good deal of himself) where this is set out. Contarini tells his father that he left college "because they taught me only words, and I wished to learn ideas." His father answers, "Few ideas are correct ones, and what are correct, no one can ascertain; but with words we govern men."

He went on acting on this belief in the power of words till he became the victim of his own phrases, just as people who talk cynically for effect grow sometimes into real cynics. When he had invented a phrase which happily expressed the aspect he wished his view, or some part of his policy, to bear, he came to believe in the phrase, and to think that the facts were altered by the colour the phrase put upon them. During the contest for the extension of the parliamentary franchise, he declared himself "in favour of popular privileges, but opposed to democratic rights." When he was accused of having assented, at the Congress of Berlin, to the dismemberment of the Turkish Empire, he said that what had been done was "not dismemberment, but consolidation." No statesman of recent times has given currency to so many quasi-epigrammatic expressions: "organised hypocrisy," "England dislikes coalitions," "plundering and blundering," "peace with honour," "*imperium et libertas,*" "a scientific frontier," "I am on the side of the angels," are a few, not perhaps the best, though the best remembered, of the many which issued from his fertile mint. This turn for epigram, not common in England, sometimes led him into scrapes which would have damaged a man of less imperturbable coolness. No one else could have ventured to say, when he had induced the Tories to pass a Reform Bill stronger than the one they had rejected from the Liberals in the preceding year, that it had been his mission "to educate his party." Some of his opponents professed to be shocked by such audacity, and many old Tories privily gnashed their teeth. But the country received the dictum in the spirit in which it was spoken. " It was Disraeli all over."

If his intellect was not of wide range, it was within its range a weapon of the finest flexibility and temper. It was ingenious, ready, incisive. It detected in a moment the weak point, if not of an argument, yet of an attitude or of a character. Its imaginative quality made it often picturesque, sometimes even impressive. Disraeli had the artist's delight in a situation for its own sake, and what people censured as insincerity or frivolity was frequently only the zest which he felt in posing, not so much because there was anything to be gained, as because he realised his aptitude for improvising a new part in the drama which he

always felt himself to be playing. The humour of
the situation was too good to be wasted. Perhaps
this love of merry mischief may have had something to do with his tendency to confer honours
on those whom the world thought least deserving.

His books are not only a valuable revelation
of his mind, but have more literary merit than
critics have commonly allowed to them, perhaps
because we are apt, when a man excels in one
walk, to deem him to have failed in any other
wherein he does not reach the same level. The
novels foam over with cleverness; indeed, *Vivian
Grey*, with all its youthful faults, gives as great
an impression of intellectual brilliance as does
anything Disraeli ever wrote or spoke. Their
easy fertility makes them seem to be only,
so to speak, a few sketches out of a large
portfolio. There is some variety in the subjects — *Contarini Fleming* and *Tancred* are
more romantic than the others, *Sybil* and *Coningsby* more political — as well as in the merits
of the stories. The two latest, *Lothair* and
Endymion, works of his old age, are markedly
inferior in spirit and invention; but the general
features are the same in all — a lively fancy, a
knack of hitting characters off in a few lines and
of catching the superficial aspects of society, a
brisk narrative, a sprightly dialogue, a keen insight
into the selfishness of men and the vanities of
women, with flashes of wit lighting up the whole

stage. It is always a stage. The brilliance
is never open-air sunshine. There is scarcely
one of the characters whom we feel we might
have met and known. Heroes and heroines
are theatrical figures; their pathos rings false,
their love, though described as passionate, does
not spring from the inner recesses of the soul.
The studies of men of the world, and particularly of heartless ones, are the most life-like;
yet, even here, any one who wants to feel the
difference between the great painter and the
clever sketcher need only compare Thackeray's
Marquis of Steyne with Disraeli's Marquis of
Monmouth, both of them suggested by the same
original. There is little intensity, little dramatic
power in these stories, as also is in his play
of *Alarcos;* and if we read them with pleasure
it is not for the sake either of plot or of character, but because they contain so many sparkling
witticisms and reflections, setting in a strong
light, yet not always an unkindly light, the seamy
side of politics and human nature. The slovenli-
ness of their style, which is often pompous, but
seldom pure, makes them appear to have been
written hastily. But Disraeli seems to have
taken the composition of them (except, perhaps,
the two latest) quite seriously. When he wrote
the earlier tales, he meant to achieve literary
greatness; while the middle ones, especially
Coningsby and *Sybil,* were designed as political

manifestoes. The less they have a purpose or
profess to be serious, the better they are; and
the most vivacious of all are two classical bur-
lesques, written at a time when that kind of
composition had not yet become common —
Ixion in Heaven and *The Infernal Marriage*
— little pieces of funning worthy of Thackeray,
I had almost said of Voltaire. They recall,
perhaps they were suggested by, similar pieces
of Lucian's. Is Semitic genius specially rich in
this mocking vein? Lucian was a Syrian from
Samosata, probably a Semite; Heinrich Heine
was a Semite; James Russell Lowell used to
insist, though he produced little evidence for his
belief, that Voltaire was a Semite.

Whether Disraeli could ever have taken high
rank as a novelist if he had thrown himself completely into the profession may be doubted, for his
defects were such as pains and practice would
hardly have lessened. That he had still less the
imagination needed by a poet, his *Revolutionary
Epick* conceived on the plains of Troy, and meant
to make a fourth to the *Iliad*, the *Æneid*, and the
Divina Commedia, is enough to show. The literary
vocation he was best fitted for was that of a
journalist or pamphleteer; and in this he might
have won unrivalled success. His dash, his
verve, his brilliancy of illustration, his scorching
satire, would have made the fortune of any newspaper, and carried dismay into the enemy's ranks.

In inquiring how far the gifts I have sought to describe qualified Disraeli for practical statesmanship, it is well to distinguish the different kinds of capacity which an English politician needs to attain the highest place. They may be said to be four. He must be a debater. He must be a parliamentary tactician. He must understand the country. He must understand Europe. This last is, indeed, not always necessary; there have been moments when England, leaving Europe to itself, may look to her own affairs only; but when the sky grows stormy over Europe, the want of knowledge which English statesmen sometimes evince may bode disaster.

An orator, in the highest sense of the word, Disraeli never was. He lacked ease and fluency. He had not Pitt's turn for the lucid exposition of complicated facts, nor for the conduct of a close argument. The sustained and fiery declamation of Fox was equally beyond his range. And least of all had he that truest index of eloquence, the power of touching the emotions. He could not make his hearers weep. But he could make them laugh; he could put them in good-humour with themselves; he could dazzle them with rhetoric; he could pour upon an opponent streams of ridicule more effective than the hottest indignation. When he sought to be profound or solemn, he was usually heavy and laboured — the sublimity often false, the diction often stilted. For wealth

of thought or splendour of language his speeches
will not bear to be compared — I will not say with
those of Burke (on whom he sometimes tried to
model himself), but with those of three or four of
his own contemporaries. Even within his own
party, Lord Derby, Lord Ellenborough, and Lord
Cairns in their several ways surpassed him. There
is not one of his longer and more finished harangues
which can be read with interest from beginning to
end. But there is hardly any among them which
does not contain some striking passage, some
image or epigram, or burst of sarcasm, which
must have been exceedingly effective when delivered. It is partly upon these isolated passages,
especially the sarcastic ones (though the witticisms
were sometimes borrowed), and still more upon
the aptness of the speech to the circumstances
under which it was made, that his parliamentary
fame rests. If he was not a great orator he was
a superb debater, who watched with the utmost
care the temper of the audience, and said just
what was needed at the moment to disconcert an
opponent or to put heart into his friends. His
repartees were often happy, and must sometimes
have been unpremeditated. As he had not the
ardent temperament of the born orator, so neither
had he the external advantages which count for
much before large assemblies. His voice was
not remarkable either for range or for quality.
His manner was somewhat stiff, his gestures few,

his countenance inexpressive. Yet his delivery was not wanting in skill, and often added point, by its cool unconcern, to a stinging epigram.

What he lacked in eloquence he made up for by tactical adroitness. No more consummate parliamentary strategist has been seen in England. He had studied the House of Commons till he knew it as a player knows his instrument — studied it collectively, for it has a collective character, and studied the men who compose it: their worse rather than their better side, their prejudices, their foibles, their vanities, their ambitions, their jealousies, above all, that curious corporate pride which they have, and which makes them resent any approach to dictation. He could play on every one of these strings, and yet so as to conceal his skill; and he so economised himself as to make them always wish to hear him. He knew how in a body of men obliged to listen to talk, and most of it tedious talk, about matters in themselves mostly uninteresting, the desire for a little amusement becomes almost a passion; and he humoured this desire so far as occasionally to err by excess of banter and flippancy. Almost always respectful to the House, he had a happy knack of appearing to follow rather than to lead, and when he made an official statement it was with the air of one who was taking them into his confidence. Much of this he may have learned from observing Lord Palmerston; but the art came more naturally to that statesman, who was an Englishman all through, than to a man of Mr. Disraeli's origin, who looked on Englishmen from outside, and never felt himself, so to speak, responsible for their habits or ideas.

As leader of his party in opposition, he was at once daring and cautious. He never feared to give battle, even when he expected defeat, if he deemed it necessary, with a view to the future, that the judgment of his party should have been pronounced in a formal way. On the other hand, he was wary of committing himself to a policy of blind or obstinate resistance. When he perceived that the time had come to yield, he knew how to yield with a good grace, so as both to support a character for reasonableness and to obtain valuable concessions as the price of peace. If difficulties arose with foreign countries he claimed full liberty of criticising the conduct of the Ministry, but ostentatiously abstained from obstructing or thwarting their acts, declaring that England must always present a united front to the foreigner, whatever penalties she might afterwards visit on those who had mismanaged her concerns. As regards the inner discipline of his party, he had enormous difficulties to surmount in the jealousy which many Tories felt for him as a

E

new man, a man whom they could not understand and only partially trusted.[1] Conspiracies
were repeatedly formed against him; malcontents
attacked him in the press, and sometimes even in
Parliament. These he seldom noticed, maintaining a cool and self-confident demeanour which
disheartened the plotters, and discharging the
duties of his post with steady assiduity. He
was always on the look-out for young men of
promise, drew them towards him, encouraged
them to help him in parliamentary sharp-shoot-
ing, and fostered in every way the spirit of party.
The bad side of that spirit was seen when he
came into office, for then every post in the
public service was bestowed either by mere
favouritism or on party grounds; and men who
had been loyal to him were rewarded by places
or titles to which they had no other claim.
But the unity and martial fervour of the Tory
party was raised to the highest point. Nor was
Disraeli himself personally unpopular with his
parliamentary opponents, even when he was most
hotly attacked on the platform and in the press.

To know England and watch the shifting

---

[1] In the *Life of Lord George Bentinck* (written shortly after Peel's
death), Disraeli, after dilating upon the loyalty which the Tory aristocracy
had displayed towards Peel, observes, " An aristocracy hesitates before it
yields its confidence, but it never does so grudgingly. . . . In political
connections the social feeling mingles with the principle of honour which
governs gentlemen. . . . Such a following is usually cordial and faithful.
An aristocracy is rather apt to exaggerate the qualities and magnify the
importance of a plebeian leader."

currents of its opinion is a very different matter from knowing the House of Commons. Indeed, the two kinds of knowledge are in a measure incompatible. Men who enter Parliament soon begin to forget that it is not, in the last resort, Parliament that governs, but the people. Absorbed in the daily contests of their Chamber, they over-estimate the importance of those contests. They come to think that Parliament is in fact what it is in theory, a microcosm of the nation, and that opinion inside is sure to reflect the opinion outside. When they are in a minority they are depressed ; when they are in a majority they fancy that all is well, forgetting their masters out-of-doors. This tendency is aggravated by the fact that the English Parliament meets in the capital, where the rich and luxurious congregate and give their tone to society. The House of Commons, though many of its members belong to the middle class by origin, belongs practically to the upper class by sympathy, and is prone to believe that what it hears every evening at dinners or receptions is what the country is thinking. A member of the House of Commons is, therefore, ill-placed for feeling the pulse of the nation, and in order to do so must know what is being said over the country, and must frequently visit or communicate with his constituents. If this difficulty is experienced by an ordinary private member, it

is greater for a minister whose time is filled
by official duties, or for a leader of opposition,
who has to be constantly thinking of his tactics
in the House. In Disraeli's case there was a
keenness of observation and discernment far
beyond the common. But he was under the
disadvantages of not being really an Englishman,
and of having never lived among the people.[1]
The detachment I have already referred to tended
to weaken his power of judging popular sentiment,
and appraising at their true value the various
tendencies that sway and divide a nation so
complex as the English. Early in life he had
formed theories about the relations of the different classes of English society — nobility, gentry,
capitalists, workmen, peasantry, and the middle
classes — theories which were far from containing
the whole truth; and he adhered to them even
when the changes of half a century had made them
less true. He had a great aversion, not to say contempt, for Puritanism, and for the Dissenters among
whom it chiefly holds its ground, and pleased himself
with the notion that the extension of the suffrage
which he carried in 1867 had destroyed their
political power. The Conservative victory at the
election of 1874 confirmed him in this belief, and
made him also think that the working classes
were ready to follow the lead of the rich. He

---

[1] When he did set himself to examine the condition of the people, the
diagnosis, if not always correct, was always suggestive, *e.g.* the account of
the manufacturing districts given in *Sybil, or the Two Nations*.

perceived that the Liberal ministry of 1868–74 had offended certain influential sections by appearing too demiss or too unenterprising in foreign affairs, and fancied that the bulk of the nation would be dazzled by a warlike mien, and an active, even aggressive, foreign policy. Such a policy was congenial to his own ideas, and to the society that surrounded him. It was applauded by some largely circulated newspapers which had previously been unfriendly to the Tory party. Thus he was more surprised than any other man of similar experience to find the nation sending up a larger majority against him in 1880 than it had sent up for him in 1874. This was the most striking instance of his miscalculation. But he had all through his career an imperfect comprehension of the English people. Individuals, or even an assembly, may be understood by dint of close and long-continued observation; but to understand a whole nation, one must also have sympathy, and this his circumstances, not less than his character, had denied him.

It was partly the same defect that prevented him from mastering the general politics of Europe. There is a sense in which no single man can pretend to understand Europe. Bismarck himself did not. The problem is too vast, the facts to be known too numerous, the undercurrents too varying. One can speak only of more or less. If Europe had been in his time what it was a century before, Disraeli would have had a far better chance of being fit to become what it was probably his dearest wish to become — its guide and arbiter. He would have taken the measure of the princes and ministers with whom he had to deal, would have seen and adroitly played on their weaknesses. His novels show how often he had revolved diplomatic situations in his mind, and reflected on the way of handling them. Foreign diplomatists are agreed that at the Congress of Berlin he played his part to admiration, spoke seldom, but spoke always to the point and with dignity, had a perfect conception of what he meant to secure, and of the means he must employ to secure it, never haggled over details or betrayed any eagerness to win support, never wavered in his demands, even when they seemed to lead straight to war. Dealing with individuals, who represented material forces which he had gauged, he was perfectly at home, and deserved the praise he obtained from Bismarck, who, comparing him with other eminent figures at the Congress, is reported to have said, bluntly but heartily, " Der alte Jude, das ist der Mann." [1] But to know what the condition of South-Eastern Europe really was, and understand how best to settle its troubles, was a far more difficult task, and Disraeli possessed neither the knowledge nor the insight required. In the Europe

[1] "The old Jew, that is the man."

of to-day, peoples count for more than the wills of individual rulers: one must comprehend the passions and sympathies of peoples if one is to forecast the future. This he seldom cared to do. He did not realise the part and the power of moral forces. Down till the outbreak of the American Civil War he maintained that the question between the North and the South was mainly a fiscal question between the Protectionist interests of the one and the Free Trade interests of the other. He always treated with contempt the national movement in Italy. He made no secret in the days before 1859 of his good-will to Austria and of his liking for Louis Napoleon — a man inferior to him in ability and in courage, but to whose character his own had some affinities. In that elaborate study of Sir Robert Peel's character,[1] which is one of Disraeli's best literary performances, he observes that Peel " was destitute of imagination, and wanting imagination he wanted prescience." True it is that imagination is necessary for prescience, but imagination is not enough to give prescience. It may even be a snare.

Disraeli's imagination, his fondness for theories, and disposition rather to cling to them than to study and interpret facts, made him the victim of his own preconceived ideas, as his indolence deterred him from following the march of change and noting how different things were in the

[1] In the *Life of Lord George Bentinck.*

seventies from what they had been in the thirties.   Mr. Gladstone said to me in 1876, " Disraeli's two leading ideas in foreign policy have always been the maintenance of the temporal power of the Pope, and the maintenance of the power of the Sultan."   Unable to save the one, he clung to the hope of saving the other.   He was possessed by the notion, seductive to a dreamy mind, that all the disturbances of Europe arose from the action of secret societies; and when the Eastern Question was in 1875 re-opened by the insurrection in Herzegovina, followed by the war of Servia against the Turks, he explained the event in a famous speech by saying, " The secret societies of Europe have declared war against Turkey " — the fact being that the societies which in Russia were promoting the Servian war were public societies, openly collecting subscriptions, while those secret " social democratic" societies of which we have since heard so much were strongly opposed to the interference of Russia, and those other secret societies in the rest of Europe, wherein Poles and Italians have played a leading part, were, if not hostile, at any rate quite indifferent to the movement among the Eastern Christians.

Against these errors there must be set several cases in which he showed profound discernment. In 1843 and 1844 he delivered, in debates on the condition of Ireland, speeches which then con-

stituted and long remained the most penetrating
and concise diagnosis of the troubles of that country ever addressed to Parliament.   Ireland has, he
said, a starving peasantry, an alien church, and an
absentee aristocracy, and he went on to add that
the function of statesmanship was to cure by peaceful and constitutional methods ills which in other
countries had usually induced, and been removed
by, revolution.   During the American Civil War of
1861-65, Disraeli was the only leading statesman
on his own side of politics who did not embrace
and applaud the cause of the South.   Whether this
arose from a caution that would not commit itself
where it recognised ignorance, or from a perception of the superior strength of the Northern
States (a perception which whoever visits the
South even to-day is astonished that so few
people in Europe should have had), it is not easy
to decide; but whatever the cause, the fact is an
evidence of his prudence or sagacity all the more
weighty because Lord Palmerston, Lord Russell,
and Mr. Gladstone, as well as Lord Derby and
Sir Hugh Cairns, had each of them expressed
more or less sympathy with, or belief in, the
success of the Southern cause.

The most striking instance, however, of Disraeli's insight was his perception that an extension of the suffrage would not necessarily injure,
and might end by strengthening, the Tory party.
The Act of 1867 was described at the time as

"a leap in the dark." But Disraeli's eyes had pierced the darkness. For half a century politicians had assumed that the masses of the people were and would remain under the Liberal banner. Even as late as 1872 it was thought on Liberal platforms a good joke to say of some opinion that it might do for Conservative working men, if there were any. Disraeli had, long before 1867, seen deeper, and though his youthful fancies that the monarchy might be revived as an effective force, and that "the peasantry" would follow with mediæval reverence the lead of the landed gentry, proved illusory, he was right in discerning that wealth and social influence would in parliamentary elections count for more among the masses than the traditions of constitutional Whiggism or the dogmas of abstract Radicalism.

In estimating his statesmanship as a whole, one must give due weight to the fact that it impressed many publicists abroad. No English minister had for a long time past so fascinated observers in Germany and Austria. Supposing that under the long reign of Liberalism Englishmen had ceased to care for foreign politics, they looked on him as the man who had given back to Britain her old European position, and attributed to him a breadth of design, a grasp and a foresight such as men had revered in Lord Chatham, greatest in the short list of ministers who have raised the fame of England abroad. I remember

seeing in a Conservative club, about 1880, a
large photograph of Lord Beaconsfield, wearing
the well-known look of mysterious fixity, under
which is inscribed the line of Homer: " He alone
is wise: the rest are fleeting shadows." [1]   It
was a happy idea to go for a motto to the
favourite poet of his rival, as it was an unhappy chance to associate the wisdom ascribed
to Disraeli with his policy in the Turkish East
and in Afghanistan, a policy now universally admitted to have been unwise and unfortunate.[2]
But whatever may be thought of the appropriate-
ness of the motto, the fact remains that this was
the belief he succeeded in inspiring.   He did it
by virtue of those very gifts which sometimes
brought him into trouble — his taste for large and
imposing theories, his power of clothing them in
vague and solemn language, his persistent faith in
them.   He came, by long posing, to impose upon
himself and to believe in his own profundity.
Few people could judge whether his ideas of
imperial policy were sound and feasible; but
every one saw that he had theories, and many
fell under the spell which a grandiose imagination
can exercise.   It is chiefly this gift, coupled with

[1] Οἴῳ πεπνῦσθαι, τοὶ δὲ σκιαὶ ἀίσσουσιν (*Od.* x. 495).   Used of Tiresias,
in the world of disembodied spirits.

[2] To defend Disraeli by arguing that his policy had not a fair chance
because his colleagues did not allow him to carry it through is to admit
another error not less grave, for the path he took was one on which no
minister ought to have entered unless satisfied that the Cabinet and the
country would let him follow it to the end.

his indomitable tenacity, which lifts him out of
the line of mere party leaders. If he failed to see
how much the English are sometimes moved by
compassion, he did see that it may be worth while
to play to their imagination.

We may now ask again the question asked at
first: How did a man, whatever his natural gifts,
who was weighted in his course by such disadvantages as Disraeli's, by his Jewish origin, by the
escapades of his early career, by the want of confidence which his habitual cynicism inspired, by the
visionary nature of so many of his views,—how did
he, in a conservative and aristocratic country like
England, triumph over so many prejudices and
enmities, and raise himself to be the head of the
Conservative and aristocratic party, the trusted
counsellor of the Crown, the ruler, almost the
dictator, of a free people?

However high be the estimate formed of
Disraeli's gifts, secondary causes must have been
at work to enable him to overcome the obstacles
that blocked his path. The ancients were not
wrong in ascribing to Fortune a great share in
human affairs. Now, among the secondary causes
of success, that "general minister and leader set
over worldly splendours," as Dante calls her,[1]
played no insignificant part. One of these causes
lay in the nature of the party to which he belonged.
The Tory party of the years between 1848 and

[1] *Inf.* vii. 77.

Lord Beaconsfield 61

1865 contained a comparatively small number of able men. When J. S. Mill once called it the stupid party, it did not repudiate the name, but pointed to its cohesion and its resolution as showing how many things besides mere talent go to make political greatness. A man of shining gifts had within its ranks few competitors; and this was signally the case immediately after Peel's defection. That statesman had carried off with him the intellectual flower of the Conservatives. Those who were left behind to form the Protectionist Opposition in the House of Commons were broad-acred squires, of solid character but slender capacity. Through this heavy atmosphere Mr. Disraeli rose like a balloon. Being practically the only member of his party in the Commons with either strategical or debating power, he became indispensable, and soon established a supremacy which years of patient labour might not have given him in a rivalry with the distinguished band who surrounded Peel. During the twenty years that followed the great Tory schism of 1846 no man arose in the Tory ranks capable of disputing his throne. The conspiracies hatched against him might well have prospered could a candidate for the leadership have been found capable of crossing swords with the chieftain in possession. Fortune, true to her nursling, suffered none such to appear.

Another favouring influence not understood outside England was to be found in the character of the party he led.   In his day the Tories, being the party of the property-holders, and having not to advance but to stand still, not to propose changes but to resist them, having bonds of interest as well as of sentiment to draw them close together, possessed a cohesion, a loyalty to their chiefs, a tenacious corporate spirit, far exceeding what was to be found among their adversaries, who were usually divided into a moderate or Whig and an advanced or Radical section. He who established himself as the Tory leader was presently followed by the rank and file with a devotion, an unquestioning submission and confidence, which placed his character and doctrines under the ægis of the party, and enforced loyalty upon parliamentary malcontents.   This corporate spirit was of infinite value to Disraeli.   The historical past of the great Tory party, its associations, the social consideration which it enjoys, all went to ennoble his position and efface the remembrance of the less creditable parts of his career. And in the later days of his reign, when no one disputed his supremacy, every Tory was, as a matter of course, his advocate and admirer, and resented assaults on him as insults to the party. When a man excites hatred by his words or deeds, attacks on his character are an inevitable relief to overcharged feelings.   Technically regarded, they

are not good politics. Misrepresentation sometimes succeeds ; vituperation seldom.   Let a man
be personally untrustworthy or dangerous, still, it
is only his own words that damage him, at least in
England and America. Even his own words, however discrediting, even his acts, however culpable,
may, if they belong to a past unfamiliar to the voter
of to-day, tell little, perhaps too little, on the voter's
mind when they are brought up against him.   The
average citizen has a short memory, and thinks
that the dead may be allowed to bury their dead.

Let it be further noted that Disraeli's career
coincided with a significant change in English
politics, a change partly in the temper of the nation,
partly in the balance of voting power.   For thirty
years after the Reform Act of 1832, not only had
the middle classes constituted the majority of
the electors, but the social influence of the great
Whig families and the intellectual influence of
the economic school of Cobden had been potent
factors. These forces were, in the later part of
Disraeli's life, tending to decline.   The working-
class vote was vastly increased in 1867.   The
old Whig light gradually paled, and many of the
Whig magnates, obeying class sympathies rather
than party traditions, drifted slowly into Toryism.
A generation arose which had not seen the Free
Trade struggle, or had forgotten the Free Trade
arguments, and which was attracted by ideals other
than those which Cobden had preached.   The

grievances which had made men reformers had been largely removed. The battle of liberty and nationality in Continental Europe had been in the main won, and Englishmen had lost the enthusiasm for freedom which had fired them in the days when the memory of their own struggle against the Crown and the oligarchy was still fresh. With none of these changes had Disraeli's personal action much to do, but they all enured to the benefit of his party, they all swelled the tide which bore him into office in 1874.

Finally, he had the great advantage of living long. Many a statesman has died at fifty, and passed from the world's memory, who might have become a figure in history with twenty years more of life. Had Disraeli's career closed in 1854, he would have been remembered as a parliamentary gladiator, who had produced a few incisive speeches, a crude Budget, and some brilliant social and political sketches. The stronger parts of his character might have remained unknown. True it is that a man must have greatness in order to stand the test of long life. Some are found out, like Louis Napoleon. Some lose their balance and therewith their influence, like Lord Brougham. Some cease to grow or learn, and if a statesman is not better at sixty than he was at thirty, he is worse. Some jog heavily on, like Metternich, or stiffen into arbitrary doctrinaires, like Guizot. Disraeli did not merely stand the test, he gained immensely by it. He gained by rising into a position where his strength could show itself. He gained also by so impressing his individuality upon people as to make them accept it as an ultimate fact, till at length they came, not so much to blame him for what he did in accord with his established reputation, as rather to relish and enter into the humour of his character. As they unconsciously took to judging him by a standard different from that which they applied to ordinary Englishmen, they hardly complained of deflections from veracity which would have seemed grave in other persons. He had given notice that he was not like other men, that his words must not be taken in their natural sense, that he was to be regarded as the skilful player of a great game, the consummate actor in a great part. And, once more, he gained by the many years during which he had opportunities of displaying his fortitude, patience, constancy under defeat, unwavering self-confidence — gifts rarer than mere intellectual power, gifts that deserve the influence they bestow. Nothing so fascinates mankind as to see a man equal to every fortune, unshaken by reverses, indifferent to personal abuse, maintaining a long combat against apparently hopeless odds with the sharpest weapons and a smiling face. His followers fancy he must have hidden resources of wisdom as well as of courage. When

F

some of his predictions come true, and the turning tide of popular feeling begins to bear them toward power, they believe that he has been all along right and the rest of the world wrong.   When victory at last settles on his crest, even his enemies can hardly help applauding a reward which seems so amply earned.   It was by this quality, more perhaps than by anything else, by this serene surface with fathomless depths below, that he laid his spell upon the imagination of observers in Continental Europe, and received at his death a sort of canonisation from a large section of the English people.

What will posterity think of him, and by what will he be remembered?   The glamour has already passed away, and to few of those who on the 19th of April deck his statue with flowers is he more than a name.

Parliamentary fame is fleeting: the memory of parliamentary conflicts soon grows dim and dull. Posterity fixes a man's place in history by asking not how many tongues buzzed about him in his lifetime, but how great a factor he was in the changes of the world, that is, how far different things would have been twenty or fifty years after his death if he had never lived.   Tried by this standard, the results upon the course of events of Disraeli's personal action are not numerous, though some of them may be deemed momentous. He was an adroit parliamentary tactician who held his followers together through a difficult time. By helping to keep the Peelites from rejoining their old party, he gave that party a colour different from the sober hues which it had worn during the leadership of Peel. He became the founder of what has in later days been called Tory democracy, winning over a large section of the humbler classes to the banner under which the majority of the wealthy and the holders of vested interests already stood arrayed. He saved for the Turkish Empire a part of its territories, yet in doing so merely prolonged for a little the death agony of Turkish power. Though it cannot be said that he conferred any benefit on India or the Colonies, he certainly stimulated the imperial instincts of Englishmen. He had occasional flashes of insight, as when in 1843 he perceived exactly what Ireland needed, and at least one brilliant flash of foresight when he predicted that a wide extension of the suffrage would bring no evil to the Tory party. Yet in the case of Ireland he did nothing, when the chance came to him, to give effect to the judgment which he had formed, while in the case of the suffrage he did but follow up and carry into effect an impulse given by others. The Franchise Act of 1867 is perhaps the only part of his policy which has, by hastening a change that induced other changes, permanently affected the course of events ; and it remains the chief monument of his parliamentary skill. There was nothing in his career to set the example of a lofty soul or a noble purpose. He did not raise, he may even have lowered, the tone of English public life.

Yet history will not leave him without a meed of admiration. When all possible explanations of his success have been given, what a wonderful career! An adventurer foreign in race, in ideas, in temper, without money or family connections, climbs, by patient and unaided efforts, to lead a great party, master a powerful aristocracy, sway a vast empire, and make himself one of the four or five greatest personal forces in the world. His head is not turned by his elevation. He never becomes a demagogue; he never stoops to beguile the multitude by appealing to sordid instincts. He retains through life a certain amplitude of view, a due sense of the dignity of his position, a due regard for the traditions of the ancient assembly which he leads, and when at last the destinies of England fall into his hands, he feels the grandeur of the charge, and seeks to secure what he believes to be her imperial place in the world. Whatever judgment history may ultimately pass upon him, she will find in the long annals of the English Parliament no more striking figure.

DEAN STANLEY[1]

In the England of his time there was no personality more attractive, nor any more characteristic of the country, than Arthur Penrhyn Stanley, Dean of Westminster. England is the only European country in which such a figure could have appeared, for it is the only country in which a man may hold a high ecclesiastical post and yet be regarded by the nation, not specially as an ecclesiastic, but rather as a distinguished writer, an active and influential man of affairs, an ornament of social life. But if in this respect he was typical of his country, he was in other respects unique. He was a clergyman untouched by clericalism, a courtier unspoiled by courts. No one could point to any one else in England who occupied a similar position, nor has any one since arisen who recalls him, or who fills the place which his departure left empty.

Stanley was born in 1815. His father, then Rector of Alderley, in Cheshire, afterwards Bishop

1 A *Life of Dean Stanley*, in two volumes, begun by Theodore Walrond, continued by Dean Bradley, and completed by Mr. R. E. Prothero, appeared in 1893.

of Norwich, belonged to the family of the Stanleys of Alderley, a branch of that ancient and famous line the head of which is Earl of Derby. His mother, Catherine Leycester, was a woman of much force of character and intellectual power. He was educated at Rugby School under Dr. Arnold, the influence of whose ideas remained great over him all through his life, and at Oxford, where he became a fellow and tutor of University College. Passing thence to be Canon of Canterbury, he returned to the University as Professor of Ecclesiastical History, and remained there for seven years. In 1863 he was appointed Dean of Westminster, and at the same time married Lady Augusta Bruce (sister of the then Lord Elgin, Governor-General first of Canada and afterwards of India). He died in 1881.

He had an extraordinarily active and busy life, so intertwined with the history of the University of Oxford and the history of the Church of England from 1850 to 1880, that one can hardly think of any salient point in either without thinking also of him. Yet it was perhaps rather in the intensity of his nature and the nobility of his sentiments than in either the compass or the strength of his intellectual faculties that the charm and the force he exercised lay. In some directions he was curiously deficient. He had no turn for abstract reasoning, no liking for metaphysics or any other form of speculation. He was equally unfitted for scientific inquiry, and could scarcely work a sum in arithmetic. Indeed, in no field was he a logical or systematic thinker. Neither, although he had a retentive memory, and possessed a great deal of various knowledge on many subjects, could he be called learned, for he had not really mastered any branch of history, and was often inaccurate in details. He had never been trained to observe facts in natural history. He had absolutely no ear for music, and very little perception either of colour or of scent. He learned foreign languages with difficulty and never spoke them well. He was so short-sighted as to be unable to recognise a face passing close in the street. Yet with these shortcomings he was a born traveller, went everywhere, saw everything and everybody worth seeing, always seized on the most characteristic features of a landscape, or building, or a person, and described them with a freshness which made one feel as if they had never been described before. Of the hundreds who have published books on the Desert of Sinai and the Holy Land, many of them skilful writers or men of profound knowledge, he is the only one who is still read and likely to continue to be read, so vivid in colour, so exquisite in feeling, are the pictures he has given. Nature alone, however, nature taken by herself, did not satisfy him, did not, indeed, in his later days (for in his boyhood he had been a passionate lover of the mountains) greatly interest him. A building or a landscape had power to rouse his imagination and call forth his unrivalled powers of description only when it was associated with the thoughts and deeds of men.

The largest part of his literary work was done in the field of ecclesiastical history, a subject naturally congenial to him, and to which he was further drawn by the professorship which he held at Oxford during a time when a great revival of historical studies was in progress. It was work which critics could easily disparage, for there were many small errors scattered through it; and the picturesque method of treatment he employed was apt to pass into scrappiness. He fixed on the points which had a special interest for his own mind as illustrating some trait of personal or national character, or some moral lesson, and passed hastily over other matters of equal or greater importance. Nevertheless his work had some distinctive merits which have not received from professional critics the whole credit they deserved. In all that Stanley wrote one finds a certain largeness and dignity of view. He had a sense of the unity of history, of the constant relation of past and present, of the similarity of human nature in one age and country to human nature in another; and he never failed to dwell upon the permanently valuable truths which history has to teach. Nothing was too small to attract him, because he discovered a meaning in everything, and he was therefore never dull, for even when he moralised he would light up his reflections by some happy anecdote. With this he possessed a keen eye, the eye of a poet, for human character, and a power of sympathy that enabled him to appreciate even those whose principles and policy he disliked. Herein he was not singular, for the sympathetic style of writing history has become fashionable among us. What was remarkable in him was that his sympathy did not betray him into the error, now also fashionable, of extenuating moral distinctions. His charity never blunted the edge of his justice, nor prevented him from reprobating the faults of the personages who had touched his heart. For one sin only he had little historical tolerance — the sin of intolerance. So there was one sin only which ever led him to speak severely of any of his contemporaries — the sin of untruthfulness. Being himself so simple and straightforward as to feel his inability to cope with deceitful men, deceit incensed him. But he did not resent the violence of his adversaries, for though he suffered much at their hands he knew many of them to be earnest, unselfish, and conscientious men.

His pictures of historical scenes are admirable, for with his interest in the study of character there went a large measure of dramatic power. Nothing can be better in its way than the description of the murder of St. Thomas of Canterbury given in the *Memorials of Canterbury*, which, after *Sinai and Palestine* and the *Life of Arnold*, may be deemed the best of Stanley's books. Whether he could, with more leisure for careful thought and study, have become a great historian, was a question which those of us who were dazzled by his Public Lectures at Oxford used often to discuss. The leisure never came, for he was throughout life warmly interested in every current ecclesiastical question, and ready to bear a part in discussing it, either in the press — for he wrote in the *Edinburgh Review*, and often sent letters to the *Times* under the signature of "Anglicanus" — or in Convocation, where he had a seat during the latter part of his career. These interruptions not only checked the progress of his studies, but gave to his compositions an air of haste, which made them seem to want system and finish. The habit of rapid writing for magazines or other ephemeral purposes is alleged to tell injuriously upon literary men: it told the more upon Stanley because he was also compelled to produce sermons rapidly. Now sermon-writing, while it breeds a tendency to the making of rhetorical points, subordinates the habit of dispassionate inquiry to the

enforcement of a moral lesson. Stanley, who
had a touch of the rhetorical temperament, and
was always eager to improve an occasion, certainly
suffered in this way. When he brings out a general
truth he is not content with it as a truth, but
seeks to turn it also to edification, or to make
it illustrate and support some view for which he
is contending at the time. When he is simply
describing, he describes rather as a dramatic artist
working for effect than as a historian solely
anxious to represent men and events as they
were. Yet if we consider how much a historian
gains, not only from an intimate knowledge of
his own time, but also, and even more
largely, from playing an active part in the
events of his own time, from swaying opinion by
his writings and his speeches, from sitting in
assemblies and organising schemes of attack and
defence, we may hesitate to wish that Stanley's
time had been more exclusively given to quiet
investigation. The freshness of his historical
portraits is notably due to the sense he carried
about with him of moving in history and being
a part of it. He never mounted his pulpit
in the Abbey or walked into the Jerusalem
Chamber when Convocation was sitting without
feeling that he was about to do something which
might possibly be recorded in the annals of his
country. I remember his mentioning, to illustrate
undergraduate ignorance, that once when he was

going to give a lecture to his class, he suddenly
recollected that Mr. Goldwin Smith, then Regius
Professor of Modern History, was announced to
deliver a public lecture at the same hour. Telling
the class that they would be better employed in
hearing Mr. Goldwin Smith than himself, he led
them all there. The next time the class met,
one of them, after making some acute comments
on the lecture, asked who the lecturer was. "I
was amazed," said Stanley, "that an intelligent
man should ask such a question, and then it
occurred to me that probably he did not know
who I was either." There was nothing of personal vanity or self-importance in this. All the
men of mark among whom he moved were to him
historical personages, and he would describe to
his friends some doing or saying of a contemporary statesman or ecclesiastic with the same
eagerness, the same sense of its being a fact to
be noted and remembered, as the rest of us feel
about a personal anecdote relating to Oliver
Cromwell or Cardinal Richelieu.

His sermons, like nearly all good sermons, will
be inadequately appreciated by those who now
peruse them, not only because they were composed
for a given audience with special reference to the
circumstances of the time, but also because the
best of them gained so much by his impassioned
delivery. They were all read from manuscript, and
his handwriting was so illegible that it was a marvel

how he contrived to read them. I once asked him, not long after he had been promoted to the Deanery of Westminster, whether he found it easy to make himself heard in the enormous nave of the Abbey church. His frame, it ought to be stated, was spare as well as small, and his voice not powerful. He answered: "That depends on whether I am interested in what I am saying. If the sermon is on something which interests me deeply I can fill the nave; otherwise I cannot." When he had got a worthy theme, or one which stimulated his own emotions, the power of his voice and manner was wonderful. His tiny body seemed to swell, his chest vibrated as he launched forth glowing words. The farewell sermon he delivered when quitting Oxford for Westminster lives in the memory of those who heard it as a performance of extraordinary power, the power springing from the intensity of his own feeling. No sermon has ever since so moved the University.

He was by nature shy and almost timid, and he was not supposed to possess any gift for extempore speaking. But when in his later days he found himself an almost solitary champion in Convocation of the principles of universal toleration and comprehension which he held, he developed a debating power which surprised himself as well as his friends. It was to him a matter of honour and conscience to defend his principles, and to defend them all the more zealously because he stood alone on their behalf in a hostile assembly. His courage was equal to the occasion, and his faculties responded to the call his courage made.

In civil politics he was all his life a Liberal, belonging by birth to the Whig aristocracy, and disposed on most matters to take rather the Whiggish than the Radical view, yet drawn by the warmth of his sympathy towards the working classes, and popular with them. One of his chief pleasures was to lead parties of humble visitors round the Abbey on public holidays. Like most members of the Whig families, he had no great liking for Mr. Gladstone, not so much, perhaps, on political grounds as because he distrusted the High Churchism and anti-Erastianism of the Liberal leader. However, he never took any active part in general politics, reserving his strength for those ecclesiastical questions which seemed to lie within his peculiar province.[1] Here he had two leading ideas: one, that the Church of England must at all hazards continue to be an Established Church, in alliance with, or subjection to, the State (for his Erastianism was unqualified), and recognising the Crown as her head; the other, that she must be a compre-

[1] When J. S. Mill was a candidate for Westminster in 1868, Stanley published a letter announcing his support, partly out of personal respect for Mill, partly because it gave him an opportunity of expressing an opinion on the Irish Church question, and of reprobating the charge of atheism which had been brought against Mill.

hensive Church, finding room in her bosom for every sort or description of Christian, however much or little he believed of the dogmas contained in the Thirty-nine Articles and the Prayer-Book, to which she is bound by statute. The former view cut him off from the Nonconformists and the Radicals; the latter exposed him to the fire not only of those who, like the High Churchmen and the Evangelicals, attach the utmost importance to these dogmas, but of those also among the laity who hold that a man ought under no circumstances to sign any test or use any form of prayer which does not express his own convictions. Stanley would, of course, have greatly preferred that the laws which regulate the Church of England should be so relaxed as to require little or no assent to any doctrinal propositions from her ministers. He strove for this; and he continued to hope that this might be ultimately won. But he conceived that in the meantime it was a less evil that men should be technically bound by subscriptions they objected to than that the National Church should be narrowed by the exclusion of those whose belief fell short of her dogmatic standards. It was remarkable that not only did he maintain this unpopular view of his with unshaken courage on every occasion, pleading the cause of every supposed heretic against hostile majorities with a complete forgetfulness of his own peace and ease, but that no

one ever thought of attributing the course he
took to any selfish or sinister motive. It was
generally believed that his own opinions were
what nine-tenths of the Church of England would
call unorthodox. But the honesty and uprightness of his character were so patent that nobody
supposed that this fact made any difference, or
that it was for the sake of keeping his own place
that he fought the cause of others.

What his theological opinions were it might
have puzzled Stanley himself to explain. His
mind was not fitted to grasp abstract propositions. His historical imagination and his early
associations attached him to the doctrines of the
Nicene Creed; but when he came to talk of
Christianity, he laid so much more stress on
its ethics than on its dogmatic side that his
clerical antagonists thought he held no creed at
all. Dr. Pusey once said that he and Stanley did
not worship the same God. The point of difference
between him and them was not so much that he
consciously disbelieved the dogmas they held —
probably he did not — as that he did not, like them,
think that true religion and final salvation depended
on believing them. And the weak point in his
imagination was that he seemed never to understand their position, nor to realise how sacred and
how momentous to them were statements which
he saw in a purely imaginative light. He never
could be got to see that a Church without any

dogmas would not be a Church at all in the sense either of mankind in the past or of mankind in the present. An anecdote was current that once when he had in Disraeli's presence been descanting on the harm done by the enforcement of dogmatic standards, Disraeli had observed, " But pray remember, Mr. Dean, no dogma, no Dean."

Those who thought him a heathen would have assailed him less bitterly if he had been content to admit his own differences from them. What most incensed them was his habit of assuming that, except in mere forms of expression, there were really no differences at all, and that they also held Christianity to consist not in any body of doctrines, but in reverence for God and purity of life. They would have preferred heathenism itself to this kind of Universalism.

As ecclesiastical preferment had not discoloured the native hue of his simplicity, so neither did the influences of royal favour. It says little for human nature that few people should be proof against what the philosopher deems the trivial and fleeting fascinations of a court. Stanley's elevation of mind was proof. Intensely interested in the knowledge of events passing behind the scenes which his relations with the reigning family opened to him, he scarcely ever referred to those relations, and seemed neither to be affected thereby, nor to care a whit more for the pomps and vanities of power or wealth, a whit less for the friends and the causes he had learned to value in his youth.

In private, that which most struck one in his intellect was the quick eagerness with which his imagination fastened upon any new fact, caught its bearings, and clothed it with colour. His curiosity remained inexhaustible. His delight in visiting a new country was like that of an American scholar landing for the first time in Europe. A friend met him a year before his death at a hotel in the north of England, and found he was going to the Isle of Man. He had mastered its geography and history, and talked about it and what he was to explore there as one might talk of Rome or Athens when visiting them for the first time. When anybody told him an anecdote his susceptible imagination seized upon points which the narrator had scarcely noticed, and discovered a whole group of curious analogies from other times or countries. Whatever you planted in this fertile soil struck root and sprouted at once. Morally, he impressed those who knew him not only by his kindness of heart, but by a remarkable purity and nobleness of aim. Nothing mean or small or selfish seemed to harbour in his mind. You might think him right or wrong, but you never doubted that he was striving after the truth. He was not merely a just man; he loved justice with passion. It was partly, perhaps, because justice, goodness, honour, charity, seemed to him of such paramount importance in life that he made little of doctrinal differences, having perceived that these virtues may exist, and may also be found wanting, in every form of religious creed or philosophical profession. When the Convocation of the Anglican Church met at Westminster, it was during many years his habit to invite a great number of its leading members to the deanery, the very men who had been attacking him most hotly in debate, and who would go on denouncing his latitudinarianism till Convocation met again. They yielded — sometimes reluctantly, but still they yielded — to the kindliness of his nature and the charm of his manner. He used to dart about among them, introducing opponents to one another, as indeed on all occasions he delighted to bring the most diverse people together, so that some one said the company you met at the deanery were either statesmen and duchesses or starving curates and briefless barristers.

He had on the whole a happy life. It is true that the intensity of his attachments exposed him to correspondingly intense grief when he lost those who were dearest to him; true also that, being by temperament a man of peace, he was during the latter half of his life almost constantly at war. But his home, first in the lifetime of his mother and then in that of his wife, had

a serene and unclouded brightness; and the care
of the Abbey, rich with the associations of nearly
a thousand years of history, provided a function
which exactly suited him and which constituted
a never failing source of enjoyment.   To dwell in
the centre of the life of the Church of England,
and to dwell close to the Houses of Parliament,
in the midst of the making of history, knowing
and seeing those who were principally concerned
in making it, was in itself a pleasure to his
quenchless historical curiosity.   His cheerfulness
and animation, although to some extent revived
by his visit to America and the reception he met
with there, were never the same after his wife's
death in 1876.   But the sweetness of his disposition and his affection for his friends knew no
diminution.   He remembered everything that
concerned them; was always ready with sympathy in sorrow or joy; and gave to all alike,
high or low, famous or unknown, the same impression, that his friendship was for themselves,
and not for any gifts or rank or other worldly
advantage they might enjoy.   The art of friendship is the greatest art in life.   To enjoy his
was to be educated in that art.

THOMAS HILL GREEN

THE name of Thomas Green, Professor of Moral Philosophy in the University of Oxford, was not, during his lifetime, widely known outside the University itself. But he is still remembered by students of metaphysics and ethics as one of the most vigorous thinkers of his time; and his personality was a striking one, which made a deep and lasting impression on those with whom he came in contact.

He was born in Yorkshire in 1836, the son of a country clergyman; was educated at Rugby School and at Balliol College, Oxford, of which he became a fellow in 1860, and a tutor in 1869. In 1867 he was an unsuccessful candidate for a chair of philosophy at St. Andrews, and in 1878 was elected Professor of Moral Philosophy in his own University, which he never thereafter quitted. He was married in 1869 and died in 1882. It was a life externally uneventful, but full of thought and work, and latterly crowned by great influence over the younger and great respect from the senior members of the University.

I can best describe Green as he was in his

undergraduate days, for it was then that I saw most of him.   His appearance was striking, and made him a familiar figure even to those who did not know him personally.   Thick black hair, a sallow complexion, dark eyebrows, deep-set eyes of rich brown with a peculiarly steadfast look, were the features which first struck one; and with these there was a remarkable seriousness of expression, an air of solidity and quiet strength.   He knew comparatively few people, and of these only a very few intimately, having no taste or turn for those sports in which university acquaintances are most frequently made, and seldom appearing at breakfast or wine parties.   This caused him to pass for harsh or unsocial; and I remember having felt a slight sense of alarm the first time I found myself seated beside him.   Though we belonged to different colleges I had heard a great deal about him, for Oxford undergraduates are warmly interested in one another, and at the time I am recalling they had an inordinate fondness for measuring the intellectual gifts and conjecturing the future of those among their comtemporaries who seemed likely to attain eminence.

Those who came to know Green intimately, soon perceived that under his reserve there lay not only a capacity for affection — no man was more tenacious in his friendships — but qualities that made him an attractive companion. His tendency to solitude sprang less from pride or coldness, than from the occupation of his mind by subjects which seldom weigh on men of his age. He had, even when a boy at school (where he lived much by himself, but exercised considerable moral influence), been grappling with the problems of metaphysics and theology, and they had given a tinge of gravity to his manner. The relief to that gravity lay in his humour, which was not only abundant but genial and sympathetic. It used to remind us of Carlyle — he had both the sense of humour and an underlying Puritanism in common with Carlyle, one of the authors who (with Milton and Wordsworth) had most influenced him — but in Green the Puritan tinge was more kindly, and, above all, more lenient to ordinary people. While averse, perhaps too severely averse, to whatever was luxurious or frivolous in undergraduate life, he had the warmest interest in, and the strongest sympathy for, the humbler classes. Loving social equality, and filled with a sense of the dignity of simple human nature, he liked to meet farmers and tradespeople on their own level, and knew how to do so without seeming to condescend; indeed nothing pleased him better than when they addressed him as one of themselves, the manner of his talk to them, as well as the extreme plainness of his dress, conducing to such mistakes. The belief in the duty of approaching

the people directly and getting them to think and
to form and express their own views in their own
way was at the root of all his political doctrines.

Though apt to be silent in general company, no one could be more agreeable when
you were alone with him. We used to say
of him — and his seniors said the same — that
one never talked to him without carrying
away something to ponder over. On everything he said or wrote there was stamped the
impress of a strong individuality, a mind that
thought for itself, a character ruggedly original,
wherein grimness was mingled with humour, and
practical shrewdness with a love for abstract
speculation. His independence appeared even in
the way he pursued his studies. With abilities of
the highest order, he cared comparatively little
for the distinctions which the University offers;
choosing rather to follow out his own line of
reading in the way he judged permanently useful
than to devote himself to the pursuit of honours
and prizes.

He was constitutionally lethargic, found it hard
to rouse himself to exertion, and was apt to let
himself be driven to the last moment in finishing
a piece of work. There was a rule in his College
that an essay should be given in every Friday
evening. His was, to the great annoyance of
the dons, never ready till Saturday. But when
it did go in, it was the weightiest and most

thoughtful, as well as the most eloquent, that the College produced. This indolence had one good result. It disposed him to brood over subjects, while others were running quickly through many books and getting up subjects for examination. It contributed to that depth and systematic quality which struck us in his thinking, and made him seem mature beside even the ablest of his contemporaries. When others were being, so to speak, blown hither and thither, picking up and fascinated by new ideas, which they did not know how to fit in with their old ones, he seemed to have already formed for himself, at least in outline, a scheme of philosophy and life coherent and complete. There was nothing random or scattered in his ideas; his mind, like his style of writing, which ran into long and complicated sentences, had a singular connectedness. You felt that all its principles were in relation with one another. This maturity in his mental attitude gave him an air of superiority, just as the strength of his convictions gave a dogmatic quality to his deliverances. Yet in spite of positiveness and tenacity he had the saving grace of a humility which distrusted human nature in himself at least as much as he distrusted it in others. Leading an introspective life, he had many "wrestlings," and often seemed conscious of the struggle between the natural man and the spiritual man, as described in the Epistle to the Romans.

In these early days, before, and to a less extent after, taking his degree, he used to speak a good deal, mostly on political topics, at the University Debating Society, where so many generations of young men have sharpened their wits upon one another. His speaking was vigorous, shrewd, and full of matter, yet it could not be called popular. It was, in a certain sense, too good for a debating society, too serious, and without the dash and sparkle which tell upon audiences of that kind. Sometimes, however, and notably in a debate on the American War of Secession in 1863, he produced, by the concentrated energy of his language and the fierce conviction with which he spoke, a powerful effect.[1]   In a business assembly, discussing practical questions, he would soon have become prominent, and would have been capable on occasions of an oratorical success.

Retired as was Green's life, he became by degrees more and more widely known beyond the

---

[1] As I have referred to the American Civil War, it is worth adding that there were no places in England where the varying fortunes of that tremendous struggle were followed with a more intense interest than in Oxford and Cambridge, and none in which so large a proportion of the educated class sympathised with the cause of the North. Mr. Goldwin Smith led the section which took that view, and which included three-fourths of the best talent in Oxford. Among the younger men Green was the most conspicuous for his ardour on behalf of the principles of human equality and freedom. He followed and watched every move in the military game. No Massachusetts Abolitionist welcomed the fall of Vicksburg with a keener joy. He used to say that the whole future of humanity was involved in the triumph of the Federal arms.

circle of his own intimates; and became also, I think, more willing to make new friends. His truthfulness appeared in this that, though powerful in argument, he did not argue for victory. When he felt the force of what was urged against him, his admissions were candid. Thus people came to respect his character, with its high sense of duty, its simplicity, its uprightness, its earnest devotion to an ideal, even more than they admired his intellectual powers. I remember one friend of my own, himself eminent in undergraduate Oxford, and belonging to another college, between which and Green's there existed much rivalry, who, having been defeated by Green in competition for a University prize, said, "If it had been any one else, I should have been vexed, but I don't mind being beaten by a man I respect so much." My friend knew Green very slightly, and had been at one time strongly prejudiced against him by rumours of his heterodox opinions.

So much for those undergraduate days on which recollection loves to dwell, but which were not days of unmixed happiness to Green, for his means were narrow and the future rose cloudy before him. When anxiety was removed by the income which a fellowship secured, he still hesitated as to his course in life. At one time he thought of journalism, or of seeking a post in the Education Office. More frequently his thoughts turned to the clerical profession. His theological

opinions would not have permitted him to enter
the service of the Church of England, but he
did seriously consider whether he should become
a Unitarian minister. It was not till he found
that his college needed him as a teacher that
these difficulties came to an end. Similarly he
had doubted whether to devote himself to history,
to theology, or to metaphysics. For history
he had unquestionable gifts. With no exceptional capacity for mastering or retaining facts,
he had a remarkable power of penetrating at once
to the dominant facts, of grasping their connection,
and working out their consequences.   He had also
a keen sense of the dramatic aspect of events, and
a turn, not unlike Carlyle's, partly perhaps formed
on Carlyle, of fastening on the details in which
character shows itself, and illumining narrative by
personal touches.   On the problems of theology
he had meditated even at school, and after taking
his degree he set himself to a systematic study of
the German critics, and I remember that when
we were living together at Heidelberg he had
begun to prepare a translation of C. F. Baur's
principal treatise.   As he worked slowly, the translation was never finished. Though not professing to be an adherent of the Tübingen school,
he had been fascinated by Baur's ingenuity and
constructive power.

Ultimately he settled down to metaphysical
and ethical inquiries, and devoted to these the

last thirteen years of his life. During his undergraduate years the two intellectual forces most
powerful at Oxford had been the writings of
J. H. Newman in the religious sphere, though
their influence was already past its meridian, and
the writings of John Stuart Mill in the sphere
of logic and philosophy. By neither of these,
save in the way of antagonism, had Green been
influenced. He heartily hated all the Utilitarian
school, and had an especial scorn for Buckle, who,
now almost forgotten, enjoyed in those days, as
being supposed to be a philosophic historian, a
brief term of popularity. Green had been led
by Carlyle to the Germans, and his philosophic
thinking was determined chiefly by Kant and
Hegel, more perhaps by the former than by the
latter, for it was always upon ethical rather than
upon purely metaphysical problems that his mind
was bent. His religious vein and his hold upon
practical life made him more interested in morals
than in abstract speculation. Thus he became
the leader in Oxford of a new philosophic school
which looked to Kant as its master, and which
for a time, partly perhaps because it effectively attacked the school of Mill, received the adhesion of
some among the most thoughtful of the younger
High Churchmen. Like Kant, he set himself to
answer David Hume, and the essay prefixed to
his edition of Hume's *Treatise on Human Nature*,
along with his *Prolegomena to Ethics*, are the only

books in which his doctrines have been given to the world, for he did not live to write the more systematic exposition he had planned. These two essays are hard reading, for his philosophical style was usually technical, and sometimes verged on obscurity. But when he wrote on less abstruse matters he was intelligible as well as weighty, full of thought, and with an occasional underglow of restrained eloquence. The force of character and convictions makes itself felt through the language.

His mind, though constructive, was not, having regard to its general power, either fertile or versatile. Like most of those who prefer solitary musings to the commerce of men, he had little facility, and found it hard to express his thoughts in any other words than those into which his musings had first flowed. Thus even his oral teaching was not easy to follow. An anecdote was current how when one day he had been explaining to a small class his theory of the origin of our ideas, the class listened in wrapt attention to his forcible rhetoric, admiring each sentence as it fell, and thinking that all their difficulties were being removed. When he ended they expressed their gratitude for the pleasure he had given them, and were quitting the room, when one, halting at the door, said timidly, " But, Mr. Green, what did you say was really the origin of our ideas ? " However, whether

they were or were not capable of assimilating
his doctrines, his pupils all joined in their respect
for him.   They felt the loftiness of his character,
they recognised the fervour of his belief.   He
was the most powerful ethical influence, and
perhaps also the most stimulative intellectual
influence, that in those years played upon the
minds of the ablest youth of the University.
But it was a singular fact, which those who
have never lived in Oxford or Cambridge may
find it hard to understand, that when he rose
from the post of a college tutor to that of a
University professor, his influence declined, not
that his powers or his earnestness waned, but
because as a professor he had fewer auditors
and less personal relation with them than he
had commanded as a college teacher.   Such is
the working of the collegiate system in Oxford,
curiously unfortunate when it deprives the ablest
men, as they rise naturally to the highest positions, of the opportunities for usefulness they had
previously enjoyed.

As his powers developed and came to be
recognised, so did those slight asperities which
had been observed in undergraduate days soften
down and disappear.   Though he lived a retired
life, his work brought him into contact with
a good many people, and he became more
genial in general company.   I remember his
saying with a smile when I had lured him into

Wales for a short excursion, "I don't know whether it is a sign of declining virtue, but I find as I grow older that I am less and less fond of my own company." From the first he had won the confidence and affection of his pupils. Many of them used long afterwards to say that his conduct and his teaching had been the one great example or one great influence they had found and felt in Oxford. The unclouded happiness of his married life made it easier for him to see the bright side of things, and he could not but enjoy the sense that the seed he sowed was falling on ground fit to receive it. Even when ill-health had fastened on him, and was checking both his studies and his public work, it did not affect the evenness of his temper nor sharpen the edge of his judgments of others. In earlier days these had been sometimes austere, though expressed in temperate and measured terms.

I must not forget to add that although Green's opinions were by no means orthodox, the influence he exerted while he remained a college tutor was in large measure a religious influence. As the clergyman used to be in the English Universities less of a clergyman than he was anywhere else, so conversely it caused no surprise there that a lay teacher should concern himself with the religious life of his pupils. Green, however, did more, for he on two occasions at least delivered to his pupils, before the celebration of the communion in the college chapel, addresses which were afterwards privately printed, and which present his view of the relations of ethics and religion in a way impressive even to those who may find it hard to follow the philosophical argument.

Metaphysicians are generally as little interested in practical politics as poets are, and not better suited for political life. Green was a remarkable exception. Politics were in a certain sense the strongest of his interests. To him metaphysics were not only the basis of theology, but also the basis of politics. Everything was to converge on the free life of the individual in a free State; rational faith and reason inspired by emotion were to have their perfect work in making the good citizen.

His interest in politics was perhaps less active in later years than it had been in his youth, but his principles stood unchanged. He was a thoroughgoing Liberal, or what used to be called a Radical, full of faith in the people, an advocate of pretty nearly every measure that tended to democratise English institutions, a friend of peace and of non-intervention. In our days he would have been called a Little Englander, for though his ideal of national life was lofty, the wellbeing of the masses was to him a more essential part of that ideal than any extension of territory or power. He once said that he would rather see the flag of England

H

trailed in the dirt than add sixpence to the taxes that weigh upon the poor. In foreign politics Louis Napoleon, as the corrupter of France and the disturber of Europe, was his favourite aversion; in home politics, Lord Palmerston, as the chief obstacle to parliamentary reform. The statesman whom he most admired and trusted was Mr. Bright. A strong sense of civic duty led him to enter the City Council of Oxford, although he could ill spare from his study and his lecture-room the time which the discharge of municipal duties required. He was the first tutor who had ever offered himself to a ward for election. The townsfolk, between whom and the University there had generally been little love, the former thinking themselves looked down upon by the latter, warmly appreciated his action in coming out of his seclusion to help them, and his influence in the Council contributed to secure some useful reforms — among others, the establishment of a "grammar" or secondary school for the city.

One of the last things he wrote was a short pamphlet on freedom of contract, intended to justify the interference with bargains between landlord and tenant which was proposed by Mr. Gladstone's Irish Land Bill of 1881. It is a vigorous piece of reasoning, which may still be read with interest in respect of its application of philosophical principles to a political controversy. Had he desired it he might have gone

to the House of Commons as member for the city
of Oxford. But he had found in the Council a
field for local public work, and apart from his
constitutional indolence and his declining health,
he had concluded that his first duty lay in ex-
pounding his philosophical system.

Green will be long remembered in the English
Universities as the strongest force in the sphere
of ethical philosophy that they have seen in the
second half of the nineteenth century, and remembered also as a singular instance of a meta-
physician with a bent towards politics and practical
life, no less than as a thinker far removed from
orthodoxy who exerted over orthodox Christians
a potent and inspiring religious influence.

ARCHBISHOP TAIT[1]

ENGLAND is now the only Protestant country in which bishops retain some relics of the dignity and influence which belonged to the episcopal office during the Middle Ages. Even in Roman Catholic countries they have been sadly shorn of their ancient importance, though the prelates of Hungary still hold vast possessions, while in France, or Spain, or the Catholic parts of Germany a man of eminent talents and energy may occasionally use his official position to become, through his influence over Catholic electors or Catholic deputies, a considerable political factor. This happens even in the United States and Canada, though in the United States the general feeling that religion must be kept out of politics obliges ecclesiastics to use their spiritual powers cautiously and sparingly. England stands alone in the fact that although the Protestant Episcopal Church is, in so far as she is established by law, the creature and subject of the State, she is nevertheless so far independent as a

---

[1] An admirable life of Archbishop Tait by his son-in-law, Dr. R. T. Davidson (now Archbishop of Canterbury), and Canon Benham appeared in 1891.

religious organisation that she retains a greater power than in other Protestant nations. State establishment, though it may have depressed, has not stifled her ecclesiastical life, and a larger proportion of her laity show an interest in ecclesiastical questions than one finds shown in Germany or the Scandinavian kingdoms. A man of shining parts has, as an English bishop, a wide field of action and influence open to him outside the sphere of theology or of purely official duty. And the opportunities of the position attain their maximum when he reaches the primatial chair of Canterbury, which is now the oldest and the most dignified of all the metropolitan sees in countries that have accepted the Reformation of the sixteenth century.

Ever since there was a bishop at Canterbury at all, that is to say, ever since the conversion of the English began in the seventh century of our era, the holder of that see has been the greatest ecclesiastical personage in these islands, with a recognised authority over all England, as well as an influence and dignity to which, in the Middle Ages, the Archbishops of Armagh and St. Andrews (primates of the Irish and Scottish Churches) practically bowed, even while refusing to admit his legal supremacy. To be the most highly placed and officially the most powerful man in the churches of Britain, in days when the Church was better organised, and in some ways stronger, than the State, meant a vast deal. The successor of Augustine was often called a Pope of his own world — that world of Britain which lay apart from the larger world of the European continent. Down till the Reformation, the English primates possessed a power which made some of them almost a match for the English kings. Dunstan, Lanfranc, Anselm, Thomas (Becket), Hubert, Stephen Langton, Arundel, Warham, were among the foremost statesmen of their time. After Henry VIII.'s breach with Rome, the Primate of England received some access of dignity in becoming independent of the Pope; but, in reality, the loss of church power and church wealth which the Reformation caused lowered his political importance. In the sixteenth and seventeenth centuries, however, there were still some conspicuous and influential prelates at Canterbury — Cranmer, Pole, Whitgift, and Laud the best remembered among them. After the Revolution of 1688, a time of smaller men begins. The office retained its dignity as the highest place open to a subject, ranking above the Lord Chancellor or the Lord President of the Council, but the Church of England, having no fightings within, nor anything to fear from without, was lapped in placid ease, so it mattered comparatively little who her chief pastor was.

Bishoprics were in those days regarded chiefly

as pieces of rich preferment with which prime
ministers bought the support of powerful adherents. But since the middle of the nineteenth
century, as the Anglican Church has become at
once more threatened and more energetic, as
more of the life of the nation has flowed into
her and round her, the office of a bishop
has risen in importance. People show more
interest in the appointments to be made, and
ministers have become proportionately careful
in making them. Bishops work harder and are
more in the public eye now than they were
eighty, or even fifty, years ago. They have
lost something of the antique dignity and social
consideration which they enjoyed. They no
longer wear wigs or ride in State coaches. They
may be seen in third-class railway carriages,
or sitting on the tops of omnibuses. But they
have gained by having countless opportunities
opened up to them for exerting influence in
philanthropic as well as in religious movements;
and the more zealous among them turn these
opportunities to excellent account.

Whatever is true of an ordinary bishop is true
a fortiori of the Archbishop of Canterbury. He
is still a great personage, but he is great in a new
way, with less of wealth and power but larger
opportunities of influence. He is also a kind
of Pope in a new way, because he is the central figure of the Anglican communion over the

whole world, with no legal jurisdiction outside England (except in India), but far over-topping all the prelates of that communion in the United States or the British Colonies.   Less deference is paid to the office, considered simply as an office, than it received in the Middle Ages, because society and thought have been tinged by the spirit of democratic equality, and people realise that offices are only artificial creations, whose occupants are human beings like themselves.   But if he is himself a man of ability and force, he may make his headship of an ancient and venerated church a vantage ground whence to address the nation as well as the members of his own com-munion.   He is sure of being listened to, which is of itself no small matter in a country where many voices are striving to make themselves heard at the same time.   The world takes his words into consideration; the newspapers repeat them.   His position gives him easy access to the ministers of the Crown, and implies a confidential intercourse with the Crown itself.   He is, or can be, "in touch" with all the political figures who can in any way influence the march of events, and is able to enforce his views upon them.   All his conduct is watched by the nation; so that if it is discreet, provident, animated by high and consistent principle, he gets full credit for whatever he does well, and acquires that in-fluence to which masses of men are eager to

bow whenever they can persuade themselves
that it is deserved. During the first half of
the nineteenth century the English people was
becoming more interested in ecclesiastical and in
theological matters than it had been during the
century preceding. It grew by slow degrees
more inclined to observe ecclesiastical persons,
to read and think about theological subjects, to
reflect upon the relations which the Church
ought to bear to civil life and moral progress.
Thus a leader of the Church of England became
relatively a more important factor than he had
been a century ago, and an archbishop, strong
by his character, rectitude, and powers of utterance, rose to occupy a more influential, if not more
conspicuous, position than his predecessors in the
days of the Georges had done.

These changes naturally made the selection
of an archbishop a more delicate and trouble-
some business than it was in those good old
days. Nobody then blamed a Prime Minister for
preferring an aspirant who had the support of
powerful political connections. Blameless in life
he must be: even the eighteenth century demanded that from candidates for English, if
not, according to Dean Swift, for Irish sees.
If he was also a man of courtly grace and
dignity, and a finished scholar, so much the
better. If he was a man of piety, that also was
well. By the time of Queen Victoria the pos-

session of piety and of gifts of speech had become more important qualifications, but the main thing was tactful moderation.   Even in apostolic days it was required that a bishop should rule his own house well, and the Popes esteemed most saintly have not always been the best, as the famous case of Celestine the Fifth attests.   An archbishop must first and foremost be a discreet and guarded man, expressing few opinions, and those not extreme ones.   His chief virtue came to be, if not the purely negative one of offending no section by expressing the distinctive views of any other, yet that of swerving so little from the *via media* between Rome and Geneva that neither the Tractarian party, who began to be feared after 1837, nor the pronounced Low Churchmen could claim the Primate as disposed to favour their opinions. In the case of ordinary bishops the plan could be adopted, and has since the days of Lord Palmerston been mostly followed, of giving every party its turn, while choosing from every party men of the safer sort.   This method, however, was less applicable to the See of Canterbury, for a man on whose action much might turn could not well be taken from any particular section. The acts and words of a Primate, who is expected to "give a line" to the clergy generally and to speak on behalf of the bench of bishops as a whole, are so closely scrutinised that he must be prudent and wary, yet not so wary as to seem

timid. He ought to be both firm and suave,
conciliatory and decided. That he may do
justice to all sections of the Church of England, he ought not to be an avowed partisan
of any. Yet he must be able and eminent, and
of course able and eminent men are apt to throw
themselves into some one line of action or set of
views, and so come to be considered partisans.
The position which the Archbishop of Canterbury holds as the representative in Parliament
of the whole Established Church, makes statesmanship the most important of all qualifications. Learning, energy, eloquence, piety, would
none of them, nor all of them together, make
up for the want of calmness and wisdom. Yet
all those qualities are obviously desirable, because
they strengthen as well as adorn the Primate's
position.

Archibald Campbell Tait (born in Scotland in
1811, died 1882) was educated at Glasgow University and at Balliol College, Oxford; worked at
his college for some years as a tutor, succeeded
Dr. Arnold as head-master of Rugby School in
1843, became Dean of Carlisle and then Bishop
of London, and was translated to Canterbury
in 1868. It has been generally understood that
Mr. Disraeli, then Prime Minister, suggested
another prelate for the post, but the Queen,
who did not share her minister's estimate of
that prelate, expressed a preference for Tait,

Her choice was amply justified, for Tait united, and indeed possessed in a high degree, the qualifications which have just been enumerated. He was, if it be not a paradox to say so, more remarkable as an archbishop than as a man. He had no original power as a thinker. He was not a striking preacher, and the more pains he took with his sermons the less interesting did they become. He was so far from being learned that you could say no more of him than that he was a sound scholar and a well-informed man. He was deeply and earnestly pious, but in a quiet, almost dry way, which lacked what is called unction, though it impressed those who were in close contact with him. He showed slight interest either in the historical or in the speculative side of theology. Though a good headmaster, he was not a stimulating teacher. Had he remained all his life in a subordinate position, as a college tutor at Oxford, or as canon of some cathedral, he would have discharged the duties of the position in a thoroughly satisfactory way, and would have acquired influence among his colleagues, but no one would have felt that Fate had dealt unfairly with him in depriving him of some larger career and loftier post. No one, indeed, who knew him when he was a college tutor seems to have predicted the dignities he was destined to attain, although he had shown in the theological strife that then

raged at Oxford the courage and independence
of his character.

In what, then, did the secret of his success
lie — the secret, that is, of his acquitting himself so excellently in those dignities as to have
become almost a model to his own and the next
generation of what an Archbishop of Canterbury
ought to be? In the statesmanlike quality of
his mind. He had not merely moderation, but
what, though often confounded with moderation, is something rarer and better, a steady
balance of mind. He was carried about by
no winds of doctrine. He seldom yielded to
impulses, and was never so seduced by any one
theory as to lose sight of other views and conditions which had to be regarded. He was, I think,
the first man of Scottish birth who ever rose to
be Primate of England, and he had the cautious
self-restraint which is deemed characteristic of his
nation. He knew how to be dignified without
assumption, firm without vehemence, prudent
without timidity, judicious without coldness.
He was, above all things, a singularly just
man, who recognised every one's rights, and
did not seek to overbear them by an exercise
of authority. He was as ready to listen to his
opponents as to his friends. Indeed, he so held
himself as to appear to have no opponents, but
to be rather a judge before whom different
advocates were stating their respective cases,

than a leader seeking to make his own views or his own party prevail. Genial he could hardly be called, for there was little warmth, little display of emotion, in his manner; and the clergy noted, at least in his earlier episcopal days, a touch of the head-master in his way of receiving them. But he was simple and kindly, capable of seeing the humorous side of things, desiring to believe the good rather than the evil, and to lead people instead of driving them. With all his caution he was direct and straightforward, saying no more than was necessary, but saying nothing he had occasion to be ashamed of. He sometimes made mistakes, but they were not mistakes of the heart, and, being free from vanity or self-conceit, he was willing in his quiet way to admit them and to alter his course accordingly. So his character by degrees gained upon the nation, and so even ecclesiastical partisanship, proverbially more bitter than political, because it springs from deeper wells of feeling, grew to respect and spare him. The influence he obtained went far to strengthen the position of the Established Church, and to keep its several parties from breaking out into more open hostility with one another. He himself inclined to what might be called a moderate Broad Church attitude, leaning more to Evangelical than to Tractarian or Romanising views in matters of doctrine. At one time the extreme

High Churchmen regarded him as an enemy. But this unfriendliness had almost died away when the death of his wife and his only son (a young man of singularly winning character), followed by his own long illness, stilled the voices of criticism.

He exerted great influence in the House of Lords by his tact, by his firmness of character, and by the consistency of his public course, as well as by powers of speech, which, matured by long practice, had risen to a high level. Without eloquence, without either imagination or passion, which are the chief elements in eloquence, he had a grave, weighty, thoughtful style which impressed that fastidious audience. His voice was strong and sonorous, his diction plain yet pure and dignified, his matter well considered. His thought moved on a high plane; he spoke as one who fully believed every word he said. The late Bishop of Winchester, the famous Dr. Samuel Wilberforce, was incomparably his superior not only as a talker but as an orator, but no less inferior in his power over the House of Lords, for so little does rhetorical brilliance count in a critical and practical assembly. Next to courage, the quality which gains trust and regard in a deliberative body is that which is familiarly described when it is said of a man, " You always know where to find him." Tait belonged to no

party.   But his principles, though not rigid, were
fixed and settled; his words and votes were the
expression of his principles.

The presence of bishops in the House of
Lords is disapproved by some sections of English
opinion, and there are those among the temporal
peers who, quite apart from any political feeling,
are said to regard them with little favour.   But
every one must admit that they have raised
and adorned the debates in that chamber.
Besides Tait and Wilberforce, two other prelates
of the same generation stood in the front
rank of speakers, Dr. Magee, whose wit and
fire would have found a more fitting theatre
in the House of Commons, and Dr. Thirlwall,
a scholar and historian whose massive intellect
and stately diction were too rarely used to raise
great political issues above the dust-storms of
party controversy.

Perhaps no archbishop since the Revolution
of 1688 has exercised so much influence as Dr.
Tait, and certainly none within living memory
is so well entitled to be credited with a definite
ecclesiastical policy.   His aim was to widen the
bounds of the Church of England, so far as the law
could, without evasion, be stretched for that purpose.   He bore a leading part in obtaining an Act of
Parliament which introduced a new and less strict
form of clerical subscription.   He realised that
the Church of England can maintain her position

as a State Church only by adapting herself to
the movements of opinion, and accordingly he
voted for the Divorce Bill of 1859, and for the
Burials Bill, which relieved Dissenters from a
grievance that exposed the Established Church
to odium. The Irish Church Disestablishment
Bill of 1869 threw upon him, at the critical
moment when it went from the House of
Commons, where it had passed by a large
majority, to the House of Lords, where a still
larger majority was hostile, a duty delicate in
itself, and such as seldom falls to the lot of a
prelate. The Queen wrote to him suggesting
that he should endeavour to effect a compromise between Mr. Gladstone, then head of the
Liberal Ministry, and the leading Tory peers
who were opposing the Bill. He conducted the
negotiation with tact and judgment, and succeeded
in securing good pecuniary terms for the Protestant Episcopal Establishment. Though he
had joined in the Letter of the Bishops which
conveyed their strong disapproval of the book
called *Essays and Reviews* (whose supposed
heretical tendencies roused such a storm in
1861), and had thereby displeased his friends,
Temple (afterwards archbishop), Jowett, and
Stanley,[1] he joined in the judgment of the Privy
Council which in 1863 dismissed the charges

---

[1] They thought his public action scarcely consistent with the language
he had used to Temple in private.

I

against the impugned Essayists. Despite his
advocacy of the Bill which in 1874 provided a
new procedure to be used against clergymen
transgressing the ritual prescribed by law, he
discouraged prosecutions, and did his utmost
to keep Ritualists as well as moderate Ration-
alists within the pale of the Church of England.
He did not succeed — no one could have succeeded, even though he had spoken with the
tongues of men and of angels — in stilling ecclesiastical strife.   The controversies of his days still
rage, though in a slightly different form.   But
in refusing to yield to the pressure of any section,
in regarding the opinion of the laity rather than
that of the clergy, in keeping close to the law yet
giving it the widest possible interpretation, he
laid down the lines on which the Anglican
Established Church can best be defended and
upheld.   That she will last, as an Establishment, for any very long time, will hardly be
expected by those who mark the direction in
which thought tends to move all over the civil-
ised world.   But Tait's policy and personality
have counted for something in prolonging the
time-honoured connection of the Anglican Church
with the English State.

Perhaps a doubtful service either to the Church
or to the State. Yet even those who regret
the connection, and who, surveying the long
course of Christian history from the days of the

Emperor Constantine down to our own, believe that the Christian Church would have been spiritually purer and morally more effective had she never become either the mistress or the servant or the ally of the State, but relied on her divine commission only, may wish that, when the day arrives for the ancient bond to be unloosed, it should be unloosed not through an embittered political struggle, but because the general sentiment of the nation, and primarily of religious men throughout the nation, has come to approve the change.

ANTHONY TROLLOPE[1]

When Mr. Anthony Trollope died (December 11, 1882) at the age of sixty-seven, he was the best known of our English writers of fiction and stood foremost among them if the double test of real merit and wide popularity be applied. Some writers, such as Wilkie Collins, may have commanded a larger sale. One writer at least, Mr. George Meredith, had produced work of far deeper insight and higher imaginative power. But the gifts of Mr. Meredith had then scarcely begun to win recognition, and not one reader knew his name for five who knew Trollope's. So Mr. Thomas Hardy had published what many continue to think his two best stories, but they had not yet caught the eye of the general public. Mrs. Oliphant, high as was the general level of her work, and inexhaustible as her fertility appeared, had not cut her name so deep upon the time as Trollope did. Everything she did was good, nothing superlatively good. No one placed

---

[1] Trollope's autobiography, published in 1883, is a good specimen of self-portraiture, candid, straightforward, and healthy, and leaves an agreeable impression of the writer. Dr. Richard Garnett has written well of him in the *Dictionary of National Biography*.

Trollope in the first rank of creative novelists beside Dickens or Thackeray, or beside George Eliot, who had died two years before. But in the second rank he stood high; and though other novelists may have had as many readers as he, none was in so many ways representative of the general character and spirit of English fiction. He had established his reputation nearly thirty years before, when Thackeray and Dickens were still in the fulness of their fame; and had maintained it during the zenith of George Eliot's. For more than a generation his readers had come from the best-educated classes as well as from those who lack patience or taste for anything heavier than a story of adventure. In this respect he stood above Miss Braddon, Mrs. Henry Wood, Ouida, and other heroines of the circulating libraries, and also above such more artistic or less sensational writers as William Black, Walter Besant, James Payn, and Whyte Melville. (The school of so-called realistic fiction had scarcely begun to appear.) None of these had, like Trollope, succeeded in making their creations a part of the common thought of cultivated Englishmen; none had, like him, given us characters which we treat as typical men and women, and discuss at a dinner-table as though they were real people. Mrs. Proudie, for instance, the Bishop of Barchester's wife, to take the most obvious instance (though not that most favourable to Trollope, for he produced better portraits than hers), or Archdeacon Grantly, was when Trollope died as familiar a name to English men and women between sixty and thirty years of age as Wilkins Micawber or Blanche Amory, or Rosamond Lydgate.   There was no other living novelist of whose personages the same could be said, and perhaps none since has attained this particular kind of success.

Personally, Anthony Trollope was a bluff, genial, hearty, vigorous man, typically English in his face, his talk, his ideas, his tastes.   His large eyes, which looked larger behind his large spectacles, were full of good-humoured life and force; and though he was neither witty nor brilliant in conversation, he was what is called very good company, having travelled widely, known all sorts of people, and formed views, usually positive views, on all the subjects of the day, views which he was prompt to declare and maintain.   There was not much novelty in them — you were disappointed not to find so clever a writer more original — but they were worth listening to for their solid common-sense, tending rather to commonplace sense, and you enjoyed the ardour with which he threw himself into a discussion.   Though boisterous and insistent in his talk, he was free from assumption or conceit, and gave the impression of liking the world he lived in, and being satisfied with his own place in it. Neither did one observe in him that erratic turn which is commonly attributed to literary men. He was a steady and regular worker, who rose every morning between five and six to turn out a certain quantity of copy for the printer before breakfast, enjoying his work, and fond of his own characters — indeed he declared that he filled his mind with them and saw them moving before him — yet composing a novel just as other people might compose tables of statistics. These methodical habits were to some extent due to his training as a clerk in the Post Office, where he spent the earlier half of his working life, having retired in 1864. He did not neglect his duties there, even when occupied in writing, and claimed to have been the inventor of the pillar letter-box. It was probably in his tours as an inspector of postal deliveries that he obtained that knowledge of rural life which gives reality to his pictures of country society. He turned his Civil Service experiences to account in some of his stories, giving faithful and characteristic sketches, in *The Three Clerks* and *The Small House at Allington*, of different types of Government officials, a class which is much more of a class in England than it is in America, though less of a class than it is in Germany or France. His favourite amusement was hunting, as readers of his novels know, and until his latest years he might have been seen, though a heavy weight, following the hounds in Essex once or twice a week.

When E. A. Freeman wrote a magazine article denouncing the cruelty of field sports, Trollope replied, defending the amusement he loved. Some one said it was a collision of two rough diamonds. But the end was that Freeman invited Trollope to come and stay with him at Wells, and they became great friends.

Like most of his literary contemporaries, he was a politician, and indeed a pretty keen one. He once contested in the Liberal interest — in those days literary men were mostly Liberals — the borough of Beverley in Yorkshire, a corrupt little place, where bribery proved too strong for him. It was thereafter disfranchised as a punishment for its misdeeds; and his costly experiences doubtless suggested the clever electioneering sketches in the story of *Ralph the Heir*. Thackeray also was once a Liberal candidate. He stood for the city of Oxford, and the story was current there for years afterwards how the freemen of the borough (not an exemplary class of voters) rose to an unwonted height of virtue by declaring that though they did not understand his speeches or know who he was, they would vote for him, expecting nothing, because he was a friend of Mr. Neate's. Trollope showed his continued interest in public affairs by appearing on the platform at the great meeting in St. James's Hall in December 1876, which was the beginning of a vehement party struggle over the Eastern Question that only ended at the general election of 1880. He was a direct and forcible speaker, who would have made his way had he entered Parliament. But as he had no practical experience of politics either in the House of Commons or as a working member of a party organisation in a city where contests are keen, the pictures of political life which are so frequent in his later tales have not much flavour of reality. They are sketches obviously taken from the outside. Very rarely do even the best writers of fiction succeed in reproducing any special and peculiar kind of life and atmosphere. Of the various stories that purport to describe what goes on in the English Parliament, none gives to those who know the social conditions and habits of the place an impression of truth to nature, and the same has often been remarked with regard to tales of English University life. Trollope, however, with his quick eye for the superficial aspects of any society, might have described the House of Commons admirably had he sat in it himself. He was fond of travel, and between 1862 and 1880 visited the United States, the West Indies, Australia and New Zealand, and South Africa, about all of which he wrote books which, if hardly of permanent value, were fresh, vigorous, and eminently readable, conveying a definite and generally correct impression of the more obvious social and economic phenomena he found then existing. His account of the United States, for instance, is excellent, and did something to make the Americans forgive the asperity with which his mother had described her experiences there many years before. Trollope's travel sketches are as much superior in truthfulness to Froude's descriptions of the same regions as they are inferior in the allurements of style.

The old classification of novels, based on the two most necessary elements of a drama, divided them into novels of plot and novels of character. To these we have of late years added novels of incident or adventure, novels of conversation, novels of manners, not to speak of "novels with a purpose," which are sermons or pamphlets in disguise. No one doubted to which of these categories Trollope's work should be referred. There was in his stories as little plot as a story can well have. The conversations never beamed with humour like that of Scott, nor glittered with aphorisms like those of George Meredith. The incidents carried the reader pleasantly along, but seldom surprised him by any ingenuity of contrivance. Character there was, and, indeed, great fertility in the creation of character, for there is hardly one of the tales in which three or four at least of the personages do not stand out as people whom you would know again if you met them years after. But the conspicuous merit of Trollope's novels, in the eyes of his own countrymen, is their value as pictures of contemporary manners. Here he may claim to have been surpassed by no writer of his own generation. Dickens, with all his great and splendid gifts, did not describe the society he lived in. His personages were too unusual and peculiar to speak and act and think like the ordinary men and women of the nineteenth century; nor would a foreigner, however much he might enjoy the exuberant humour and dramatic power with which they are presented, learn from them much about the ways and habits of the average Englishman. The everyday life to which the stories are most true is the life of the lower middle class in London ; and some one has observed that although this class changes less quickly than the classes above it, it is already unlike that which Dickens saw when in the thirties he was a police-court reporter. Critics have, indeed, said that Dickens was too great a painter to be a good photographer, but the two arts are not incompatible, as appears from the skill with which Walter Scott, for instance, portrayed the peasantry of his own country in the *Antiquary*. Thackeray, again, though he has described certain sections of the upper or upper middle class with far more power and delicacy than Trollope ever reached, does not go beyond those sections, and has little to tell us about the middle class generally, still less about the classes beneath them. Trollope was thoroughly at home in the English middle class and also (though less perfectly) in the upper class; and his pictures are all the more true to life because there is not that vein of stern or cynical reflection which runs through Thackeray, and makes us think less of the story than of the moral. Trollope usually has a moral, but it is so obvious, so plainly and quietly put, that it does not distract attention from the minor incidents and little touches of every day which render the sketches lifelike. If even his best-drawn characters are not far removed from the commonplace this helps to make them fairly represent the current habits and notions of their time. They are the same people we meet in the street or at a dinner-party; and they are mostly seen under no more exciting conditions than those of a hunting meet, or a lawn-tennis match, or an afternoon tea. They are flirting or talking for effect, or scheming for some petty temporary end; they are not under the influence of strong passions, or forced into striking situations, like the leading characters in Charlotte Brontë's or George Eliot's novels; and for this reason again they represent faithfully the ordinary surface of English upper and upper middle class society:

its prejudices, its little pharisaisms and hypocri-
sies, its snobbishness, its worship of convention-
alities, its aloofness from or condescension to those
whom it deems below its own level; and therewith also its public spirit, its self-helpfulness,
its neighbourliness, its respect for honesty and
straightforwardness, its easy friendliness of manner
towards all who stand within the sacred pale of
social recognition.   Nor, again, has any one more
skilfully noted and set down those transient
tastes and fashions which are, so to speak, the
trimmings of the dress, and which, transient
though they are, and quickly forgotten by contemporaries, will have an interest for one who,
a century or two hence, feels the same curiosity
about our manners as we feel about those of
the subjects of King George the Third.   That
Trollope will be read at all fifty years after
his death one may hesitate to predict, considering how comparatively few in the present
generation read Richardson, or Fielding, or Miss
Edgeworth, or Charlotte Brontë, and how much
reduced is the number of those who read even
Walter Scott and Thackeray.   But whoever
does read Trollope in 1930 will gather from his
pages better than from any others an impression
of what everyday life was like in England in the
"middle Victorian" period.   The aspects of that
life were already, when his latest books were
written, beginning to change, and the features

he drew are fast receding into history. Even the clergy of 1852-1862 are no longer, except in quiet country districts, the same as the clergy we now see.

People have often compared the personal impressions which eminent writers make on those who talk to them with the impressions previously derived from their works. Thomas Carlyle and Robert Browning used to be taken as two instances representing opposite extremes. Carlyle always talked in character: had there been phonographs in his days, the phonographed "record" might have been printed as part of one of his books. Browning, on the other hand, seemed unlike what his poems had made a reader expect: it was only after a long *tête à tête* with him that the poet whose mind had been learned through his works stood revealed. Trollope at first caused a similar though less marked surprise. This bluff burly man did not seem the kind of person who would trace with a delicate touch the sunlight sparkling on, or a gust of temper ruffling, the surface of a youthful soul in love. Upon further knowledge one perceived that the features of Trollope's talent, facile invention, quick observation, and a strong common-sense view of things, with little originality or intensity, were really the dominant features of his character as expressed in talk. Still, though the man was more of a piece with his books than he had seemed, one could never quite recognise in him the delineator of Lily Dale.

As a painter of manners he recalls two of his predecessors — one greater, one less great than himself. In his limitations and in his fidelity to the aspects of daily life as he saw them, he resembles Miss Austen. He is inferior to her in delicacy of portraiture, in finish, in atmosphere. No two of his books can be placed on a level with *Emma* and *Persuasion*. On the other hand, while he has done for the years 1850-1870 what Miss Burney did for 1770-1790, most critics will place him above her both in fertility and in naturalness. Her characters are apt either to want colour, like the heroines of *Evelina* and *Cecilia*, or to be so exaggerated, like Mr. Briggs and Miss Larolles, as to approach the grotesque. Trollope is a realist in the sense of being, in all but a few of his books, on the lines of normal humanity, though he is seldom strong enough to succeed, when he pierces down to the bed-rock of human nature, in rendering the primal passions either solemn or terrible. Like Miss Austen, he attains actuality by observation rather than by imagination, hardly ever entering the sphere of poetry.

His range was not wide, for he could not present either grand characters or tragical situations, any more than he could break out into the splendid humour of Dickens. His wings never raised him far above the level floor of earth. But within that limited range he had surprising fertility. His clerical portrait-gallery is the most complete that any English novelist has given us. No two faces are exactly alike, and yet all are such people as one might see any day in the pulpit. So, again, there is scarcely one of his stories in which a young lady is not engaged, formally or practically, to two men at the same time, or one man more or less committed to two women; yet no story repeats exactly the situation, or raises the problem of honour and duty in quite the same form as it appears in the stories that went before. Few people who have written so much have so little appeared to be exhausting their invention.

It must, however, be admitted that Trollope's fame might have stood higher if he had written less. The public which had been delighted with his earlier groups of novels, and especially with that group in which *The Warden* comes first and *Barchester Towers* second, began latterly to tire of what they had come to deem the mannerisms of their favourite, and felt that they now knew the compass of his gifts. Partly, perhaps, because he feared to be always too like himself, he once or twice attempted to represent more improbable situations and exceptional personages. But the attempt was not successful. He lost his touch of ordinary life without getting into any higher region of poetical truth; and in his latest stories he had begun to return to his earlier and better manner.

New tendencies, moreover, embodying themselves in new schools, were already beginning to appear. R. L. Stevenson as leader of the school of adventure, Mr. Henry James as the apostle of the school of psychological analysis, soon to be followed by Mr. Kipling with a type of imaginative directness distinctively his own, were beginning to lead minds and tastes into other directions. The influence of France was more felt than it had been when Trollope began to write. And what a contrast between Trollope's manner and that of his chief French contemporaries, such as Octave Feuillet or Alphonse Daudet or Guy de Maupassant! The French novelists, be their faculty of invention greater or less, at any rate studied their characters with more care than English writers had usually shown. The characters were fewer, almost as few as in a classical drama; and the whole action of the story is carefully subordinated to the development of these characters, and the placing of them in a critical position which sets their strength and weakness in the fullest light. There was more of a judicious adaptation of the parts to the whole in French fiction than in ours, and therefore more unity of impression was attained. Trollope, no

K

doubt, set a bad example in this respect. He crowded his canvas with figures; he pursued the fortunes of three or four sets of people at the same time, caring little how the fate of the one set affected that of the others; he made his novel a sort of chronicle which you might open anywhere and close anywhere, instead of a drama animated by one idea and converging towards one centre. He neglected the art which uses incidents small in themselves to lead up to the *dénoûment* and make it more striking. He took little pains with his diction, seeming not to care how he said what he had to say. These defects strike those who turn over his pages to-day. But to those who read him in the fifties or sixties, the carelessness was redeemed by, or forgotten in, the vivacity with which the story moved, the freshness and faithfulness of its pictures of character and manners.

JOHN RICHARD GREEN [1]

John Richard Green was born in Oxford
on 12th December 1837, and educated first
at Magdalen College School, and afterwards,
for a short time, at a private tutor's. He
was a singularly quick and bright boy, and at
sixteen obtained by competition a scholarship
at Jesus College, Oxford, where he began to
reside in 1856. The members of that college
were in those days almost entirely Welshmen, and
thereby somewhat cut off from the rest of the
University. They saw little of men in other
colleges, so that a man might have a reputation
for ability in his own society without gaining
any in the larger world of Oxford. It so happened with Green. Though his few intimate
friends perceived his powers, they had so little
intercourse with the rest of the University, either
by way of breakfasts and wine-parties, or at the
University debating society, or in athletic sports,

[1] This sketch was written in 1883. A volume of Green's Letters, with
a short connecting biography by Sir Leslie Stephen, was published in
1901. The letters are extremely good reading, the biography faithful and
graceful.

that he remained unknown even to those among his contemporaries who were interested in the same things, and would have most enjoyed his acquaintance. The only eminent person who seems to have appreciated and influenced him was Dean Stanley, then Professor of Ecclesiastical History and Canon of Christ Church. Green had attended Stanley's lectures, and Stanley, whose kindly interest in young men never failed, was struck by him, and had some share in turning his studies towards history. He graduated in 1860, having refused to compete for honours, because he had not received from those who were then tutors of the college the recognition to which he was entitled.

In 1860 he was ordained, and became curate in London at St. Barnabas, King's Square, whence, after two years' experience, and one or two temporary engagements, including the sole charge of a parish in Hoxton, he was appointed in 1865 to the incumbency of St. Philip's, Stepney, a district church in one of the poorest parts of London, where the vicar's income was ill-proportioned to the claims which needy parishioners made upon him. Here he worked with zeal and assiduity for about three years, gaining an insight into the condition and needs of the poor which scholars and historians seldom obtain. He learnt, in fact, to know men, and the real forces that sway them; and he used to say in later life that he was conscious how much this had helped him in historical writing. Gibbon, as every one knows, makes a similar remark about his experience as a captain in the Hampshire militia.

Green threw the whole force of his nature into the parish schools, spending some part of every day in them; he visited incessantly, and took an active part in the movement for regulating and controlling private charity which led to the formation of the Charity Organisation Society. An outbreak of cholera and period of distress among the poor which occurred during his incumbency drew warm-hearted men from other parts of London to give their help to the clergy of the East End. Edward Denison, who was long affectionately remembered by many who knew him in Oxford and London, chose Green's parish to work in, and the two friends confirmed one another in their crusade against indiscriminate and demoralising charity. It was at this time that Green, who spent upon the parish nearly all that he received as vicar, found himself obliged to earn some money by other means, and began to write for the *Saturday Review*. The addition of this labour to the daily fatigues of his parish duties told on his health, which had always been delicate, and made him willingly accept from Archbishop Tait, who had early marked and learned to value

his abilities, the post of librarian at Lambeth.
He quitted Stepney, and never took any other
clerical work.

Although physical weakness was one of the
causes which compelled this step, there was also
another. He had been brought up in Tractarian
views, and is said to have been at one time on
the point of entering the Church of Rome. This
tendency passed off, and before he went to St.
Philip's he had become a Broad Churchman, and
was much influenced by the writings of Mr. F.
D. Maurice, whom he knew and used frequently
to meet, and whose pure and noble character,
even more perhaps than his preaching, had profoundly impressed him. However, his restless
mind did not stop long at that point. The same
tendency which had carried him away from
Tractarianism made him feel less and less at
home in the ministry of the Church of England,
and would doubtless have led him, even had his
health been stronger, to withdraw from clerical
duties. After a few years his friends ceased to
address letters to him under the usual clerical
epithet; but he continued to interest himself in
ecclesiastical affairs, and always retained a marked
dislike to Nonconformity. Aversions sometimes
outlive attachments.

On leaving Stepney he went to live in lodgings
in Beaumont Street, Marylebone, and divided
his time between Lambeth and literary work.

He now during several years wrote a good deal for the *Saturday Review*, and his articles were among the best which then appeared in that organ. The most valuable of them were reviews of historical books, and descriptions from the historical point of view of cities or other remarkable places, especially English and French towns. Some of these are masterpieces. Other articles were on social, or what may be called occasional, topics, and attracted much notice at the time from their gaiety and lightness of touch, which sometimes seemed to pass into flippancy. He never wrote upon politics, nor was he in the ordinary sense of the word a journalist, for with the exception of these social articles, his work was all done in his own historical field, and done with as much care and pains as others would bestow on the composition of a book. Upon this subject I may quote the words of one of his oldest and most intimate friends (Mr. Stopford Brooke), who knew all he did in those days.

The real history of this writing for the *Saturday Review* has much personal, pathetic, and literary interest.

It was when he was vicar of St. Philip's, Stepney, that he wrote the most. The income of the place was, I think, £300 a year, and the poverty of the parish was very great. Mr. Green spent every penny of this income on the parish. And he wrote — in order to live, and often when he was wearied out with the work of the day and late into the night — two, and often three, articles a week for the *Saturday Review*. It was less of a strain to him than it would have been to many others, because he wrote with such speed, and because his capacity for rapidly throwing his subject into form and his memory were so remarkable. But it was a severe strain, nevertheless, for one who, at the time, had in him the beginnings of the disease of which he died.

I was staying with him once for two days, and the first night he said to me, " I have three articles to write for the *Saturday Review,* and they must all be done in thirty-six hours." " What are they?" I said; " and how have you found time to think of them ? " " Well," he answered, " one is on a volume of Freeman's *Norman Conquest,* another is a ' light middle,' and the last on the history of a small town in England; and I have worked them all into form as I was walking to-day about the parish and in London." One of these studies was finished before two o'clock in the morning, and while I talked to him ; the other two were done the next day. It is not uncommon to reach such speed, but it is very uncommon to combine this speed with literary excellence of composition, and with permanent and careful knowledge. The historical reviews were of use to, and gratefully acknow-ledged by, his brother historians, and frequently extended, in two or three numbers of the *Saturday Review,* to the length of an article in a magazine. I used to think them master-pieces of reviewing, and their one fault was the fault which was then frequent in that *Review* — over-vehemence in slaughtering its foes. Such reviewing cannot be fairly described as journalism. It was an historical scholar speaking to scholars.

Another class of articles written by Mr. Green were articles on towns in England, France, or Italy. I do not know whether it was he or Mr. Freeman who introduced this custom of bringing into a short space the historical aspect of a single town or of a famous building, and showing how the town or the building recorded its own history, and how it was linked to general history, but Mr. Green, at least, began it very early in his articles on Oxford. At any rate, it was his habit, at this time, whenever he travelled in England, France, or Italy, to make a study of any town he visited.

Articles of this kind — and he had them by fifties in his

head — formed the second line of what has been called his journalism. I should prefer to call them contributions to history. They are totally different in quality from ordinary journalism. They are short historical essays.

As his duties at Lambeth made no great demands on his time, he was now able to devote himself more steadily to historical work. His first impulse in that direction seems, as I have said, to have been received from Dean Stanley at Oxford. His next came from E. A. Freeman, who had been impressed by an ingenious paper of his at a meeting of the Somerset archæological society, and who became from that time his steadfast friend. Green was a born historian, who would have been eminent without any help except that of books. But he was wise enough to know the value of personal counsel and direction, and generous enough to be heartily grateful for what he received. He did not belong in any special sense to what has been called Freeman's school, differing widely from that distinguished writer in many of his views, and still more in style and manner. But he learnt much from Freeman, and he delighted to acknowledge his debt. He learnt among other things the value of accuracy, the way to handle original authorities, the interpretation of architecture, and he received, during many years of intimate intercourse, the constant sympathy and encouragement of a friend whose affection was never blind to faults, while

his admiration was never clouded by jealousy.
It was his good fortune to win the regard and
receive the advice of another illustrious historian,
Dr. Stubbs, who has expressed in language
perhaps more measured, but not less emphatic
than Freeman's, his sense of Green's services
to English history. These two he used to call
his masters; but no one who has read him and
them needs to be told that his was one of those
strong and rich intelligences which, in becoming
more perfect by the study of others, loses nothing
of its originality.

His first continuous studies had lain among the
Angevin kings of England, and the note-books
still exist in which he had accumulated materials
for their history. However, the book he planned
was never written, for when the state of his lungs
(which forced him to spend the winter of 1870-71
at San Remo) had begun to alarm his friends,
they urged him to throw himself at once into
some treatise likely to touch the world more than
a minute account of so remote a period could
do. Accordingly he began, and in two or three
years, his winters abroad sadly interrupting work,
he completed the *Short History of the English
People*. When a good deal of it had gone
through the press, he felt, and his friends agreed
with him, that the style of the earlier chapters
was too much in the eager, quick, sketchy,
"point-making" manner of his *Saturday Review*

articles, " and did not possess " (says the friend
whom I have already quoted) " enough historical
dignity for a work which was to take in the whole
history of England. It was then, being convinced
of this, that he cancelled a great deal of what
had been stereotyped, and re-wrote it, re-creating,
with his passionate facility, his whole style." In
order to finish it he gave up the *Saturday
Review* altogether, though he could ill spare what
his writing there brought him in. It is seldom
that one finds such swiftness and ease in composition as his, united to so much fastidiousness.
He went on remoulding and revising till his
friends insisted that the book should be published
anyhow, and published it accordingly was, in
1874. Feeling that his time on earth might be
short, for he was often disabled even by a catarrh,
he was the readier to yield.

The success of the *Short History* was rapid
and overwhelming. Everybody bought it. It was
philosophical enough for scholars, and popular
enough for schoolboys. No historical book since
Macaulay's *History* has made its way so fast, or
been read with so much avidity. And Green was
under disadvantages from which his great predecessor did not suffer. Macaulay's name was
famous before his *History of England* appeared,
and Macaulay's scale was so large that he could
enliven his pages with a multitude of anecdotes
and personal details. Green was known only to a

small circle of friends, having written nothing under his own signature except one or two papers in magazines or in the Transactions of archæological societies ; and the plan of his book, which dealt, in eight hundred and twenty pages, with the whole fourteen centuries of English national life, obliged him to handle facts in the mass, and touch lightly and briefly on personal traits. A summary is of all kinds of writing that which it is hardest to make interesting, because one must speak in general terms, one must pack facts tightly together, one must be content to give those facts without the delicacies of light and shade, or the subtler tints of colour. Yet such was his skill, both literary and historical, that his outlines gave more pleasure and instruction than other people's finished pictures.

In 1876 he took, for the only time in his life, except when he had supported a working man's candidate for the Tower Hamlets at the general election of 1868, an active part in practical politics. Towards the end of that year, when war seemed impending between Russia and the Turks, fears were entertained that England might undertake the defence of the Sultan, and a body called the Eastern Question Association was formed to organise opposition to the pro-Turkish policy of Lord Beaconsfield's Ministry. Green threw himself warmly into the movement, was chosen to serve on the Executive Committee of the Association, and was one of a sub-committee of five (which included also Mr. Stopford Brooke and Mr. William Morris the poet [1]) appointed to draw up the manifesto convoking the meeting of delegates from all parts of the country, which was held in December 1876, under the title of the Eastern Question Conference. The sub-committee met at my house and spent the whole day on its work. It was a new and curious experience to see these three great men of letters drafting a political appeal. Morris and Green were both of them passionately anti-Turkish, and Morris indeed acted for the next two years as treasurer of the Association, doing his work with a business-like efficiency such as poets seldom possess. Green continued to attend the general committee until, after the Treaty of Berlin, it ceased to meet, and took the keenest interest in its proceedings. But his weak health and frequent winter absences made public appearances impossible to him. He was all his life an ardent Liberal. His sympathy with national movements did not confine itself to Continental Europe, but embraced Ireland and made him a Home Ruler long before Mr. Gladstone and the Liberal party adopted that policy. It ought to be added that though he had ceased to belong to the Church of England, he remained strongly opposed to disestablishment.

[1] Sir George Young and I were the other members.

When he had completed the re-casting of his *Short History* in the form of a larger book, which appeared under the title of *A History of the English People*, he addressed himself with characteristic activity to a new project. He had for a long time meditated upon the *origines* of English history, the settlement of the Teutonic invaders in Britain, followed by the consolidation of their tribes into a nation with definite institutions and a settled order; and his desire to treat this topic was stimulated by the way in which some critics had sought to disparage his *Short History* as a mere popularising of other people's ideas. The criticism was unjust, for, if there had been no rummaging in MS. sources for the *Short History*, there was abundant originality in the views the book contained. However, these carpings disposed his friends to recommend an enterprise which would lead him to deal chiefly with original authorities, and to put forth those powers of criticism and construction which they knew him to possess. Thus he set to work afresh at the very beginning, at Roman Britain and the Saxon Conquest. He had not advanced far when, having gone to spend the winter in Egypt, he caught an illness which so told on his weak frame that he was only just able to return to London in April, and would not have reached it at all but for the care with which he was tended by his wife. (He had married Miss Alice Stopford in 1877.) In a few weeks he so far recovered as to be able to resume his studies, though now forbidden to give to them more than two or three hours a day. However, what he could not do alone he did with and through his wife, who consulted the original sources for him, investigated obscure points, and wrote at his dictation. In this way, during the summer and autumn months of 1881, when often some slight change of weather would throw him back and make work impossible for days or weeks, the book was prepared, which he published in February 1882, under the title of *The Making of England*. Even in those few months it was incessantly rewritten; no less than ten copies were made of the first chapter. It was warmly received by the few persons who were capable of judging its merits. But he was himself far from satisfied with it as a literary performance, thinking that a reader would find it at once too speculative and too dry, deficient in the details needed to make the life of primitive England real and instructive. If this had been so it would have been due to no failing in his skill, but to the scantiness of the materials available for the first few centuries of our national history. But he felt it so strongly that he was often disposed to recur to his idea of writing a history of the last seventy or eighty years, and was only induced by the encouragement of a few friends to pursue the narrative which, in *The Making of England*, he had carried

down to the reign of Egbert.   The winter of 1881
was spent at Mentone, and the following summer
in London.   He continued very weak, and was
sometimes unable for weeks together to go out
driving or to work at home.   But the moment
that an access of strength returned, the note-
books were brought out, and he was again busy
going through what his wife's industry had
tabulated, and dictating for an hour or two till
fatigue forced him to desist.   Those who saw
him during that summer were amazed, not only
at the brave spirit which refused to yield to
physical feebleness, but at the brightness and
clearness of his intellect, which was not only
as active as it had ever been before, but as
much interested in whatever passed in the world.
When one saw him sitting propped up with
cushions on the sofa, his tiny frame worn to
skin and bone, his voice interrupted by frequent
fits of coughing, it seemed wrong to stay, but,
after a little, all was forgotten in the fascination of his talk, and one found it hard to
realise that where thought was strong speech
might be weak.

   In October, when he returned to Mentone,
the tale of early English history had been completed, and was in type down to the death of
Earl Godwine in A.D. 1052.   He had hesitated
as to the point at which the book should end,
but finally decided to carry it down to A.D. 1085,

the date of the dispersion of the last great Scandinavian armament which threatened England. As the book dealt with both the Danish and Norman invasions, he called it *The Conquest of England.* It appeared after his death, wanting, indeed, those expansions in several places which he had meant to give it, but still a book such as few but he could have produced, full of new light, and equal in the parts which have been fully handled to the best work of his earlier years.

Soon after he returned to Mentone he became rapidly worse, and unfit for any continuous exertion. He could barely sit in the garden during an hour or two of morning sunshine. There I saw him in the end of December, fresh and keen as ever, aware that the most he could hope for was to live long enough to complete his *Conquest,* but eagerly reading every new book that came to him from England, starting schemes for various historical treatises sufficient to fill three life-times, and ranging in talk over the whole field of politics, literature, and history. It seemed as if the intellect and will, which strove to remain till their work was done, were the only things which held the weak and wasted body together. The ardour of his spirit prolonged life amid the signs of death. In January there came a new attack, and in February another unexpected rally. On the 2nd of March he remarked that it was no use fighting longer,

L

and expired five days afterwards at the age of forty-six.

Short as his life was, maimed and saddened by an ill health which gave his powers no fair chance, it was not an unhappy life, for he had that immense power of enjoyment which so often belongs to a vivacious intelligence. He delighted in books, in travel, in his friends' company, in the constant changes and movements of the world. No satiety dulled his taste for these things, nor was his spirit, except for passing moments, darkened by the shadows which to others seemed to lie so thick around his path. He enjoyed, though without boasting, the fame his books had won, and the sense of creative power. And the last six years of his life were brightened by the society and affection of one who entered into all his tastes and pursuits with the fullest sympathy, and enabled him, by her unwearied diligence, to prosecute labours which physical weakness must otherwise have arrested.

He might have won fame as a preacher or as a political journalist. It was, however, towards historical study that the whole current of his intellect set, and as it is by what he did in that sphere that he will be remembered, his special gifts for it deserve to be examined.

A historian needs four kinds of capacity. First of all, accuracy, and a desire for the exact truth, which will grudge no time and pains in tracing out even what might seem a trivial matter. Secondly, keen observation, which can fasten upon small points, and discover in isolated data the basis for some generalisation, or the illustration of some principle. Thirdly, a sound and calm judgment, which will subject all inferences and generalisations, both one's own and other people's, to a searching review, and weigh in delicate scales their validity. These two last mentioned qualifications taken together make up what we call the critical faculty, *i.e.* the power of dealing with evidence as tending to establish or discredit statements of fact, and those general conclusions which are built on the grouping of facts. Neither acuteness alone nor the judicial balance alone is enough to make the critic. There are men quick in observation and fertile in suggestion whose conclusions are worthless, because they cannot weigh one argument against another, just as there are solid and well-balanced minds that never enlighten a subject because, while detecting the errors of others, they cannot combine the data and propound a luminous explanation. To the making of a true critic, in history, in philosophy, in literature, in psychology, even largely in the sciences of nature, there should go not only judgment, but also a certain measure of creative power. Fourthly, the historian must have imagination, not indeed with that intensity which

makes the poet, but in sufficient volume to let
him feel the men of other ages and countries to be
living and real like those among whom he moves,
to present to him a large and full picture of a
world remote from himself in time, as a world
moving, struggling, hoping, fearing, enjoying, believing, like the near world of to-day — a world in
which there went on a private life of thousands or
millions of men and women, vaster, more complex,
more interesting than that public life which is
sometimes all that the records of the past have
transmitted to us. Our imaginative historian
may or may not be able to reconstruct for us the
private and personal as well as the public or
political life of the past. If he can, he will. If
the data are too scanty, he may cautiously for-
bear. Yet he will still feel that those whose
movements on the public stage he chronicles
were steeped in an environment of natural
and human influences which must have affected
them at every turn; and he will so describe
them as to make us feel them human, and give
life to the pallid figures of far-off warriors and
lawgivers.

To these four aptitudes one need hardly add
the faculty of literary exposition, for whoever
possesses in large measure the last three, or
even the last alone, cannot fail to interest his
readers; and what more does literary talent
mean?

Distinguishing these several aptitudes, historians will be found to fall into two classes, according as there predominates in them the critical or the imaginative faculty. Though no one can attain greatness without both gifts, still they may be present in very unequal degrees. Some will investigate tangible facts and their relations with special care, occupying themselves chiefly with that constitutional and diplomatic side of history in which positive conclusions are (from the comparative abundance of records) most easily reached. Others will be drawn towards the dramatic and personal elements in history, primarily as they appear in the lives of famous individual men, secondarily as they are seen, more dimly but not less impressively, in groups and masses of men, and in a nation at large, and will also observe and dwell upon incidents of private life or features of social and religious custom, which the student of stately politics passes by.

As Coleridge, when he divided thinkers into two classes, took Plato as the type of one, Aristotle of the other, so we may take as representatives of these two tendencies among historians Thucydides for the critical and philosophical, Herodotus for the imaginative and picturesque. The former does not indeed want a sense of the dramatic grandeur of a situation; his narrative of the later part of the Athenian expedition against Syracuse is like a

piece of Æschylus in prose. So too Herodotus
is by no means without a philosophical view of
things, nor without a critical instinct, although
his generalisations are sometimes vague or
fanciful, and his critical apparatus rudimentary.
Each is so splendid because each is wide, with
the great gifts largely, although not equally,
developed.

Green was an historian of the Herodotean
type. He possessed capacities which belong to
the other type also; he was critical, sceptical,
perhaps too sceptical, and philosophical. Yet
the imaginative quality was the leading and distinctive quality in his mind and writing. An
ordinary reader, if asked what was the main
impression given by the *Short History of the
English People*, would answer that it was the
impression of picturesqueness and vividity —
picturesqueness in attention to the externals of
the life described, vividity in the presentation
of that life itself.

I remember to have once, in talking with
Green about Greek history, told him how I
had heard Mr. Jowett, in discussing the ancient
historians, disparage Herodotus and declare him
unworthy to be placed near Thucydides. Green
answered, almost with indignation, that to say
such a thing showed that eminent scholars might
have little feeling for history. "Great as Thucydides is," he said, "Herodotus is far greater, or

at any rate far more precious. His view was so much wider." I forget the rest of the conversation, but what he meant was that Herodotus, to whom everything in the world was interesting, and who has told us something about every country he visited or heard of, had a more fruitful conception of history than his Athenian successor, who practically confined himself to politics in the narrower sense of the term, and that even the wisdom of the latter is not so valuable to us as the flood of miscellaneous information which Herodotus pours out about everything in the early world — a world about which we should know comparatively little if his book had not been preserved.

This deliverance was thoroughly characteristic of Green's own view of history. Everything was interesting to him because his imagination laid hold of everything. When he travelled, nothing escaped his quick eye, perpetually ranging over the aspects of places and society. When he went out to dinner, he noted every person present whom he had not known before, and could tell you afterwards something about them. He had a theory, so to speak, about each of them, and indeed about every one with whom he exchanged a dozen words. When he read the newspaper, he seemed to squeeze all the juice out of it in a few minutes. Nor was it merely the large events that fixed his mind; he drew from stray notices of minor current matters evidence of principles or tendencies which escaped other people's eyes. You never left him without having new light thrown upon the questions of the hour. His memory was retentive, but more remarkable was the sustained keenness of apprehension with which he read, and which made him fasten upon everything in a book or in talk which was significant, and could be made the basis for an illustration of some view. He had the Herodotean quality of reckoning nothing, however small or apparently remote from the main studies of his life, to be trivial or unfruitful. His imagination vitalised the small things, and found a place for them in the pictures he was always sketching out.

As this faculty of discerning hidden meanings and relations was one index and consequence of his imaginative power, so another was found in that artistic gift to which I have referred. To give literary form to everything was a necessity of his intellect. He could not tell an anecdote or repeat a conversation without unconsciously dramatising it, putting into people's mouths better phrases than they would have themselves employed, and giving a finer point to the moral which the incident expressed. Verbal accuracy suffered, but what he thought the inner truth came out the more fully.

Though he wrote very fast, and in the most familiar way, the style of his more serious letters was as good, I might say as finished, as that of his

books. Every one of them had a beginning,
middle, and end. The ideas were developed in an
apt and graceful order, the sentences could all be
construed, the diction was choice. It was the
same with the short articles which he at one time
used to write for the *Saturday Review.* They
are little essays, some of them worthy to live not
only for the excellent matter they contain, but
for the delicate refinement of their form. Yet
they were all written swiftly, and sometimes in
the midst of physical exhaustion. The friend I
have previously quoted describes the genesis of
one. Green had reached the town of Troyes
early one morning with two companions, and
immediately started off to explore it, darting
hither and thither through the streets like a dog
trying to find a scent. In two or three hours the
examination was complete. The friends lunched
together, took the train on to Basel, got there
late, and went off to bed. Green, however, wrote
before he slept, and laid on the breakfast-table
next morning, an article on Troyes, in which its
characteristic features were brought out and connected with its fortunes and those of the Counts
of Champagne during some centuries, an article
which was really a history in miniature. Then they
went out together to look at Basel, and being asked
some question about that city he gave on the spur
of the moment a sketch of its growth and character
equally vivid and equally systematic, grouping all

he had to say round two or three leading theories.
Yet he had never been in either place before, and
had not made a special study of either. He could
apparently have done the same for many another
town in France or the Rhineland.

Nothing struck one so much in daily intercourse with him as his passionate interest in
human life. The same quickness of sympathy
which had served him well in his work among
the East End poor, enabled him to pour feeling
into the figures of a bygone age, and become
the most human, and in so far the most real and
touching, of all who have dealt with English
history. Whether or not his portraits are true,
they always seem to breathe.

Men and women — that is to say, such of them
as have characteristics pronounced enough to
make them classifiable — may be divided into
those whose primary interests are in nature and
what relates to nature, and those whose primary
interests are in and for man. Green was the most
striking type I have known of the latter class,
not merely because his human interests were
strong, but also because they excluded, to a
degree singular in a mind so versatile, interests
in purely natural things. He did not seem to
care for or seek to know any of the sciences of
nature[1] except in so far as they bore directly

---

[1] At one time, however, he learnt a little geology from his friend
Professor Dawkins, perceiving its bearings on history.

upon man's life, and were capable of explaining it or of serving it. He had a keen eye for country, for the direction and character of hills, the position and influence of rivers, forests, and marshes, of changes in the line of land and sea. Readers of *The Making of England* will recall the picture of the physical aspects of Britain when the Teutonic invaders entered it as an unsurpassed piece of reconstructive description. So on a battle-field or in an historical town, his vision of the features of the ground or the site was unerring. But he perceived and enjoyed natural beauty chiefly in reference to human life. The study of the battle-field and the town site were aids to the comprehension of historical events. The exquisite landscape was exquisite because it was associated with the people dwelling there, with the processes of their political growth, with their ideas or their social usages. I remember to have had from him the most vivid descriptions of the towns of the Riviera and of Capri, where he used to pass the winter, but he never touched on anything which did not illustrate or intertwine itself with the life of the people, leaving one uninformed on matters purely physical. Facts about the character of the mountains, the relation of their ranges to one another, or their rocks, or the trees and flowers of their upper regions, the prospects their summits command, the scenes of beauty in their glens, or beside their wood-embosomed lakes, all, in fact, which the mountain lover delights in, and which are to him a part of the mountain ardour, of the passion for pure nature unsullied by the presence of man — all this was cold to him. But as soon as a touch of human life fell like a sunbeam across the landscape, all became warm and lovable.

It was the same with art. With an historian's delight in the creative ages and their work, he had a fondness for painting and sculpture, and could so describe what he saw in the galleries and churches of Italy as to bring out meanings one had not perceived before. But here, too, it was the human element that fascinated him. Technical merits, though he observed them, as he observed most things, were forgotten; he dwelt only on what the picture expressed or revealed. Pure landscape painting gave him little pleasure.

It seems a truism to say that one who writes history ought to care for all that bears upon man in the present in order that he may comprehend what bore upon him in the past. This roaring loom of Time, these complex physical and moral forces playing round us, and driving us hither and thither by such a strange and intricate interlacement of movements that we seem to perceive no more than what is next us, and are unable to say whither we are tending, ought to be always before the historian's mind.

But there are few who have tried, as Green
tried, to follow every flash of the shuttle, and to
discover a direction and a relation amidst apparent confusion, for there are few who have taken
so wide a view of the historian's functions, and
have so distinctly set before them as their object
the comprehension and realisation and description of the whole field of bygone human life.
The Past was all present to him in this sense,
that he saw and felt in it not only those large
events which annalists or state papers have recorded, but the everyday life of the people, their
ideas, their habits, their external surroundings.
And the Present was always as if past to him
in this sense, that in spite of his strong political
feelings, he looked at it with the eye of a
philosophical observer, trying to disengage principles from details, permanent tendencies from
passing outbursts. His imagination visualised,
so to speak, the phenomena as in a picture; his
speculative faculty tried to harmonise them,
measure them, and forecast their effects. Hence
it was a necessity to him to know what was
passing in the world. The first thing he did
every day, whatever other pressure there might
be on him, was to read the daily newspaper.
The last thing that he ceased to read, when what
remained of life began to be counted by hours,
was the daily newspaper. This warm interest in
mankind is the keynote of his *History of the*

English People. It is the whole people that is ever present to him, as it had been present before to few other historians.

Such power of imagination and sympathy as I have endeavoured to describe is enough to make a brilliant writer, yet not necessarily a great historian. One must see how far the other qualifications, accuracy, acuteness of observation, and judgment, are also brought into action.

His accuracy has been much impeached. When the first burst of applause that welcomed the *Short History* had subsided, several critics began to attack it on the score of minor errors. They pointed out a number of statements of fact which were doubtful, and others which were incorrect, and spread in some quarters the impression that Green was a careless and untrustworthy writer. I do not deny that there are in the first editions of the *Short History* some assertions made more positively than the evidence warrants, some pictures drawn from exceedingly slender materials. Mr. Skene remarks of the account given of the battle between the Jutes and the Britons which took place in the middle of the fifth century, somewhere near Aylesford in Kent, and about which we really know scarcely anything, " Mr. Green describes it as if he had been present." The temptation to such liberties is strong where the treatment of a period is summary. A writer who compresses the whole history of England into eight hundred pages of small octavo, making his narrative not a bare narrative but a picture full of colour and incident — incident which, for brevity's sake, must often be given by allusion — cannot be always interrupting the current of the story to indicate doubts or quote authorities for every statement in which there may be an element of conjecture; and it is probable that when the authorities are scrutinised their result will sometimes appear different from that which the author has presented. On this head the *Short History* may be admitted to have occasionally purchased vividity at the price of exactitude. Of mistakes, strictly so called — *i.e.* statements demonstrably incorrect and therefore ascribable to haste or carelessness — there are enough to make a show under the hands of a hostile critic, yet not more than one is prepared to expect from any but the most careful scholars. The book falls far short of the accuracy of Thirlwall or Ranke or Stubbs, short even of the accuracy of Gibbon or Carlyle; but it is not greatly below the standard of Grote or Macaulay or Robertson, it is equal to the standard of Milman, above that of David Hume. I take famous names, and could put a better face on the matter by choosing for comparison divers contemporary writers whose literary eminence is higher than their historical. And Green's mistakes, although pretty numerous, were (for they have been corrected in later editions) nearly all in small matters. He puts an event, let us say, in 1340 which happened in the November of 1339; he calls a man John whose name was William.   These are mistakes to the eye of a civil service examiner, but they seldom make any difference to the general reader, for they do not affect the doctrines and pictures which the book contains, and in which lies its permanent value as well as its literary charm.   As Bishop Stubbs says, " Like other people, Green makes mistakes sometimes; but scarcely ever does the correction of his mistakes affect either the essence of the picture or the force of the argument. . . . All his work was real and original work; few people besides those who knew him well would see under the charming ease and vivacity of his style the deep research and sustained industry of the laborious student." It may be added that Green's later and more detailed works, *The Making of England* and *The Conquest of England*, though they contain plenty of debatable matter, as in the paucity of authentic data any such book must do, have been charged with few errors in matters of fact.

In considering his critical gift, it is well to distinguish those two elements of acute perception and sober judgment which I have already specified, for he possessed the former in larger measure than the latter.   The same activity of mind which made

him notice everything while travelling or entering a company of strangers, played incessantly
upon the historical data of his work, and supplied
him with endless theories as to the meaning of
a statement, the source it came from, the way it
had been transmitted, the conditions under which
it was made.   No one could be more acute and
penetrating in what the Germans call *Quellen-
forschung*, the collection and investigation and
testing of the sources of history, nor could any
one be more painstaking.   Errors of view, apart
from those trivial inaccuracies already referred to,
did not arise from an indolence that left any
stone unturned, but rather from an occupation
with the leading idea which had drawn his
attention away from the details of time and place.
The ingenuity with which he built up theories
was as admirable as the art with which he
stated them.   People whom that art fascinated
sometimes fancied that the charm lay entirely in
the style.   But the style was only a part of the
craftsmanship.   The facility in theorising, the
power of grouping facts under new aspects, the
skill in gathering and sifting evidence, were
as remarkable as those artistic qualities which
expressed themselves in the paragraphs and
sentences and phrases.   What danger there was
arose from this fecundity.   His mind was so
fertile, could see so much in a theory and apply
it so dexterously, that his judgment was some-

M

times dazzled by the brilliance of his ingenuity. I do not think he loved his theories specially because they were his own, for he often modified them, and was ready to consider any one else's suggestions; but he had a passion for light, and when a new view seemed to him to explain things previously dark, he wanted the patience to suspend his judgment and abide in uncertainty. Some of his hypotheses he himself dropped. Some others he probably would have dropped, as the authorities he respected have not embraced them.   Others have made their way into general acceptance, and may become still more useful as future research works them out.   But, whether right or wrong, they were instructive.   Every one of them is based upon facts whose importance had not been so fully seen before, and suggests a point of view worth considering. Green's view may sometimes appear fanciful: it is never foolish, or superficial, or perverse.   And so far from being credulous, his natural tendency was towards doubt.

Inventive as his mind was, it was also solvent and sceptical.   Seldom is a strong imagination coupled with so unsparing a criticism as that which he applied to the materials on which the constructive faculty had to work.   His later tendencies were rather towards scepticism, and towards what one may call a severe and ascetic view of history.   While writing *The Making of*

England and *The Conquest of England,* he used
to lament the scantiness of the data and the
barren dryness which he feared the books would
consequently show. "How am I to make anything of these meagre entries of marches and
battles which are the only materials for the history
of whole centuries? Here are the Norsemen
and Danes ravaging and occupying the country;
we learn hardly anything about them from English
sources, and nothing at all from Danish. How
can one conceive and describe them? how have
any comprehension of what England was like in
the districts the Northmen took and ruled?" I
tried to get him to work at the Norse Sagas, and
remember in particular to have entreated him
when he came to the battle of Brunanburh to
eke out the pitifully scanty records of that fight
from the account given of it in the story of
the Icelandic hero, Egil, son of Skallagrim.
But he answered that the Saga was unhistorical,
a bit of legend written down more than a
century after the events, and that he could not,
by using it in the text, appear to trust it, or to
mix up authentic history with what was possibly
fable. It was urged that he could guard himself in a note from being supposed to take it
for more than what it was, a most picturesque
embellishment of his tale. But he stood firm.
Throughout these two last books, he steadily
refrained from introducing any matter, however

lively or romantic, which could not stand the
test of his stringent criticism, and used laughingly
to tell how Dean Stanley had long ago said to
him, after reading one of his earliest pieces, " I
see you are in danger of growing picturesque.
Beware of it. I have suffered for it."

If in these later years he reined in his
imagination more tightly, the change was due
to no failing in his ingenuity. Nothing in
his work shows higher constructive ability than
The Making of England. He had to deal
with a time which has left us scarcely any
authentic records, and to piece together his narrative and his picture of the country out of these
records, and the indications, faint and scattered,
and often capable of several interpretations, which
are supplied by the remains of Roman roads and
villas, the names of places, the boundaries of local
divisions, the casual statements of writers many
centuries later. What he has given us remains
an enduring witness to his historical power.
For here it is not a question of mere brilliance
of style. The result is due to patience, penetration, and the careful weighing of evidence,
joined to that faculty of realising things in
the concrete by which a picture is conjured up
out of a mass of phenomena, everything falling
into its place under laws which seem to prove
themselves as soon as they are stated.

Of his style nothing need be said, for his

readers have felt its charm. But it deserves
to be remarked that this accomplished master
of words had little verbal memory. He used
to say that he could never recollect a phrase in
its exact form, and in his books he often unconsciously varied, writing from memory, some expression whose precise form is on record. Nor
had he any turn for languages. German he knew
scarcely at all, a fact which makes the range of his
historical knowledge appear more striking; and
though he had spent several winters in Italy, he
could not speak Italian except so far as he
needed it for the inn or the railway. The want
of mere verbal memory partly accounts for this
deficiency, but it was not unconnected with the
vehemence of his interest in the substance of
things. He was so anxious to get at the kernel
that he could not stop to examine the nut. In
this absence of linguistic gifts, as well as in the
keenness of his observation (and in his short-
sightedness), he resembled Dean Stanley, who,
though he had travelled in and brought back all
that was best worth knowing from every country
in Europe, had no facility in any language but his
own.

Green was not one of those whose personality
is unlike their books, for there was in both
the same fertility, the same vivacity, the same
quickness of sympathy. Nevertheless, his conversation seemed to give an even higher impres-

sion of intellectual power than did his writings, because it was so swift and so spontaneous. Such talk has rarely been heard in our time, so gay was it, so vivid, so various, so full of anecdote and illustration, so acute in criticism, so candid in consideration, so graphic in description, so abundant in sympathy, so flashing in insight, so full of colour and emotion as well as of knowledge and thought. One had to forbid one's self to visit him in the evening, because it was impossible to get away before two o'clock in the morning.   And, unlike many famous talkers, he was just as willing to listen as to speak. One of the charms of his company was that it made a man feel better than his ordinary self. His appreciation of whatever had any worth in it, his comments and replies, so stimulated the interlocutor's mind that it moved faster and could hit upon apter expressions than at any other time. The same gifts which shone in his conversation, lucid arrangement of ideas, ready command of words, and a power in perceiving the tendencies of those whom he addressed, would have made him an admirable public speaker. I do not remember that he ever did speak, in his later years, to any audience larger than a committee of twenty. But he was an eloquent preacher. The first time I ever saw him was in St. Philip's Church at Stepney about 1866, and I shall never forget the impression made on me by the impassioned sentences that rang through the church from the fiery little figure in the pulpit with its thin face and bright black eyes.

What Green accomplished seems to those who used to listen to him little in comparison with what he might have done had longer life and a more robust body been granted him. Some of his finest gifts would not have found their full scope till he came to treat of a period where the materials for history are ample, and where he could have allowed himself space to deal with them — such a period, for instance, as that of his early choice, the Angevin kings of England. Yet, even basing themselves on what he has done, they may claim for him a place among the foremost writers of his time. He left behind him no one who combined so many of the best gifts. There were among his contemporaries historians more learned and equally industrious. There were two or three whose accuracy was more scrupulous, their judgment more uniformly sober and cautious. But there was no one in whom so much knowledge and so wide a range of interests were united to such ingenuity, acuteness, and originality, as well as to such a power of presenting results in rich, clear, pictorial language. A master of style may be a worthless historian. We have instances. A skilful investigator and sound reasoner may be unreadable. The conjunction of fine gifts for investigation with fine gifts for exposition is a rare conjunction, which cannot be prized too highly, for while it advances historical science, it brings historical methods, as well as historical facts, within the horizon of the ordinary reader.

Of the services Green rendered to English history, the first, and that which was most promptly appreciated, was the intensity with which he realised, and the skill with which he portrayed, the life of the people of England as a whole, and taught his readers that the exploits of kings and the intrigues of ministers, and the struggles of parties in Parliament, are, after all, secondary matters, and important chiefly as they affect the welfare or stimulate the thoughts and feelings of the great mass of undistinguished humanity in whose hands the future of a nation lies. He changed the old-fashioned distribution of our annals according to reigns and dynasties into certain periods, showing that such divisions often obscure the true connection of events, and suggesting new and better conceptions of the periods into which the record of English progress naturally falls. And, lastly, he laid, in his latest books, a firm and enduring foundation for our mediæval history by that account of the Teutonic occupation of England, of the state of the country as they found it, and the way they conquered and began to organise it, which I have already dwelt on as a signal proof of his constructive faculty.

Many readers will be disposed to place him
near Macaulay, for though he was less weighty
he was more subtle, and not less fascinating. To
fewer perhaps will it occur to compare him with
Gibbon, yet I am emboldened by the opinion of
one of our greatest contemporary historians to
venture on the comparison. There are indeed
wide differences between the two.   Green is
as completely a man of the nineteenth century
as Gibbon was a man of the eighteenth. Green's
style has not the majestic march of Gibbon: it
is quick and eager almost to restlessness. Nor is
his judgment so uniformly grave and sound.
But one may find in his genius what was
characteristic of Gibbon's also, the combination
of a mastery of multitudinous details, with a large
and luminous view of those far-reaching forces and
relations which govern the fortunes of peoples and
guide the course of empire. This width and com-
prehensiveness, this power of massing for the purposes of argument the facts which his literary
art has just been clothing in its most brilliant
hues, is the highest of a historian's gifts, and is
the one which seems most surely to establish
Green's position among the leading historical
minds of his time.

SIR GEORGE JESSEL, MASTER OF THE ROLLS

THERE is hardly any walk of English life in which brilliant abilities win so little fame for their possessor among the public at large as that of practice at the Chancery bar. A leading ecclesiastic, or physician, or surgeon, or financier, or manufacturer, or even a great man of science, unless his work is done in some sphere which, like pure mathematics, is far removed from the comprehension of ordinary educated men, is sure, in a time like ours, to become well known to the world and acquire influence in it. A great advocate practising in the Common-law Courts is, of course, still more certain to become a familiar figure. But the cases which are dealt with by the Courts of Equity, though they often involve vast sums of money and raise intricate and important points of law, mostly turn on questions of a technical kind, and are seldom what the newspapers call sensational. Thus it may happen that a practitioner or a judge in these Courts enjoys an extraordinary reputation within his profession, and is by them regarded as one of the ornaments of his time, while the rest of his fellow-country-men know nothing at all about his merits.

This was the case with Sir George Jessel, though towards the end of his career the admiration which the Bar felt for his powers began so far to filter through to the general public that his premature death was felt to be a national misfortune.

Jessel (born in 1824, died in 1883) was only one among many instances England has lately seen of men of Jewish origin climbing to the highest distinction. But he was the first instance of a Jew who, continuing to adhere to the creed of his forefathers, received a very high office; for Mr. Disraeli, as every one knows, had been baptized as a boy, and always professed to be a Christian. Jessel's career was not marked by any remarkable incidents. He rose quickly to eminence at the bar, being in this aided by his birth; for the Jews in London, as elsewhere, hold together. There are among them many solicitors in large practice, and these take a natural pleasure in pushing forward any specially able member of their community. His powers were more fully seen and appreciated when he became (in 1865) a Queen's Counsel, and brought him with unusual speed to the front rank. He came into Parliament at the general election of 1868 on the Liberal side, and three years later was made Solicitor-General in Mr. Gladstone's first Government, retaining, as was then usual, his private practice, which had become so large that there was scarcely any case of first-rate importance brought into the Chancery Courts in which he did not appear. Although a decided Liberal, as the Jews mostly were until Lord Beaconsfield's foreign policy had begun to lead them into other paths, he had borne little part in politics till he took his seat in the House of Commons; and when he spoke there, he obtained no great success. Lawyers in the English Parliament are under the double disadvantage of having had less leisure than most other members to study and follow political questions, and of having contracted a manner and style of speaking not suited to an assembly which, though deliberative, is not deliberate, and which listens with impatience to a technical or forensic method of treating the topics which come before it.

Jessel's ability would have soon overcome the former difficulty, but less easily the latter. Though he was lucid and powerful in his treatment of legal topics, and made a quite admirable law officer in the way of advising ministers and the public departments, he was never popular with the House of Commons, for he presented his views in a hard, dry, dogmatic form, with no graces of style or delivery. However, he did not long remain in that arena, but on the retirement of Lord Romilly from the office of Master of the Rolls, was in 1873 appointed to succeed him. In this post his extraordinary gifts found their amplest sphere. The equity judges in England used always to sit, and in nearly all cases do still sit, without a jury to hear causes, with or without witnesses, and they despatch a great deal of the heaviest business that is brought into the courts. Commercial causes of the first importance come before them, no less than those which relate to trusts or to real property; and the granting of injunctions, a specially serious matter, rests chiefly in their hands. Each equity judge sits alone, and the suitor may choose before which of them he will bring his case. Among the four — a number subsequently increased to five — equity judges of first instance, Jessel immediately rose to the highest reputation, so that most of the heavy and difficult cases were brought into his court. He possessed a wonderfully quick, as well as powerful, mind, which got to the kernel of a matter while other people were still hammering at the shell, and which applied legal principles just as swiftly and surely as it mastered a group of complicated facts.

The Rolls Court used to present, while he presided over it, a curious and interesting sight, which led young counsel, who had no business to do there, to frequent it for the mere sake of watching the Judge. When the leading counsel

for the plaintiff was opening his case, Jessel
listened quietly for the first few minutes only,
and then began to address questions to the
counsel, at first so as to guide his remarks in a
particular direction, then so as to stop his course
altogether and turn his speech into a series of
answers to the Judge's interrogatories. When,
by a short dialogue of this kind, Jessel had
possessed himself of the vital facts, he would
turn to the leading counsel for the defendant
and ask him whether he admitted such and such
facts alleged by the plaintiff to be true. If these
facts were admitted, the Judge proceeded to
indicate the view he was disposed to take of the
law applicable to the facts, and, by a few more
questions to the counsel on the one side or the
other, as the case might be, elicited their respective legal grounds of contention. If the facts
were not admitted, it of course became necessary to call the witnesses or read the affidavits,
processes which the vigorous impatience of
the Judge considerably shortened, for it was a
dangerous thing to read to him any irrelevant
or loosely drawn paragraph. But more generally
his searching questions and the sort of pressure
he applied so cut down the issues of fact that
there was little or nothing left in controversy
regarding which it was necessary to examine the
evidence in detail, since the counsel felt that
there was no use in putting before him a conten-

tion which they could not sustain under the fire
of his criticism. Then Jessel proceeded to deliver
his opinion and dispose of the case.   The affair
was from beginning to end far less an argument
and counter-argument by counsel than an investigation directly conducted by the Judge himself, in which the principal function of the counsel
was to answer the Judge's questions concisely
and exactly, so that the latter might as soon as
possible get to the bottom of the matter.   The
Bar in a little while came to learn and adapt
themselves to his ways, and few complained of
being stopped or interrupted by him, because
his interruptions, unlike those of some judges,
were neither inopportune nor superfluous.   The
counsel (with scarcely an exception) felt themselves his inferiors, and recognised not only that
he was better able to handle the case than they
were, but that the manner and style in which they
presented their facts or arguments would make
little difference to the result, because his penetration was sure to discover the merits of each con
tention, and neither eloquence nor pertinacity
would have the slightest effect on his resolute
and self-confident mind.   Thus business was
despatched before him with unexampled speed,
and it became a maxim among barristers that,
however low down in the cause-list at the
Rolls your cause might stand, it was never
safe to be away from the court, so rapidly

were cases "crumpled up" or "broken down" under the blows of this vigorous intellect. It was more surprising that the suitors, as well as the Bar and the public generally, acquiesced, after the first few months, in this way of doing business. Nothing breeds more discontent than haste and heedlessness in a judge. But Jessel's speed was not haste. He did as much justice in a day as others could do in a week; and those few who, dissatisfied with these rapid methods, tried to reverse his decisions before the Court of Appeal, were very seldom successful, although that court then contained in Lord Justice James and Lord Justice Mellish two unusually strong men, who would not have hesitated to differ even from the redoubtable Master of the Rolls.

As I have mentioned Lord Justice Mellish, I may turn aside for a moment to say a word regarding that extraordinary man, who stood along with Cairns and Roundell Palmer in the foremost rank of Jessel's professional contemporaries. Mellish held for some years before his elevation to the Bench in 1869 a position unique at the English Common-law Bar as a giver of opinions on points of law. As the Israelites in King David's day said of Ahithophel that his counsel was as if a man had inquired at the oracle of God,[1] so the legal profession deemed Mellish

[1] 2 Sam. xvi. 23.

practically infallible, and held an opinion signed by him to be equal in weight to a judgment of the Court of Exchequer Chamber (the then court of appeal in common-law cases). He was not effective as an advocate addressing a jury, being indeed far too good for any jury; but in arguing a point of law his unerring logic, the lucidity with which he stated his position, the cogency and precision with which he drew his inferences, made it a delight to listen to him. The chain of ratiocination seemed irrefragable:

Ἐν δ' ἔθετ' ἀκμοθέτῳ μεγὰν ἄκμονα, κόπτε δε δεσμούς
Ἀρρήκτους ἀλύτους, ὄφρ' ἔμπεδον αὖθι μένοιεν.[1]

He had, indeed, but one fault as an arguer. He could not argue a point whose soundness he doubted as effectively as one in which he had faith; and when it befell that several points arose in a case, and the Court seemed disposed to lay more stress on the one for which he cared little than on the one he deemed conclusive, he refused to fall in with their view and continued to insist upon that which his own mind approved.

I remember to have once heard him and Cairns argue before the House of Lords (sitting as the final Court of Appeal) a case relating to a vessel called the *Alexandra* — it was a case

[1] *Odyss.* viii. 274 : "And upon the anvil-stand he set the mighty anvil ; and he forged the links that could be neither broken nor loosed, so that they should stay firm in their place."

N

arising out of an attempt of the Confederates, during the American War of Secession, to get out of a British port a cruiser they had ordered. Cairns spoke first with all his usual power, and seemed to have left nothing to be added. But when Mellish followed on the same side, he set his points in so strong a light, and placed his contention on so solid a basis, that even Cairns's speech was forgotten, and it seemed impossible that any answer could be found to Mellish's arguments. One felt as if the voice of pure reason were speaking through his lips.

Such an intellect might seem admirably qualified for judicial work. But as a judge, Mellish, admirable though he was in temper, in fairness, in learning, and in logic, did not win so exceptional a reputation as he had won at the Bar. People used to ascribe this partly to his weak health, partly to the fact that he, who had been a common-law practitioner, was sitting in a court which heard equity appeals, and alongside of a quick and strong colleague reared in the equity courts.[1] But something may have been due to the fact that he needed the stimulus of conflict to bring out the full force of his splendid intelligence. A circumstance attending the appointment of

[1] Lord Justice James said of his colleague that he had only one defect as a judge : " He was too anxious to convince counsel that they were wrong, when he thought their contention unsound, seeming to forget that counsel are paid not to be convinced."

Mellish illustrates the remark already made that a great counsel whose work lies apart from so-called "sensation cases" may remain unknown to his contemporaries. When Mr. Gladstone, being then Prime Minister, and having to select a Lord Justice of Appeal, was told that Mellish was the fittest man for the post, he asked, "Can that be the boy who was my fag at Eton?" He had not heard of Mellish during the intervening forty years!

However, I return to the Master of the Rolls. In dealing with facts, Jessel has never had a superior, and in our days, perhaps, no rival. He knew all the ways of the financial and commercial world. In his treatment of points of law, every one admitted and admired both an extraordinary knowledge and mastery of reported cases, and an extremely acute and exact appreciation of principles, a complete power of extracting them from past cases and fitting them to the case in hand. He had a memory which forgot nothing, and which, indeed, wearied him by refusing to forget trivial things. When he delivered an elaborate judgment it was his delight to run through a long series of cases, classifying and distinguishing them. His strength made him bold; he went further than most judges in readiness to carry a principle somewhat beyond any decided case, and to overrule an authority which he did not

respect. The fault charged on him was his
tendency, perhaps characteristic of the Hebrew
mind, to take a somewhat hard and dry view
of a legal principle, overlooking its more delicate shades, and, in the interpretation of
statutes or documents, to adhere too strictly to
the letter, overlooking the spirit. An eminent
lawyer said, " If all judges had been like
Jessel, there might have been no equity." In
that respect many deemed him inferior to
Lord Cairns, the greatest judge among his contemporaries, who united to an almost equally
wide and accurate knowledge of the law a grasp
of principles even more broad and philosophical
than Jessel's was. Be this as it may, the
judgments of the Master of the Rolls, which
fill so many pages of the recent English Law
Reports, are among the best that have ever gone
to build up the fabric of the English law. Except
on two occasions, when he reserved judgment
at the request of his colleagues in the Court
of Appeal, they were delivered on the spur of
the moment, after the conclusion of the arguments, or of so much of the arguments as he
allowed counsel to deliver; but they have all the
merits of carefully-considered utterances, so clear
and direct is their style, so concisely as well as
cogently are the authorities discussed and the
grounds of decision stated. The bold and sweeping character which often belongs to them makes

them more instructive as well as more agreeable reading than the judgments of most modern judges, whose commonest fault is a timidity which tries to escape, by dwelling on the details of the particular case, from the enunciation of a definite general principle. Positive and definite Jessel always was. As he put it himself: " I may be wrong, but I never have any doubts."

At the Bar, Jessel had been far from popular; for his manners were unpolished, and his conduct towards other counsel overbearing. On the Bench he improved, and became liked as well as respected. There was a sort of rough *bonhomie* about him, and though he could be disagreeable on occasions to a leading counsel, especially if brought from the common-law bar into his court, he showed a good-humoured wish to deal gently with young or inexperienced barristers. There was also an obvious anxiety to do justice, an impatience of mere technicalities, and a readiness, remarkable in so strong-willed a man, to hear what could be said against his own opinion, and to reconsider it. Besides, a profession is naturally proud of any one whose talents adorn it, and whose eminence seems to be communicated to the whole body.

Ever since, under the Plantagenet kings, the Chancery became a law court, the office of Master of the Rolls had been that of a judge of first

instance. In 1881 its character was changed,
and its occupant placed at the head of the
Court of Appeal. Thus it was as an appellate
judge that Jessel latterly sat, giving no less
satisfaction in that capacity than in his former
one, and being indeed confessedly the strongest
judicial intellect (except Lord Cairns) on the
Bench. Outside his professional duties, his chief
interest was in the University of London, at
which he had himself graduated. He was a
member of its senate, and busied himself with its
examinations, being up till the last excessively
fond of work, and finding that of a judge who
sits for five or six hours daily insufficient to
satisfy his appetite. He was not what would
be called a highly cultivated man, although he
knew a great deal beyond the field of law,
mathematics, for instance, and Hebrew literature
and botany, for he had been brought up in a
not very refined circle, and had been absorbed
in legal work during the best years of his life.
But his was an intelligence of extraordinary power
and flexibility, eminently practical, as the Semitic
intellect generally is, and yet thoroughly scientific.
And he was also one of those strong natures who
make themselves disliked while they are fighting
their way to the top, but grow more genial and
more tolerant when they have won what they
sought, and perceive that others admit their pre-
eminence. The services which he rendered as a

judge illustrate not only the advantage of throwing open all places to all comers — the bigotry of an elder day excluded the Jews from judicial office altogether — but also the benefit of having a judge at least equal in ability to the best of those who practise before him. It was because Jessel was so easily master in his court that so large and important a part of the judicial business of the country was, during many years, despatched with a swiftness and a success seldom equalled in the annals of the English Courts.

LORD CHANCELLOR CAIRNS

HUGH M'CALMONT CAIRNS, afterwards Earl Cairns (born 1819, died 1885), was one of three remarkable Scoto-Irishmen whom the north-east corner of Ulster gave to the United Kingdom in one generation, and each of whom was foremost in the career he entered. Lord Lawrence was the strongest of Indian or Colonial administrators, and did more than any other man to save India for England in the crisis of the great Mutiny of 1857. Lord Kelvin has been, since the death of Charles Darwin, the first among British men of science. Lord Cairns was unquestionably the greatest judge of the Victorian epoch, perhaps of the nineteenth century.[1] His name and family were of Scottish origin, but he combined with the shrewd sense and grim persistency of Scotland some measure of the keen partisanship which marks the Irish Orangeman. Born an Episco-

---

[1] No biography of Lord Cairns has (so far as I know) appeared — a singular fact, considering the brilliancy of his career, and considering the tendency which now prevails to bestow this kind of honour on many persons of the second or even the third rank. One reason may be that Cairns, great though he was, never won personal popularity even with his own political party or among his contemporaries at the bar, and was to the general public no more than a famous name.

palian, he grew up a Tory in politics, an earnest Low-Church Evangelical in religion; nor did his opinions in either respect ever seem to alter during his long life. His great abilities were perceived both at school (he was educated at the Academy in Belfast) and at college (Trinity College, Dublin), and so much impressed the counsel in whose chambers he studied for a year in London, that he strongly dissuaded the young man from returning to Dublin to practise at the Irish bar, promising him a brilliant career on the wider theatre of England. The prediction was verified by the rapidity with which Cairns, who had, no doubt, the advantage of influential connections in the City of London, rose into note. He obtained (as a Conservative) a seat in Parliament for his native town of Belfast when only thirty-three years of age, and was appointed Solicitor-General to Lord Derby's second Ministry six years later — a post which few eminent lawyers have reached before fifty. In the House of Commons, though at first somewhat diffident and nervous, he soon proved himself a powerful as well as ready speaker, and would doubtless have remained in an assembly where he was rendering such valuable services to his party but for the weakness of his lungs and throat, which had threatened his life since boyhood. He therefore accepted, in 1867, the office of Lord Justice of Appeal, with a seat in

the House of Lords, and next year was made
Lord Chancellor by Mr. Disraeli, then Prime
Minister, who dismissed Lord Chelmsford, then
Chancellor, in order to have the benefit of Cairns's
help as a colleague. Disraeli subsequently caused
him to be raised to an earldom.

After Lord Derby's death, Cairns led the
Tory party in the House of Lords for a time
(replacing the Duke of Richmond when the latter
quitted the leadership), but his very pronounced
Low-Church proclivities, coupled perhaps with a
certain jealousy felt toward him as a newcomer,
prevented him from becoming popular there, so
that ultimately the leadership of that House settled
itself in the hands of Lord Salisbury, a statesman
not superior to Cairns in political judgment or
argumentative power, but without the disadvantage of being a lawyer, possessing a wider range
of political experience, and in closer sympathy
with the feelings and habits of the titled order.
There were, however, some peers who, when
Lord Beaconsfield died in 1881, desired to see
Cairns chosen to succeed him in the leadership
of the Tory party, then in opposition, in the
Upper Chamber. Whether in opposition or in
power, Cairns took a prominent part in all "full-
dress" political debates in the House of Lords
and in the discussion of legal measures, and was
indeed so absolutely master of the Chamber when
such measures came under discussion, that the

Liberal Government, during the years from 1868 to 1874, and again from 1880 till 1885, could carry no legal reforms through the House of Lords except by his permission, which, of course, was never given when such reforms could seem to affect any political issue. Yet the vehemence of his party feeling did not overcast his judgment. It was mainly through his interposition (aided by that of Archbishop Tait) that the House of Lords consented to pass the Irish Church Bill of 1869, a measure which Cairns, of course heartily disliking it, accepted for the sake of saving to the disestablished Church a part of her funds, since these might have been lost had the Bill been rejected then and passed next year by an angrier House of Commons. Of all the members of Disraeli's two Cabinets, he was the one whom Disraeli himself had been wont most to trust and most to rely on. In January 1874, when Mr. Gladstone's suddenly announced dissolution of Parliament startled all England one Saturday morning, Disraeli, who heard of it while still in bed, was at first frightened, thinking that the Liberal leader had played his cards boldly and well, and would carry the elections. When his chief party manager came to see him he was found restless and dejected, and cried out, " Send for Cairns at once." Lord Cairns was sent for, came full of vigour, hope, and counsel, and after an hour's talk so restored the confidence of his ally that Disraeli sat down in the best spirits to compose his electoral manifesto. As everybody knows, Cairns's forecast was right, and the Tories won the general election by a large majority.

For political success Cairns had several qualities of the utmost value — a stately presence, a clear head, a resolute will, and splendid oratorical gifts. He was not an imaginative speaker, nor fitted to touch the emotions; but he had a match-less power of statement, and a no less matchless closeness and cogency in argument. In the famous controversies of 1866, he showed himself the clearest and most vigorous thinker among the opponents of reform, more solid, if less brilliant, than was Robert Lowe. His diction, without being exceptionally choice, was pure and precise, and his manner had a dignity and weight which seemed to compel your attention even when the matter was uninteresting. A voice naturally neither strong nor musical, and some-times apt to sound hollow (for the chest was weak), was managed with great skill ; action and gesture were used sparingly but effectively, and the tall well-built figure and strongly-marked, somewhat Roman features, with their haughty and distant air, deepened the impression of power, courage, and resolution which was characteristic of the whole man.

The qualities of oratory I have described

may seem better fitted to a comparatively sober
and sedate assembly like the House of Lords
than to a changeful and excitable assembly
like the House of Commons. Yet, in point of
fact, Cairns spoke better in the Commons than he
did afterwards in the Lords, and would have left
an even higher oratorical reputation had his
career in the popular House been longer and his
displays more numerous. The reason seems to be
that the heat of that House warmed his somewhat
chilly temperament, and roused him to a more
energetic and ardent style of speaking than was
needed in the Upper Chamber, where he and
his friends, commanding a large majority, had
things all their own way. In the House of
Commons he confronted a crowd of zealous
adversaries, and put forth all the forces of his
logic and rhetoric to overcome them. In the more
languid House of Lords he was apt to be didactic,
sometimes even prolix. He overproved his own
case without feeling the need, which he would have
felt in the Commons, of overthrowing the case of
the other side; his manner wanted animation and
his matter variety. Still, he was a great speaker,
greater as a speaker upon legal topics, where a
power of exact statement and lucid exposition is
required, than any one he left behind him.

Why, it may be asked, with these gifts, and
with so much firmness and energy of character,
did he not play an even more conspicuous part

in politics, and succeed, after Lord Beaconsfield's death, to the chieftaincy of the Tory party? The answer is to be found partly in the prejudice which still survives in England against legal politicians, partly in certain defects of his own personality. Although sincerely pious, and exemplary in all the relations of domestic life, he was ungenial and unbending in social intercourse. Few equally eminent men of our time have had so narrow a circle of personal friends. There was a dryness, a coldness, and an appearance of reserve and hauteur about his manner which repelled strangers, and kept acquaintanceship from ripening into friendship. To succeed as a political leader, a man must usually (I do not say invariably, because there are a few remarkable instances— Mr. Parnell's would appear to be one of them — to the contrary) at least seem sympathetic; must be able to enter into the feelings of his followers, and show himself interested in them not merely as party followers, but as human beings. There must be a certain glow, a certain effluence of feeling about him, which makes them care for him and rally to him as a personality. Whether Lord Cairns wanted warmth of heart, or whether it was that an inner warmth failed to pierce the cloak of reserve and pride which he habitually wore, I do not attempt to determine. But the defect told heavily against him. He never became a familiar figure to the mass of his party, a person whose features they knew, at whose name they would cheer; and nowadays all leaders, to whatever party they belong, find a source of strength in winning this kind of popularity. The quality which Americans call magnetism is perhaps less essential in England than in the country which distinguished and named it; but it is helpful even in England. Cairns, though an Irishman, was wholly without it.

In the field of law, where passion has no place, and even imagination must be content to move with clipped wings along the ground, the merits of Lord Cairns's intellect showed to the best advantage. At the Chancery bar he was one of a trio who had not been surpassed, if ever equalled, during the nineteenth century, and whom none of our now practising advocates rivals. The other two were Mr., afterwards Lord Justice, Rolt, and Mr. Roundell Palmer, afterwards Lord Chancellor Selborne. All were admirable lawyers, but, of the three, Rolt excelled in his spirited presentation of a case and in the lively vigour of his arguments. Palmer was conspicuous for exhaustless ingenuity, and for a subtlety which sometimes led him away into reasonings too fine for the court to follow. Cairns was broad, massive, convincing, with a robust urgency of logic which seemed to grasp and fix you, so that while he spoke you could fancy no conclusion possible save that toward which he moved. His habit was to seize upon what he deemed the central and vital point of the case, throwing the whole force of his argument upon that one point, and holding the judge's mind fast to it.

All these famous men were raised to the judicial bench. Rolt remained there for a few months only, so his time was too short to permit him to enrich our jurisprudence and leave a memory of himself in the Reports. Palmer sat in the House of Lords from his accession to the Chancellorship in 1872 till his death in 1896, and, while fully sustaining his reputation as a man of eminent legal capacity, was, on the whole, less brilliant as a judge than he had been as an advocate, because a tendency to over-refinement is more dangerous in the judicial than in the forensic mind. He made an admirable Chancellor, and showed himself more industrious and more zealous for law reform than did Cairns. But Cairns was the greater judge, and became to the generation which argued before him a model of judicial excellence. In hearing a cause he was singularly patient, rarely interrupting counsel, and then only to put some pertinent question. His figure was so still, his countenance so impassive, that people sometimes doubted whether he was really attending to all that was urged at the bar. But when the time came for him to deliver judgment, which in the House of Lords is done in the form of a speech addressed to the House in moving or supporting a motion that is to become the judgment of the tribunal, it was seen how fully he had apprehended the case in all its bearings. His deliverances were never lengthy, but they were exhaustive. They went straight to the vital principles on which the question turned, stated these in the most luminous way, and applied them with unerring exactitude to the particular facts. It is as a storehouse of fundamental doctrines that his judgments are so valuable. They disclose less knowledge of case-law than do those of some other judges; but Cairns was not one of the men who love cases for their own sake, and he never cared to draw upon, still less to display, more learning than was needed for the matter in hand. It was in the grasp of the principles involved, in the breadth of view which enabled him to see these principles in their relation to one another, in the precision of the logic which drew conclusions from the principles, in the perfectly lucid language in which the principles were expounded and applied, that his strength lay. Herein he surpassed the most eminent of contemporary judges, the then Master of the Rolls, for while Jessel had perhaps a quicker mind than Cairns, he had not so wide a mind, nor one so thoroughly philosophical in the methods by which it moved.

Outside the spheres of law and politics, Cairns's only interest was in religion. He did not seem, although a good classical scholar and a competent

o

mathematician, to care either for letters or for science. But he was a Sunday-school teacher nearly all his life. Prayer-meetings were held at his house, at which barristers, not otherwise known for their piety, but believed to desire county court judgeships, were sometimes seen. He used to take the chair at missionary and other philanthropic meetings. He was surrounded by evangelisers and clergymen. But nothing softened the austerity or melted the ice of his manners. Neither did the great position he had won seem to give a higher and broader quality to his statesmanship. It is true that in law he was wholly free from the partisanship which tinged his politics. No one was more perfectly fair upon the Bench; no one more honestly anxious to arrive at a right decision. And as a law reformer, although he effected less than might have been hoped from his abilities or expected from the absolute sway which he exercised while Chancellor in Lord Beaconsfield's Government from 1874 to 1880, he was free from prejudice, and willing to sweep away antiquated rules or usages if they seemed to block the channel of speedy justice. But in politics this impartiality and elevation vanished even after he had risen so high that he did not need to humour the passions or confirm the loyalty of his own associates. He seemed to be not merely a party man, which an English politician is forced to be, because if he stands outside party he cannot effect anything, but a partisan — that is, a man wholly devoted to his party, who sees everything through its eyes, and argues every question in its interests. He gave the impression of being either unwilling or unable to rise to a higher and more truly national view, and sometimes condescended to arguments whose unsoundness his penetrating intellect could hardly have failed to detect. His professional tone had been blameless, but at the bar the path of rectitude is plain and smooth, and a scrupulous mind finds fewer cases of conscience present themselves in a year than in Parliament within a month. Yet if in this respect Cairns failed to reach a level worthy of his splendid intellect, the defect was due not to any selfish view of his own interest, but rather to the narrowness of the groove into which his mind had fallen, and to the atmosphere of Orange sentiment in which he had grown up. As a politician he is already beginning to be forgotten; but as a judge he will be held in honourable remembrance as one of the five or six most brilliant luminaries that have adorned the English Bench since those remote days [1] in which the beginning of legal memory is placed.

[1] The reign of King Richard the First.

BISHOP FRASER

JAMES FRASER, Bishop of Manchester from 1870 till 1885, was born in Gloucestershire, of a Scottish family, in 1818, and died at Manchester in 1885.[1] He took no prominent part in ecclesiastical politics, and no part at all in general politics. Though a sound classical scholar in the old-fashioned sense of the term—he won the Ireland University Scholarship at Oxford, then and still the most conspicuous prize in the field of classics — he was not an exceptionally cultivated man, and he never wrote anything except official reports and episcopal charges. Neither was he, although a ready and effective speaker, gifted with the highest kind of eloquence. Neither was he a profound theologian. Yet his character and career are of permanent interest, for he created not merely a new episcopal type, but (one may almost say) a new ecclesiastical type within the Church of England.

Till some sixty or seventy years ago the normal English bishop was a rich, dignified, and

---

[1] Two Lives of Dr. Fraser have been published, one (in 1887) by the late Judge Hughes, the other, which gives a fuller impression of his personal character, by the Rev. J. W. Diggle (1891).

rather easy-going magnate, aristocratic in his tastes and habits, moderate in his theology, sometimes to the verge of indifferentism, quite as much a man of the world as a pastor of souls. He had usually obtained his preferment by his family connections, or by some service rendered to the court or a political chief — perhaps even by solicitation or intrigue. Now and then eminence in learning or literature raised a man to the Bench: there were, for instance, the " Greek play " bishops, such as Dr. Monk of Gloucester, whose fame rested on their editions of the Attic dramatists; and the *Quarterly Review* bishops, such as Dr. Copleston, of Llandaff, whose powerful pen, as well as his wise administration of the great Oxford College over which he long presided, amply justified his promotion. So even in the eighteenth century the illustrious Butler had been Bishop of Durham, as in Ireland the illustrious Berkeley had been Bishop of Cloyne. But, on the whole, the bishops of our grandfathers' days were more remarkable for their prudence and tact, their adroitness or suppleness, than for intellectual or moral superiority to the rest of the clergy. Their own upper-class world, and the middle class which, in the main, took its view of English institutions from the upper class, respected them as a part of the solid fabric of English society, but they were a mark for Radical invective and for literary sneers.

Their luxurious pomp and ease were incessantly contrasted with the simplicity of the apostles and the poverty of curates, and the abundance among them of the gifts that befit the senate or the drawing-room was compared with the rarity of the graces that adorn a saint. The comparison was hardly fair, for saints are scarce, and a good bishop needs some qualities which a saint may lack.

That revival within the Church of England which went on in various forms from 1800 till 1870, at first Low Church or Evangelical in its tendencies, latterly more conspicuously High Church and Ritualist, began from below and worked upwards till at length it reached the bishops. Lord Palmerston, influenced by Lord Shaftesbury, filled the vacant sees that fell to him with earnest men, sometimes narrow, sometimes deficient in learning, but often good preachers, and zealous for the doctrines they held. When the High Churchmen found their way to the Bench, as they did very largely under Lord Derby's and Mr. Gladstone's rule, they showed as much theological zeal as the Evangelicals, and perhaps more talent for administration. The popular idea of what may be expected from a bishop rose, and the bishops rose with the idea. As Bishop of Oxford, Dr. Samuel Wilberforce was among the first to make himself powerfully felt through his diocese. His example told upon other prelates, and prime ministers grew more anxious to select energetic

and popular men. So it came to pass that the
bishops began to be among the foremost men in
the Church of England. Some, like Dr. Magee
of Peterborough, and afterwards of York, were
brilliant orators; some, like Dr. Lightfoot of
Durham, profound scholars; some, like Dr.
Temple of Exeter, able and earnest administrators. There remained but few who had not
some good claim to the dignity they enjoyed.
So it may be said, when one compares the later
Victorian bishops with their Georgian predecessors, that no class in the country has improved
more. Few now sneer at them, for no set of men
take a more active and more creditable part in the
public business of the country. Their incomes,
curtailed of late years in the case of the richer
sees, are no more than sufficient for the expenses
which fall upon them, and they work as hard as
any other men for their salaries. Though the
larger sees have been divided, the reduction of
the toil of bishops thus effected has been less than
the addition to it due to the growth of population
and the increased activity of the clergy. The
only defect which the censorious still impute to
them is a certain episcopal conventionality, a disposition to try to please everybody by the use of
vague professional language, a tendency to think
too much about the Church as a church establishment, and to defer to clerical opinion when they
ought to speak and act with an independence

born of their individual opinions. Some of them, as, for instance, the three I have just mentioned, were not open to this reproach. It was one of the merits and charms of Fraser that he was absolutely free from any such tendency. Other men, such as Bishop Lightfoot, have been not less eminent models of the virtues which ought to characterise a great Christian pastor; but Fraser (appointed some time before Lightfoot) was the first to be an absolutely unconventional and, so to speak, unepiscopal bishop. His career marked a new departure and set a new example.

Fraser spent the earlier years of his manhood in Oxford, as a tutor in Oriel College, teaching Thucydides and Aristotle. Like many of his Oxford contemporaries, he continued through life to think on Aristotelian lines, and one could trace them in his sermons. He then took in succession two college livings, both in quiet nooks in the south of England, and discharged for nearly twenty years the simple duties of a parish priest, unknown to the great world, but making himself beloved by the people, and doing his best to improve their condition. The zeal he had shown in promoting elementary education caused him to be appointed (in 1865) by the Schools Inquiry Commissioners to be their Assistant Commissioner to examine the common-school system of the United States, and the excellence of his report thereon attracted the notice of the late Lord

Lyttelton, one of those Commissioners who were then sitting to investigate the state of secondary education in England. His report long remained by far the best general picture of American schools, conspicuous for its breadth of view, its clearness of statement, its sympathetic insight into conditions unlike those he had known in England. On the recommendation (as has been generally believed) of Lord Lyttelton and of the then Bishop of Salisbury, who was a friend of Dr. Fraser's, Mr. Gladstone, at that time Prime Minister, appointed him Bishop of Manchester in 1870. The diocese of Manchester, which included all Lancashire except Liverpool and a small district in the extreme north of the county, had been under a bishop who, although an able and learned man, capable of making himself agreeable when he pleased, was personally un-popular, and had done little beyond his formal duties. He lived in a large and handsome country-house some miles from the city, and was known by sight to very few of its inhabitants. (I was familiar with Lancashire in those days, for I had visited all its grammar-schools as Assistant Commissioner to the Commission just referred to, and there was hardly a trace to be found in it of the bishop's action.) Fraser had not been six months in the county before everything was changed. The country mansion was sold, and he procured a modest house in one of the less fashion-

able suburbs of the city. He preached twice
every Sunday, usually in some parish church, and
spent the week in travelling up and down his
diocese, so that the days were few in which he
was not on the railway. He stretched out the
hand of friendship to the Dissenters (numerous
and powerful in the manufacturing districts), who
had hitherto regarded a bishop as a sort of natural
enemy, gained their confidence, and soon became
as popular with them as with the laity of his
own Church. He associated himself with all
the works of benevolence or public utility which
were in progress, subscribed to all so far as his
means allowed, and was always ready to speak
at a meeting on behalf of any good enterprise.
He dealt in his sermons with the topics of the
day, avoiding party politics, but speaking his
mind on all social and moral questions with a
freedom which sometimes involved him in passing
difficulties, but stimulated the minds of his hearers,
and gave the impression of his own perfect
candour and perfect courage. He used to say
that as he felt it his duty to speak wherever he
was asked to do so, he must needs speak without
preparation, and must therefore expect sometimes
to get into hot water; that this was a pity, but
it was not his fault that he was reported, and
that it was better to run the risk of making
mistakes and suffering for them than to refuse
out of self-regarding caution to give the best of

himself to the diocese. He had that true modesty
which makes a man willing to do a thing imperfectly, at the risk of lowering his intellectual reputation. He knew that he was neither a deep
thinker nor a finished preacher, and was content
to be what he was, so long as he could perform
the work which it was in him to do. He lost
no opportunity of meeting the working men,
would go and talk to them in the yards of the
mills or at the evening gatherings of mechanics'
institutes; and when any misfortune befell, such
as a colliery accident, he was often among the
first who reached the spot to help the survivors
and comfort the widows. He made no difference
between rich and poor, showed no wish to be a
guest in the houses of the great, and treated the
poorest curate with as much courtesy as the most
pompous county magnate. His work in Lancashire seldom allowed him to appear in the House
of Lords; and this he regretted, not that he
desired to speak there, but because, as he said,
"Whether or not bishops do Parliament good,
Parliament does bishops good."

Such a simple, earnest, active course of conduct
told upon the feelings of the people who read of
his words and doings. But even greater was the
impression made by his personality upon those
who saw him. He was a tall, well-built man,[1]

[1] He was a good judge of horses, and had in his youth been fond of
hunting.

erect in figure, with a quick eye, a firm step, a ruddy face, an expression of singular heartiness and geniality. He seemed always cheerful, and, in spite of his endless labours, always fresh and strong. His smile and the grasp of his hand put you into good-humour with yourself and the world; if you were dispirited, they led you out of shadow into sunlight. He was not a great reader, and had no time for sustained and searching thought; yet he seemed always abreast of what was passing in the world, and to know what the books and articles and speeches of the day contained, although he could not have found time to peruse them. With strong opinions of his own, he was anxious to hear yours; a ready and eager talker, yet a willing listener. His oratory was plain, with few flights of rhetoric, but it was direct and vigorous, free from conventional phrases, charged with clear good sense and genuine feeling, and capable, when his feeling was exceptionally strong, of rising to eloquence. He had a ready sense of humour, the best proof of which was that he relished a joke against himself.[1]

[1] A clergyman of his diocese had once, under the greatest provocation, knocked down a person who had insulted him, and the bishop wrote him a letter of reproof pointing out (among other things) that, exposed as the Church of England was to much criticism on all hands, her ministers ought to be very careful in their demeanour. The offender replied by saying, "I must regretfully admit that being grossly insulted, and forgetting in the heat of the moment the critical position of the Church of England, I did knock the man down, etc." Fraser, delighted with this turning of the tables on himself, told me the anecdote with great glee, and invited the clergyman to stay with him not long afterwards.

However, the greatest charm, both of his public
and private talk, was the transparent sincerity
and honesty that shone through it. His mind
was like a crystal pool of water in a mountain
stream. You saw everything that was in it, and
saw nothing that was mean or unworthy. This
sincerity and freshness made his character not
only manly, but lovable and beautiful, beautiful
in its tenderness, its loyalty to his friends, its
devotion to truth.

His conscientious anxiety to say nothing more
than he thought was apt to make him an em-
barrassing ally. It happened more than once
that when he came to speak at a public meeting
on behalf of some enterprise, he was not content,
like most men, to set forth its merits and claims,
but went on to dwell upon possible drawbacks
or dangers, so that the more ardent friends of
the scheme thought he was pouring cold water
on them, and called him a Balaam reversed. In
a political assembly he would have been an *enfant
terrible* whom his party would have feared to put
up to speak; but as people in the diocese got to
know that this was his way, they only smiled at
his too ingenuous honesty. As he spoke with no
preparation, and was naturally impulsive, he now
and then spoke unadvisedly, and received a good
deal of newspaper censure. But he was never
involved in real trouble by these speeches. As
Dean Stanley wrote to him, " You have a singular

gift of going to the very verge of imprudence and yet never crossing it."

No one will wonder that such a character, set in a conspicuous place, and joined to extraordinary activity and zeal, should have produced an immense effect on the people of his city and diocese. Since Nonconformity arose in England in the seventeenth century, no bishop, perhaps, indeed no man, whether cleric or layman, had done so much to draw together people of different religious persuasions and help them to realise their common Christianity. Densely populated South Lancashire is practically one huge town, and he was its foremost citizen; the most instant in all good works; the one whose words were most sure to find attentive listeners. This was because he spoke, I will not say as a layman, but simply as a Christian, never claiming for himself any special authority in respect either of his sacerdotal character or his official position. No English prelate before him had been so welcome to all classes and sections; none was so much lamented by the masses of the people. But it is a significant fact that he was from first to last more popular with the laity than with the clergy. Not that there was ever any slur on his orthodoxy. He began life as a moderate High Churchman, and gradually verged, half unconsciously, toward what would be called a Broad-Church position; maintaining the claim of the Anglican Church to undertake, and her duty to hold herself responsible for, the education of the people, and upholding her status as an establishment, but dwelling little on minor points of doctrinal difference, and seeming to care still less for external observances or points of ritual. This displeased the Anglo-Catholic party, and even among other sections of the clergy there was a kind of feeling that the Bishop was not sufficiently clerical, did not set full store by the sacerdotal side of his office, and did not think enough about ecclesiastical questions.

He was, I think, the first bishop who greeted men of science as fellow-workers for truth, and declared that Christianity had not, and could not have, anything to fear from scientific inquiry. This has often been said since, but in 1870 it was so novel that it drew from Huxley a singularly warm and impressive recognition. He was one of the first bishops to condemn the system of theological tests in the English universities. He even declared that " it was an evil hour when the Church thought herself obliged to add to or develop the simple articles of the Apostles' Creed." These deliverances, which any one can praise now, alarmed a large section of the Church of England then ; nor was the bishop's friendliness to Dissenters favourably regarded by those who deny to Dissenting pastors the title of Christian ministers.[1]

---

[1] He was himself aware that this caused displeasure. In his latest

The gravest trouble of his life arose in connection with legal proceedings which he felt bound to take in the case of a Ritualist clergyman who had persisted in practices apparently illegal. Fraser, though personally the most tolerant of men to those who differed from his own theological views, felt bound to enforce the law, because it was the law, and was at once assailed unjustly, as well as bitterly, by those who sympathised with the offending clergyman, and who could not, or would not, understand that a bishop, like other persons in an official position, may hold it his absolute duty to carry out the directions of the law whether or no he approves the law, and at whatever cost to himself. These attacks were borne with patience and dignity. He was never betrayed into recriminations, and could the more easily preserve his calmness, because he felt no animosity.

A bishop may be a power outside his own religious community even in a country where

Charge, delivered some months before his death, he said: "I am charged, amongst other grievous sins, with that of thinking not unkindly, and speaking not unfavourably, of Dissenters. I don't profess to love dissent, but I have received innumerable kindnesses from Dissenters. Why should I abuse them? Why should I call them hard names? Remembering how Nonconformity was made — no doubt sometimes by self-will and pride and prejudice and ignorance, but far more often by the Church's supineness, neglect, and intolerance in days long since gone by, of which we have not yet paid the full penalty — though, as I have said, I love not the thing, I cannot speak harshly of it."

That a defence was needed may seem strange to those who do not know England.

the clergy are separated as a caste from the lay people. Such men as Dupanloup in France show that. So too he may be a mighty moral and religious force outside his own religious community in a country where there is no church established or endowed by the State. The example of Dr. Phillips Brooks in the United States shows that. But Dupanloup would have been eminent and influential had he not been a clergyman at all; and Dr. Brooks was the most inspiring preacher and the most potent leader of religious thought in America long before, in the last years of his life, he reluctantly consented to accept the episcopal office. Fraser, not so gifted by nature as either of those men, would have had little chance of doing the work he did save in a country where the existence of an ancient establishment secures for one of its dignitaries a position of far-reaching influence. When the gains and losses to a nation of the retention of a church establishment are reckoned up, this may be set down among the gains.

If the Church of England possessed more leaders like Tait, Fraser, and Lightfoot — the statesman, the citizen, and the scholar — in the characters and careers of all of whom one finds the common mark of a catholic and pacific spirit, she would have no need to fear any assaults of political foes, no temptation to ally herself with any party, but might stand as an establishment

P

until, after long years, by the general wish of her own people, as well as of those who are without, she passed peaceably into the position of being the first in honour, numbers, and influence among a group of Christian communities, all equally free from State control.

Fraser's example showed how much an attitude of unpretending simplicity and friendliness to all sects and classes may do to mitigate the jealousy and suspicion which still embitter the relations of the different religious bodies in England, and which work for evil even in its politics. He created, as Dean Stanley said, a new type of episcopal excellence: and why should not originality be shown in the conception and discharge of an office as well as in the sphere of pure thought or of literary creation?

SIR STAFFORD HENRY NORTHCOTE, EARL OF IDDESLEIGH[1]

SIR STAFFORD NORTHCOTE (born 1818, died 1887) belonged to a type of politician less common among us than it used to be, and likely to become still more rare as England grows more democratic — the county gentleman of old family and good estate, who receives and profits by a classical education at one of the ancient universities, who is at an early age returned to Parliament in respect of his social position in his county, who has leisure to cultivate himself for statesmanship, who has tastes and resources outside the sphere of politics. Devonshire, whence he came, has preserved more of the old features of English country life than the central and northern parts of England, where manufactures and the growth of population have swept away the venerable remains of feudalism. In Devonshire the old families are still deeply respected by the people. They are so intermarried that most of them have ties of

---

[1] A *Life of Lord Iddesleigh*, written by Mr. Andrew Lang, presents Northcote's character and career with fairness and discrimination.

kinship with all their neighbours. Few rich
parvenus have intruded among them; society is
therefore exceptionally easy, simple, and unosten-
tatious. There is still a strong local patriotism,
which makes every Devonshire man, whatever
his political prepossessions, proud of other Devonshire men who rise to eminence, and which
exerts a wholesome influence on the tone of
manners and social intercourse. Northcote was a
thorough Devonshire man, who loved his county
and knew its dialect: his Devonshire stories,
told with the strong accent he could assume,
were the delight of any company that could
tempt him to repeat them. He was immensely
popular in the county, and had well earned his
popularity by his pleasant neighbourly ways, as
well as by his attention to county business and
to the duties of a landowner.

He had the time-honoured training of the
good old English type, was a schoolboy at
Eton, went thence to Oxford, won the highest
distinctions as a scholar, and laid the foundations of a remarkably wide knowledge of modern
as well as ancient literature. He served his
apprenticeship to statesmanship as private secretary to Mr. Gladstone, who was then (1843)
a member of Sir Robert Peel's Government.
When the great schism in the Tory party took
place over the question of free trade in corn, he
was not yet in Parliament, and therefore was

not driven to choose between Peel and the
Protectionists. In 1855, when he first entered
the House of Commons, that question was settled
and gone, so there was no inconsistency in his
entering the Tory ranks, although himself a decided Free Trader. He was not a man who
would have elbowed his way upward. But elbows
were not needed. His abilities, as well as his industry and the confidence he inspired, speedily
brought him to the top. He was appointed
Secretary to the Treasury in 1859, entered the
Cabinet in 1866, when a new Tory Ministry
was formed under Lord Derby; and when in
1876 Mr. Disraeli retired to the House of Lords,
he became, being then Chancellor of the Exchequer, leader of the majority in the House
of Commons, while Mr. Gathorne Hardy, the
only other person who had been thought of
as suitable for that post, received a peerage.
Mr. Hardy was a more forcible and rousing
speaker, but Northcote had more varied accomplishments and a fuller mastery of official work.
Disraeli said that he had "the largest parliamentary knowledge of any man he had met."

As an administrator, Sir Stafford Northcote
was diligent, judicious, and free from any taint
of jobbery. He sought nothing for himself;
did not abuse his patronage; kept the public
interests steadily before his mind. He was considerate to his subordinates, and gracious to all

men.   He never grudged labour, although there
might be no prospect of winning credit by it.
Scrupulous in discharging his duties to his
party, he overtaxed his strength by speaking
constantly at public meetings in the country, a
kind of work he must have disliked, and for
which he was ill fitted by the moderation of his
views and of his language.   Parliament is not a
good place for the pursuit of pure truth, but the
platform is still less favourable to that quest.   It
was remarked of him that even in party gatherings, where invective against political opponents
is apt to be expected and relished, he argued
fairly, and never condescended to abuse.

As a Parliamentarian he had two eminent
merits — immense knowledge and admirable
readiness.   He had been all his life a keen
observer and a diligent student; and as his
memory was retentive, all that he had observed or read stood at his command.   In
questions of trade and finance, questions which,
owing, perhaps, to their increasing intricacy,
seem to be less and less frequently mastered
by practical politicians in England, he was
especially strong.   No other man on his own
side in politics spoke on such matters with equal
authority, and the brunt of the battle fell on
him whenever they came up for discussion.
As he had now his old master for his chief
antagonist, the conflict was no easy one; but he

never shrank from it. Not less remarkable was
his alertness in debate. His manner was indeed
somewhat ineffective, for it wanted both force and
variety. Sentence followed sentence in a smooth
and easy stream, always clear, always grammati-
cally correct, but with a flow too equably un-
broken. There were few impressive phrases,
few brilliant figures, few of those appeals to
passion with which it is necessary to warm and
rouse a large assembly. When the House grew
excited at the close of a long full-dress debate,
and Sir Stafford rose in the small hours of the
morning to wind it up on behalf of his party, men
felt that the ripple of his sweet voice, the softness
of his gentle manner, were not what the occasion
called for. But what he said was always to the
point and well worth hearing. No facts or
arguments suddenly thrown at him by opponents disconcerted him; for there was sure to
be an answer ready. However weak his own
case might seem, his ingenuity could be relied
upon to strengthen it; however powerfully the
hostile case had been presented, he found weak
places in it and shook it down by a succession
of well-planted criticisms, each apparently small,
but damaging when taken all together, because
no one of them could be dismissed as irrelevant.

It was interesting to watch him as he sat on
the front bench, with his hat set so low on his brow
that it hid all the upper part of his face, while the

lower part was covered by a thick yellowish-brown
beard, perfectly motionless, rarely taking a note
of what was said, and, to all appearance, the most
indifferent figure in the House.   The only sign
of feeling which he gave was to be found in
his habit of thrusting each of his hands up the
opposite sleeve of his coat when Mr. Gladstone,
the only assailant whom he needed to fear, burst
upon him in a hailstorm of declamation.   But
when he rose, one perceived that nothing had
escaped him.   Every point which an antagonist
had made was taken up and dealt with; no point
that could aid his own contention was neglected;
and the fluent grace with which his discourse
swept along, seldom aided by a reference to
notes, was not more surprising than the unfailing
skill with which he shunned dangerous ground,
and put his propositions in a form which made
it difficult to contradict them.   I remember to
have heard a member of the opposite party
remark, that nothing was more difficult than
to defend your argument from Northcote, because
he had the art of nibbling it away, admitting
a little in order to evade or overthrow the rest.

So much for his parliamentary aptitudes, which
were fully recognised before he rose to leadership.
But as it was his leadership that has given him a
place in history, I may dwell for a little upon the
way in which he filled that most trying as well
as most honourable post.   He led the House —

that is to say, the Ministerial majority — for four
sessions (1877-1880), and the Tory Opposition for
five and a half sessions (1880 to middle of 1885).
To lead the House of Commons a man must have,
over and above the qualities which make a good
debater, an unusual combination of talents.   He
must be both bold and cautious, combative and
cool.   He must take on his own responsibility,
and on the spur of the moment, decisions which
commit the whole Ministry, and yet, especially if
he be not Prime Minister, he must consider how
far his colleagues will approve and implement his
action.   He must put enough force and fire
into his speeches to rouse his own ranks and
intimidate (if he can) his opponents, yet must
have regard to the more timorous spirits among
his own supporters, going no further than he
feels they will follow, and must sometimes throw
a crafty fly over those in the Opposition whom
he thinks wavering or disaffected.   Under the
fire of debate, perhaps while composing the
speech he has to make in reply, he must
consider not merely the audience before him
but also the effect his words will have when
they are read next morning in cold blood,
and, it may be, the effect not only in England
but abroad.   Being responsible for the whole
conduct of parliamentary business, he must keep
a close watch upon every pending bill, and determine how much of Government time shall be

allotted to each, and in what order they shall be taken, and how far the general feeling of the House will let him go in seizing the hours usually reserved for private members, and in granting or refusing opportunities for discussing topics he would prefer to have not discussed at all.

So far as prudence, tact, and knowledge of business could enable him to discharge these duties, Northcote discharged them admirably. It was his good fortune to have behind him in Lord Beaconsfield, who had recently gone to the House of Lords, a chief of the whole party who trusted him, and with whom he was on the best terms. The immense authority of that chief secured his own authority. His party was — as the Tory party usually is — compact and loyal; and his majority ample, so he had no reason to fear defeat. In the conflicts that arose over Eastern affairs in 1877-79, affairs at some moments highly critical, he was cautious and adroit, more cautious than Lord Beaconsfield, sometimes repairing by moderate language the harm which the latter's theatrical utterances had done. When a group of Irish Nationalist members, among whom Mr. Parnell soon came to the front, began to evade the rules and paralyse the action of the House by obstructive tactics, he was less successful. Their ingenuity baffled the Ministry, and brought the House into sore straits. But it may be doubted whether any leader could have overcome the difficulties of the position. It was a new position. The old rules framed under quite different conditions were not fit to check members who, far from regarding the sentiments of the House, avowed their purpose to reduce it to impotence, and thereby obtain that Parliament of their own, which could alone, as they held, cure the ills of Ireland.

After ten years of struggle and experiment, drastic remedies for obstruction were at last devised; but in the then state of opinion within the House, those remedies could not have been carried. Members accustomed to the old state of things could not for a good while make up their minds to sacrifice part of their own privileges in order to deal with a difficulty the source of which they would not attempt to cure. On the whole, therefore, though he was blamed at the time, Northcote may be deemed to have passed creditably through his first period of leadership.

It was when he had to lead his party in Opposition, after April 1880, that his severest trial came. To lead the minority is usually easier than to lead the majority. A leader of the Opposition also must, no doubt, take swift decisions in the midst of a debate, must consider how far he is pledging his party to a policy which they may be required to maintain when next they come into power, must endeavour to judge, often on scanty data, how many of his usual or nominal supporters will follow him into the lobby when a division is called, and how best he can draw off some votes from among his opponents. Still, delicate as this work is, it is not so hard as that of the leader of the Government, for it is rather critical than constructive, and a mistake can seldom do irreparable mischief. Northcote, however, had special difficulties to face. Mr. Gladstone, still full of energy and fire, was leading the majority. After a few months Lord Beaconsfield's mantle no longer covered Northcote (that redoubtable strategist died in April 1881), and a small but active group of Tory members set up an irregular skirmishing Opposition on their own account, paying little heed to his moderate counsels. The Tory party was then furious at its unexpected defeat at the election of 1880. It was full of fight, burning for revenge, eager to denounce every trifling error of the Ministry, and to give battle on small as well as great occasions. Hence it resented the calm and cautiously critical attitude which Northcote took up. He had plenty of courage; but he thought, as indeed most impartial observers thought, that little was to be gained by incessantly worrying an enemy so superior in force and flushed with victory; that premature assaults might consolidate a majority within which there existed elements of discord; and that it was wiser to wait till the Ministry should begin to make mistakes and incur misfortunes in the natural course of events, before resuming the offensive against them. There is a natural tendency to reaction in English popular opinion, and a tendency to murmur against whichever party may be in power. This tendency must soon have told in favour of the Tories, with little effort on their own part; and when it was already manifest, a Parliamentary attack could have been delivered with effect. Northcote's view and plan were probably right, but, being too prone to yield to pressure, and finding his hand forced, he allowed himself to be drawn by the clamour of his followers into aggressive operations, which, nevertheless, himself not quite approving them, he conducted in a half-hearted way. He had not Mr. Gladstone's power of doing excellently what he hated to have to do. And it must be admitted that from 1882 onwards, when troubles in Ireland and oscillations in Egyptian policy had begun to shake the credit of the Liberal Ministry, he showed less fire and pugnacity than the needs of the time required from a party leader. In one thing the young men, who, like Zulu warriors, wished to wash their spears, were right and he was wrong. He conceived that frequent attacks and a resort to obstructive tactics would damage the Opposition in the eyes of the country. Experience has shown that parties do not greatly suffer from the way they fight their Parliamentary battles. Few people follow the proceedings closely enough to know when an Opposition deserves blame for prolonging debate, or a Ministry for abuse of the closure. So, too, in the United States it would seem that neither the tyrannical action of a majority nor filibustering by a minority shocks the nation.

Not only was Northcote's own temper pacific, but he was too sweetly reasonable and too dispassionate to be a successful leader in Opposition. He felt that he was never quite a party man. His mind was almost too judicial, his courtesy too unfailing, his temper too unruffled, his manner too unassuming. He did not inspire awe or fear. Not only did he never seek to give pain, even where pain might have been a wholesome discipline for pushing selfishness — he seemed incapable of irritation, and bore with vexatious obstruction from some members of the House, and mutinous attacks from others who belonged to his own party, when a spirit less kindly and forgiving might have better secured his own authority and the dignity of the assembly. He proceeded on the assumption, an unsafe one, as he had too much reason to know, that every one else was a gentleman like himself, penetrated by the old traditions of the House of Commons.

While superior to the prejudices of the old-

fashioned wing of his party, he was too cautious
and conscientious to join those who sought to
lead it into demagogic courses. So far as
political opinions went, he might, had fortune
sent him into the world as the son of a Whig
family, have made an excellent Whig, removed
as far from high Toryism on the one hand as
from Radicalism on the other. There was, therefore, a certain incompatibility between the man
and the position. Average partisans felt that a
leader so very reasonable was not in full sympathy with them. Even his invincible optimism
displeased them. " Hang that fellow Northcote,"
said one of them, " he's always seeing blue sky."
The militant partisans, whatever their opinions,
desired a pugnacious chief. That a leader
should draw the enemy's fire does him good with
his followers, and makes them rally to him. But
the fire of his opponents was hardly ever directed
against Northcote, even when controversy was
hottest. Had he possessed a more imperious
will, he might have overcome these difficulties,
because his abilities and experience were of
the highest value to his party, and his character stood so high that the mass of sensible
Tories all over the country might perhaps have
rallied to him, if he had appealed to them
against the intrigues by which it was sought to
supplant him. He did not lack courage. But
he lacked what men call " backbone." For

practical success, it is less fatal to fail in wisdom than to fail in resolution. He had not that unquenchable self-confidence which I have sought to describe in Disraeli, and shall have to describe in Parnell and in Gladstone. He yielded to pressure, and people came to know that he would yield to pressure.

The end of it was that the weakened prestige and final fall of the Liberal Ministry were not credited to his generalship, but rather to those who had skirmished in advance of the main army. That fall was in reality due neither to him nor to them, but partly to the errors or internal divisions of the Ministry itself, partly to causes such as the condition of Ireland and the revolt of Arabi in Egypt, for which Mr. Gladstone's Cabinet was no more, perhaps less, to blame than many of its predecessors. No Ministry of recent years seemed, when it was formed, to have such a source of strength in the abilities of the men who composed it as did the Ministry of 1880. None proved so persistently unlucky.

The circumstances under which Northcote's leadership came to an end by his elevation to the Upper House (June 1885) as Earl of Iddesleigh, as well as those under which he was subsequently (1887) removed from the post of Foreign Secretary in the then Tory Ministry, evoked much comment at the time, but some of the incidents attending them have not yet been disclosed, and they could not be discussed without bringing in other persons with whom I am not here concerned. Conscious of his own loyalty to his party, and remembering his long and laborious services, he felt those circumstances deeply ; and they may have hastened his death, which came very suddenly in February 1887, and called forth a burst of sympathy such as had not been seen since Peel perished by an accident nearly forty years before.

In private life Northcote had the charm of unpretending manners, coupled with abundant humour, a store of anecdote, and a geniality which came straight from the heart. No man was a more agreeable companion. In 1884, when the University of Edinburgh celebrated its tercentenary, he happened to be Lord Rector, and in that capacity had to preside over the festivities. Although a stranger to Scotland, and as far removed (for he was a decided High Churchman) from sympathy with Scottish Presbyterianism as he was removed in politics from the Liberalism then dominant in Edinburgh, he won golden opinions from the Scotch, as well as from the crowd of foreign visitors, by the tact and grace he showed in the discharge of his duties, and the skill with which, putting off the politician, he entered into the spirit of the occasion as a lover of letters and learning. Though political eminence had secured his election to the office, every one felt that it would have been hard to find

Q

in the ranks of literature and science any one
fitter to preside over such a gathering.

He left behind few in whom the capacities
of the administrator were so happily blended with
a philosophic judgment and a wide culture. It is
a combination which was inadequately appreciated
in his own person. Vehemence in controversy,
domineering audacity of purpose, the power of
moving crowds by incisive harangues, were the
qualities which the younger generation seemed
disposed to cultivate. They are qualities apt to be
valued in times of strife and change, times when
men are less concerned to study and apply principles than to rouse the passions and consolidate
the organisation of their party, while dazzling the
nation by large promises or bold strokes of policy.
For such courses Northcote was not the man.
Were it to be observed of him that he was too
good for the work he had to do, it might be
answered that political leadership is work for
which no man can be too good, and that it was
rather because his force of will and his combativeness were not commensurate with his other gifts,
that those other gifts did not have their full effect
and win their due success. Yet this at least may
be said, that if he had been less amiable, less fair-
minded, and less open-minded, he would have
retained his leadership to the end.

CHARLES STEWART PARNELL

THOUGH I do not propose to write even the brief-
est narrative of Parnell's life, but only to note certain salient features of his intellect and character,
it may be well to state a few facts and dates; for
in these days of rapid change and hasty reading,
facts soon pass out of most men's memories,
leaving only vague impressions behind.[1]

He belonged to a family which, established at
Congleton in Cheshire, had at the time of the
Restoration migrated to Ireland, had settled on
an estate in Wicklow, and had produced in every
subsequent generation a person of distinction.
Thomas Parnell, the friend of Pope and Swift,
is still remembered by his poem of *The Hermit.*
Another Parnell (Sir John) was Chancellor of
the Irish Exchequer in the days of Henry
Grattan, whose opinions he shared. Another
(Sir Henry) was a leading Irish Liberal member of the House of Commons, and died by his
own hand in 1842. Charles's father and grand-

---

[1] The *Life of Parnell,* by Mr. R. Barry O'Brien, has taken rank among
the best biographies of the last half-century.

father figured less in the public eye. But his mother was a remarkable woman, and the daughter of a remarkable man, Commodore Charles Stewart, one of the most brilliant naval commanders on the American side in the War of 1812. Stewart was the son of a Scoto-Irishman from Ulster, who had emigrated to America in the middle of the eighteenth century; so there was a strain of Scottish as well as a fuller strain of English blood in the most powerful Irish leader of recent times.

Parnell was born at Avondale, the family estate in Wicklow, in 1846, and was educated mostly at private schools in England. He spent some months at Magdalene College, Cambridge, but, having been rusticated for an affray in the street, refused to return to the College, and finished his education for himself at home. It was a very imperfect education. He cared nothing for study, and indeed showed interest only in mathematics and cricket. In 1874 he stood as a candidate for Parliament, but without success. When he had to make a speech he broke down utterly. In 1875 he was returned as member for the county of Meath, and within two years had made his mark in the House of Commons. In 1880 he was elected leader of the Irish Parliamentary party, and ruled it and his followers in Ireland with a rod of iron until he was deposed, in 1890, at the instance of the leaders of the English Liberal party, who thought that the verdict against him in a divorce suit in which he was co-respondent had fatally discredited him in the eyes of the bulk of the English Liberal party, and made co-operation with him impossible. Refusing to resign his leadership, he conducted a campaign in Ireland against the majority of his former followers with extraordinary energy till November 1891, when he died of rheumatic fever after a short illness. A constitution which had never been strong was worn out by the ceaseless exertions and mental tension of the last twelve months.

The whole of his political activity was comprised within a period of sixteen years, during ten of which he led the Irish Nationalist party, exercising an authority more absolute than any Irish leader had exercised before.

It has often been observed that he was not Irish, and that he led the Irish people with success just because he did not share their characteristic weaknesses. But it is equally true that he was not English. One always felt the difference between his temperament and that of the normal Englishman. The same remark applies to some other famous Irish leaders. Wolfe Tone, for instance, and Fitzgibbon (afterwards Lord Clare) were unlike the usual type of Irishman — that is, the Irishman in whom the Celtic element predominates; but they were also unlike Englishmen. The Anglo-Irish Protestants, a strong race who have produced a number of remarkable men in excess of the proportion they bear to the whole population of the United Kingdom, fall into two classes — the men of North-Eastern Ulster, in whom there is so large an infusion of Scottish blood that they may almost be called "Scotchmen with a difference," and the men of Leinster and Munster, who are true Anglo-Celts. It was to this latter class that Parnell belonged. They are a group by themselves, in whom some of the fire and impulsiveness of the Celt has been blended with some of the firmness, the tenacity, and the close hold upon facts which belong to the Englishman. Mr. Parnell, however, though he might be reckoned to the Anglo-Irish type, was not a normal specimen of it. He was a man whom you could not refer to any category, peculiar both in his intellect and in his character generally.

His intellect was eminently practical. He did not love speculation or the pursuit of abstract truth, nor had he a taste for literature, still less a delight in learning for its own sake. Even of the annals of Ireland his knowledge was most slender. He had no grasp of constitutional questions, and was not able to give any help in the construction of a Home Rule scheme in 1886. His general reading had been scanty, and his speeches show no acquaintance either with history, beyond the commonest facts, or with

any other subject connected with politics.   Very
rarely did they contain a maxim or reflection of
general applicability, apart from the particular
topic he was discussing.   Nor did he ever
attempt to give to them the charm of literary
ornament.   All was dry, direct, and practical,
without so much as a graceful phrase or a
choice epithet.   Sometimes, when addressing a
great public meeting, he would seek to rouse the
audience by vehement language; but though there
might be a glow of suppressed passion, there
were no flashes of imaginative light.   Yet he
never gave the impression of an uneducated man.
His language, though it lacked distinction, was
clear and grammatical.   His taste was correct.
It was merely that he did not care for any of
those things which men of ability comparable to
his usually do care for.   His only interests, outside politics, lay in mechanics and engineering
and in the development of the material resources
of his country.   He took pains to manage his
estate well, and was specially anxious to make
something out of his stone quarries, and to learn
what could be done in the way of finding and
working minerals.

Those who observed that he was almost
always occupied in examining and attacking the
measures or the conduct of those who governed
Ireland were apt to think his talent a purely
critical one.   They were mistaken.   Critical,

indeed, it was, in a remarkable degree; keen, penetrating, stringently dissective of the arguments of an opponent, ingenious in taking advantage of a false step in administration or of an admission imprudently made in debate.   But it had also a positive and constructive quality.   From time to time he would drop his negative attitude and sketch out plans of legislation which were always consistent and weighty, though not made attractive by any touch of imagination.   They were the schemes not so much of a statesman as of an able man of business, who saw the facts, especially the financial facts, in a sharp, cold light, and they seldom went beyond what the facts could be made to prove.   And his ideas struck one as being not only forcible but independent, the fruit of his own musings.   Although he freely used the help of others in collecting facts or opinions, he did not seem to be borrowing the ideas, but rather to have looked at things for himself, and seen them as they actually were, in their true perspective, not (like many Irishmen) through the mists of sentiment or party feeling. The impression made by one of his more elaborate speeches might be compared to that which one receives from a grey sunless day with an east wind, a day in which everything shows clear, but also hard and cold.

To call his mind a narrow one, as people sometimes did, was to wrong it.   If the range of his interests was limited, his intelligence was not. Equal to any task it undertook, it judged soundly, appreciating the whole phenomena of the case, men and things that had no sort of attraction for it. There was less pleasure in watching its activities than the observation of a superior mind generally affords, for it was always directed to immediate aims, and it wanted the originality which is fertile in ideas and analogies. It was not discursive, not versatile, not apt to generalise. It did not rejoice in the exercise of thought for thought's sake, but felt itself to be merely a useful instrument for performing the definite practical work which the will required of it.

If, however, the intellect of the man could not be called interesting, his character had at least this interest, that it gave one many problems to solve, and could not easily be covered by any formulæ. An observer who followed the old method of explaining every man by ascribing to him a single ruling passion, would have said that his ruling passion was pride. The pride was so strong that it almost extinguished vanity. Parnell did not appear to seek occasions for display, frequently neglecting those which other men would have chosen, seldom seeming to be elated by the applause of crowds, and treating the House of Commons with equal coolness whether it cheered

him or howled at him.   He cared nothing for
any social compliments or attentions, rarely
accepted an invitation to dinner, dressed with
little care and often in clothes whose style and
colour seemed unworthy of his position.   He
was believed to be haughty and distant to his
followers; and although he could occasionally
be kindly and even genial, scarcely any were
admitted to intimacy, and few of the ordinary
signs of familiarity could be observed between
him and them.   Towards other persons he was
sufficiently polite but warily reserved, showing no desire for the cultivation of friendship, or, indeed, for any relations but those
of business.   Of some ordinary social duties,
such as opening and answering letters, he was,
especially in later years, more neglectful than
good breeding permits; and men doubted
whether to ascribe this fault to indolence or to
a superb disregard of everybody but himself.
Such disregard he often showed in greater
matters, taking no notice of attacks made
upon him which he might have refuted, and
intimating to the English his indifference to
their praise or blame.   On one remarkable
occasion, at the beginning of the session of
1883, he was denounced by Mr. W. E. Forster
in a long and bitter speech, which told powerfully upon the House.   Many instances were
given in which Irish members had palliated

or failed to condemn criminal acts, and Parnell
was arraigned as the head and front of this line
of conduct, and thus virtually responsible for the
outrages that had occurred. The Irish leader,
who had listened in impassive silence, broken
only by one interjected contradiction, to this
fierce invective, did not rise to reply, and was
with difficulty induced by his followers to deliver his defence on the following day. To the
astonishment of every one, that defence consisted in a declaration, delivered in a cold,
careless, almost scornful way, that for all he
said or did in Ireland he held himself responsible to his countrymen only, and did not in
the least regard what Englishmen thought of
him. It was an answer not of defence but of
defiance.

Even to his countrymen he could on occasion
be disdainful, expecting them to defer to his own
judgment of his own course. He would sometimes remain away from Parliament for weeks
together, although important business might be
under consideration, perhaps would vanish altogether from public ken. Yet this lordly attitude
and the air of mystery which surrounded him
did not seem to be studied with a view to effect.
They were due to his habit of thinking first and
chiefly of himself. If he desired to indulge his
inclinations, he indulged them. Some extremely
strong motive of passion or interest might in-

terpose to restrain this desire and stimulate
him to an unwelcome exertion; but no respect
for the opinion of others, nor fear of censure
from his allies or friends, would be allowed to
do so.

This boundless self-confidence and independence greatly contributed to his success as a leader.
His faith in his star inspired a conviction that
obstacles whose reality his judgment recognised
would ultimately yield to his will, and gave him in
moments of crisis an undismayed fortitude which
only once forsook him — in the panic which was
suddenly created by the Phœnix Park murders of
May 1882. The confidence which he felt, or appeared to feel, reacted upon his party, and became
a chief ground of their obedience to him and their
belief in his superior wisdom. His calmness, his
tenacity, his patience, his habit of listening quietly
to every one, but deciding for himself, were all
evidences of that resolute will which imposed
itself upon the Irish masses no less than upon
his Parliamentary following, and secured for him
a loyalty in which there was little or nothing of
personal affection.

In these several respects his overweening pride
was a source of strength. In another direction,
however, it proved a source of weakness. There
are men in whom the want of moral principle,
of noble emotions, or of a scrupulous conscience
and nice sense of honour, is partly replaced by

deference to the opinion of their class or of the world. Such men may hold through life a tolerably upright course, neither from the love of virtue nor because they are ambitious and anxious to stand well with those whom they aspire to influence or rule, but because, having a sense of personal dignity, combined with a perception of what pleases or offends mankind, they are resolved to do nothing whereby their good name can be tarnished or an opening given to malicious tongues. But when pride towers to such a height as to become a law to itself, disregarding the judgment of others, it may not only lead its possessor into an attitude of defiance which the world resents, but may make him stoop to acts of turpitude which discredit his character. Mr. Parnell was certainly not a scrupulous man. Without dwelling upon the circumstances attending the divorce case already referred to, or upon his betrayal of Mr. Gladstone's confidences, and his reckless appeals during the last year of his life to the most inflammable elements in Ireland, there are facts enough in his earlier career to show that he had little regard for truth and little horror for crime. A revolution may extenuate some sins, but even in a revolution there are men (and sometimes the strongest men) whose moral excellence shines through the smoke of conflict and the mists of detraction. In Mr. Parnell's nature the moral

element was imperfectly developed. He seemed
cynical and callous; and it was probably his
haughty self-reliance which prevented him from
sufficiently deferring to the ordinary moralities
of mankind. His pride, which ought to have
kept him free from the suspicion of dishonour,
made him feel himself dispensed from the usual
restraints. Whatever he did was right in his
own eyes, and no other eyes need be regarded.
Phenomena somewhat similar were observable in
Napoleon. But Napoleon, though he came of a
good family, was obviously not a gentleman in
the common sense of the term. Mr. Parnell
was a gentleman in that sense. He had the
bearing, the manners, the natural easy dignity
of a man of birth who has always moved in
good society. He rarely permitted any one to
take liberties with him, even the innocent liberties of familiar intercourse. This made his departures from what may be called the inner
and higher standard of gentlemanly conduct all
the more remarkable.

He has been accused of a want of physical
courage. He did no doubt after the Phœnix
Park murders ask the authorities in England for
police protection, being, not unnaturally, in fear
for his life; and he habitually carried firearms.
He was at times in danger, and there was every
reason why he should be prepared to defend himself. An anecdote was told of another member

of the House of Commons whose initials were the same as his own, and who, taking what he supposed to be his own overcoat from the peg on which it hung in the cloak room of the House, was startled when he put his hand into the pocket to feel in it the cold iron of a pistol. Moral courage he showed in a high degree during his whole public career, facing his antagonists with an unshaken front, even when they were most numerous and bitter. Though he intensely disliked imprisonment, the terms on which he came out of Kilmainham Gaol left no discredit upon him. He behaved with perfect dignity under the attacks of the press in 1887, and in the face of the use made of letters attributed to him which turned out to have been forged by Richard Pigott — letters which the bulk of the English upper classes had greedily swallowed. With this courage and dignity there was, however, little trace of magnanimity. He seldom said a generous word, or showed himself responsive to such a word spoken by another. Accustomed to conceal his feelings, except in his most excited moments, he rarely revealed, but he certainly cherished, vindictive sentiments. He never forgave either Mr. W. E. Forster or Mr. Gladstone for having imprisoned him in 1881;[1] and though

---

[1] An anecdote was told at the time that when he found himself in the prison yard at Kilmainham, he said, in a sort of soliloquy, "I shall live yet to dance upon those two old men's graves."

he stood in some awe of the latter, whom he considered the only really formidable antagonist he had ever had to confront, he bore a grudge which smouldered under the reconciliation of 1886 and leapt into flame in the manifesto of November 1890.

The union in Mr. Parnell of intense passion with strenuous self-control struck all who watched him closely, though it was seldom that passion so far escaped as to make the contrast visibly dramatic.   Usually he was cold, grave, deliberate, repelling advances with a sort of icy courtesy. He hardly ever lost his temper in the House of Commons, even in his last session under the sarcasms of his former friends, though the low, almost hissing tones of his voice sometimes betrayed an internal struggle.   But during the electoral campaign in Kilkenny, in December 1890, when he was fighting for his life, he was more than once so swept away by anger that those beside him had to hold him back from jumping off the platform into the crowd to strike down some one who had interrupted him.   Suspended for a moment, his mastery of himself quickly returned.   Men were astonished to observe how, after some of the stormy passages at the meetings of Irish members held in one of the House of Commons committee rooms in December 1890, he would address quietly, perhaps lay his hand upon the shoulder of, some one

of the colleagues who had just been denouncing
him, and on whom he had poured all the vitriol
of his fierce tongue. As this could not have
been good-nature, it must have been either
calculated policy or a pride that would not
accept an injury from those whom he had been
wont to deem his subjects. Spontaneous kindliness was never ascribed to him; nor had he,
so far as could be known, a single intimate
friend.

Oratory is the usual avenue to leadership in a
democratic movement, and Mr. Parnell is one of
the very few who have arrived at power neither
by that road nor by military success. So far
from having by nature any of the gifts or graces
of a popular speaker, he was at first conspicuously
deficient in them, and became at last effective
only by constant practice, and by an intellectual
force which asserted itself through commonplace-
ness of language and a monotonous delivery.
Fluency was wanting, and even moderate ease
was acquired only after four or five years' practice.
His voice was neither powerful nor delicate in its
modulations, but it was clear, and the enunciation
deliberate and distinct, quiet when the matter
was ordinary, slow and emphatic when an important point arrived. With very little action of the
body, there was often an interesting and obviously
unstudied display of facial expression. So far from
glittering with the florid rhetoric supposed to

R

characterise Irish eloquence, his speeches were
singularly plain, bare, and dry. Neither had
they any humour. If they ever raised a smile,
which seldom happened, it was by some touch of
sarcasm or adroit thrust at a point left unguarded
by an adversary. Their merit lay in their
lucidity, in their aptness to the matter in hand,
in the strong practical sense which ran through
them, coupled with the feeling that they came
from one who led a nation, and whose forecasts
had often fulfilled themselves. They were carefully prepared, and usually made from pretty
full notes; but the preparation had been given
rather to the matter and the arrangement than to
the diction, which had rarely any ornament or
literary finish. Of late years he spoke infre-
quently, whether from indolence or from weak
health, or because he thought little was to be
done in the face of a hostile majority, now that
the tactics of obstruction had been abandoned.
When he interposed without preparation in a
debate which had arisen unexpectedly, he was
short, pithy, and direct; indeed, nothing was
more characteristic of Parnell than his talent
for hitting the nail on the head, a talent which
always commands attention in deliberative assemblies. No one saw more clearly or conveyed in
terser language the course which the circumstances
of the moment required ; and as his mastery of
parliamentary procedure and practice came next

to that of Mr. Gladstone, any advice that he
gave to the House on a point of order carried
weight.   It would indeed be no exaggeration to
say that during the sessions of 1889 and 1890
he was distinctly the second man in the House
of Commons, surpassed in debating power by
five or six others, but inferior to Mr. Gladstone
alone in the interest which his speeches excited
and in the impression they produced.   Along
with this access of influence his attitude and the
spirit of his policy appeared to rise and widen.
There was less of that hard attorneyism which
had marked his criticisms of the Tory Government
and their measures up till March 1880, and of the
Liberal Government and their measures during
the five following years.   He seemed to grow
more and more to the full stature of a statesman,
with constructive views and a willingness to make
the best of the facts as he found them.   Yet even
in this later and better time one note of greatness was absent from his speeches.   There was
nothing genial or generous or elevated about
them.   They never soared into an atmosphere
of lofty feeling, worthy of the man who was by
this time deemed to be leading his nation to
victory, and who had begun to be admired and
honoured by one of the two great historic English
parties.

Parnell was not only versed in the rules of
parliamentary procedure, but also a consummate

master of parliamentary tactics.   Soon after he
entered the House of Commons he detected its
weak point, and perfected a system of obstruction which so destroyed the efficiency of its time-
honoured modes of doing business that new sets
of rules, each more stringent than the preceding,
had to be devised between 1878 and 1888.   The
skill with which he handled his small but well-
disciplined battalion was admirable.   He was
strict with individuals, requiring absolute obedience
to the party rules, but ready to gratify any pre-
vailing current of feeling when he saw that
this could be done without harm to the cause.
More than once, when English members who
happened to be acting with him on some particular
question pressed him to keep his men quiet and
let a division be taken at once, he answered that
they were doubtless right in thinking that the
moment for securing a good division had arrived,
but that he must not muzzle his followers when
they wanted to have their fling.   The best
proof of the tact with which he ruled a section
comprising many men of brilliant talents lies
in the fact that there was no serious revolt,
or movement towards revolt, against him until
the breach of 1890 between himself and the
Liberal party had led to the belief that his continued leadership would mean defeat at the polls
in Great Britain, and the postponement, perhaps
for many years, of Home Rule for Ireland.

Parnell's political views and tendencies were
eagerly canvassed by those who had studied
him closely.   Many, among both Englishmen
and Irishmen, held that he was at heart a Conservative, valuing strong government and attached
to the rights of property.   They predicted that
if an Irish Parliament had been established, as
proposed by Mr. Gladstone in 1886, and an
Irish cabinet formed to administer the affairs
of the island, Parnell would have been the inevitable and somewhat despotic leader of the
party of authority and order.   His co-operation with the agrarian agitators from 1879 onwards was in this view merely a politic expedient
to gain support for the Home Rule campaign.
For this theory there is much to be said.   Though
he came to lead a revolution, and was willing,
as appeared in the last few months of his life, to
appeal to the genuine revolutionary party, Parnell
was not by temper or conviction a revolutionist.
Those who were left in Ireland of the old Fenian
group, and especially that section of the extreme
Fenians out of which the secret insurrectionary
and dynamitard societies were formed, never
liked or trusted him.   The passion which originally carried him into public life was hatred of
England, and a wish to restore to Ireland, if
possible, her national independence (though he
rarely if ever avowed this), or at least her
own Parliament.   But he was no democratic

leveller, and still less inclined to those socialistic
doctrines which the section influenced by Mr.
Davitt had espoused. He did not desire the
"extinction of landlordism," and would probably have been a restraining and moderating
force in an Irish legislature. That he was genu-
inely attached to his native country need not
be doubted. But his patriotism had little of a
sentimental quality, and seemed to spring as
much from dislike of England as from love of
Ireland.

It may excite surprise that a man such as has
been sketched, with so cool a judgment and so
complete a self-control, a man (as his previous
career had shown) able to endure temporary
reverses in the confidence of ultimate success,
should have committed the fatal error, which
blasted his fame and shortened his life, of clinging to the headship of his party when prudence prescribed retirement. When he sought
the advice of Mr. Cecil Rhodes, retirement for
a time was the counsel he received. His
absence need not have been of long duration.
Had he, after the sentence of the Divorce
Court in November 1890, gone abroad for
eight or ten months, allowing some one to
be chosen in his place chairman of the Irish
party for the session, he might thereafter have
returned to the House of Commons, and would
doubtless, after a short lapse of time, have

naturally recovered the leadership. No one else
could have resisted his claims. Unfortunately
the self-reliant pride which had many a time
stood him in good stead, made him refuse to
bow to the storm. Probably he could not
understand the indignation which the proceedings in the divorce case had awakened in
England, being morally somewhat callous, and
knowing that his offence had been no secret to
many persons in the House of Commons. He
had been accustomed to despise English opinion,
and had on former occasions suffered little
for doing so. He bitterly resented both Mr.
Gladstone's letter and the movement to depose
him which it roused in his own party. Having
often before found defiant resolution lead to
success, he determined again to rely on the
maxim which has beguiled so many to ruin, just
because it has so much truth in it — "*De l'audace,
encore de l'audace, toujours de l'audace.*" The
affront to his pride disturbed the balance of his
mind, and made him feel as if even a temporary
humiliation would destroy the prestige that had
been won by his haughty self-confidence. It
was soon evident that he had overestimated his
power in Ireland, but when the schism began
there were many besides Lord Salisbury — many
in Ireland as well as in England — who predicted
triumph for him. Nor must it be thought that
it was pure selfishness which made him resolve

rather to break with the English Liberals than allow the Nationalist bark to be steered by any hands but his own. He was a fatalist, and had that confidence in his star and his mission which is often characteristic of minds in which superstition — for he was superstitious — and a certain morbid taint may be discerned. There were others who believed that no one but himself could hold the Irish party together and carry the Irish cause to triumph. No wonder that this belief should have filled and perhaps disordered his own brain.

The swiftness of his rise is a striking instance of the power which intellectual concentration and a strenuous will can exert, for he had no adventitious help from wealth or family connection or from the reputation of having suffered for his country. *Ergo vivida vis animi pervicit.* When he entered Parliament he was only thirty, with no experience of affairs and no gift of speech; but the quality that was in him of leading and ruling men, of taking the initiative, of seeing and striking at the weak point of the enemy, and fearlessly facing the brunt of an enemy's attack, made itself felt in a few months, and he rose without effort to the first place. With some intellectual limitations and some great faults, he will stand high in the long and melancholy series of Irish leaders: less lofty than Grattan, less romantic than Wolfe Tone, less attractive than O'Connell, less brilliant

than any of these three, yet entitled to be
remembered as one of the most remarkable
characters that his country has produced in her
struggle of many centuries against the larger
isle.

CARDINAL MANNING

HENRY EDWARD MANNING, Archbishop of Westminster and Cardinal of the Holy Roman Church,
was born in 1808, eight years after Cardinal
Newman, and died in 1892. He was one of the
most notable figures of his generation; and, indeed, in a sense, an unique figure, for he contributed a new type to the already rich and
various ecclesiastical life of England. If he
could scarcely be described as intellectually a man
of the first order, he held a considerable place
in the history of his time, having effected what
greater men might perhaps have failed to effect,
for the race is not always to the swift, and time
and chance favoured Manning.

He was the son of wealthy parents, his father
a City of London merchant; was educated at
Harrow and at Oxford, where he obtained high
classical honours and a Fellowship at Merton
College; was ordained a clergyman, and soon rose
to be Archdeacon of Chichester; and, having by
degrees been led further and further from his
original Low Church position into the Tractarian
movement, ultimately, at the age of forty-three,

went over to the Church of Rome.   Having some time before lost his wife, he was at once re-ordained a priest, was appointed Archbishop of Westminster on Cardinal Wiseman's death in 1865, and raised to the Cardinalate by Pope Pius IX. in 1875.

He was not a great thinker nor a man of wide learning.   His writings show no trace of originality, nor indeed any conspicuous philo-sophical acuteness or logical power.   So far as purely intellectual gifts are concerned, he was not to be named with Cardinal Newman or with several other of the ablest members of the English Tractarian party, such as were the two metaphysicians W. G. Ward and Dalgairns, both of whom passed over to Rome, or such as was Dean Church, an accomplished historian, and a man of singularly beautiful character, who re-mained an Anglican till his death in 1890.   Nor, though he had won a high reputation at his University, was Manning a leading spirit in the famous " Oxford Movement."   It was by his win-ning manners, his graceful rhetoric, and his zealous discharge of clerical duties, rather than by any commanding talents that he rose to eminence in the Church of England.   Neither had his character the same power either to attract or to awe as that of Newman.   Nobody in those days called him great, as men called Newman.   Nobody felt compelled to follow where he led.   There was

not, either in his sermons or in his writings, or
in his bodily presence and conversation, anything which could be pronounced majestic, or
lofty, or profound. In short, he was not in the
grand style, either as a man or as a preacher, and
wanted that note of ethereal purity or passionate
fervour which marks the two highest forms of
religious character.

Intelligent, however, skilful, versatile he was
in the highest degree; cultivated, too, with a
knowledge of all that a highly educated man
ought to know; dexterous rather than forcible
in theological controversy; an admirable rhetorician, handling language with something of that
kind of art which Roman ecclesiastics most
cultivate, and in their possession of which the
leading Tractarians showed their affinity to
Rome, an exact precision of phrase and a subtle
delicacy of suggestion. Newman had it in the
fullest measure. Dean Church had it, with less
brilliance than Newman, but with no less grace and
dignity. Manning equalled neither of these, but
we catch in him the echo. He wrote abundantly
and on many subjects, always with cleverness
and with the air of one who claimed to belong
to the *âmes d'élite*, yet his style never attained
the higher kind of literary merit. There was no
imaginative richness about it, neither were there
the weight and penetration that come from sustained and vigorous thinking. Similarly, with a

certain parade of references to history and to out-of-the-way writers, he gave scant evidence of solid learning. He was an accomplished disputant in the sense of knowing thoroughly the more obvious weaknesses of the Protestant (and especially of the Anglican) position, and of being able to contrast them effectively with the external completeness and formal symmetry of the Roman system. But he never struck out a new or illuminative thought; and he seldom ventured to face — one could indeed sometimes mark him seeking to elude — a real difficulty.

What, then, was the secret of his great and long-sustained reputation and influence? It lay in his power of dealing with men. For the work of an ecclesiastical ruler he had three inestimable gifts — a resolute will, captivating manners, and a tact equally acute and vigilant, by which he seemed not only to read men's characters, but to discern the most effective means of playing on their motives. To call him an intriguer would be unjust, because the word, if it does not imply the pursuit of some mean or selfish object, does generally connote a resort to unworthy arts; and the Cardinal was neither dishonourable nor selfish. But he had the talents which an intriguer needs, though he used them in a spirit of absolute devotion to the interests of his Church, and though he was too much of a gentleman to think that the interests of the Church, which might justify a good deal, could be made to justify any and every means. In conversation he had the art of seeming to lay his mind alongside of yours, wishful to know what you had to say, and prepared to listen respectfully to it, even though you might be much younger and of no personal consequence. Yet you sometimes felt, if your own power of observation had not been lulled to sleep by the winning manner, that he was watching you, and watching, in conformity to a settled habit, the effect upon you of whatever he said. It was hard not to be flattered by this air of kindly deference, and natural to admire the great man who condescended without condescension, even though one might be secretly disappointed at the want of freshness and insight in his conversation. Like his famous contemporary, Bishop Samuel Wilberforce, Manning was all things to all men. He was possessed, no doubt, of far less wit and far less natural eloquence than that brilliant but variable creature. But he gave a more distinct impression of earnest and un-questioning loyalty to the cause he had made his own.

In the government of his diocese, Manning showed himself a finished ruler and manager of men, flexible in his power of adapting himself to any character or society, yet inflexible when firm-ness was needed, usually tactful if not always gentle in his methods, but tenacious in his purposes, demanding rightfully from others the simplicity of life and the untiring industry of which he set an example himself. Over women his influence was still greater than over men, because women are more susceptible to the charm of presence and address; nor could any other ecclesiastic count so many conversions among ladies of high station, his dignified carriage and ascetic face according admirably with his sacerdotal rank and his life of strict observance. For some years it was his habit to go to Rome early in Lent and remain till after Easter. Promising subjects, who had doubts as to their probabilities of salvation in the Anglican communion, used to be invited to dinner to meet him, and they fell in swift succession before his skilful presentation of the peace and bliss to be found within the Roman fold.

In his public appearances, it was neither the solid substance of his discourses that struck one, nor the literary quality of their style, but their judicious adaptation to the audience, and the grace with which they were delivered. For this reason — originality being rarer and therefore more precious in the pulpit, where well-worn themes have to be handled, than on a platform, where the topic is one of the moment — his addresses at public meetings were better than his sermons, and won for him the reputation of a speaker whom it was well worth while to secure

at any social or philanthropic gathering. At the
Vatican Œcumenical Council of 1870 it was less
by his speeches than by his work in private among
the assembled prelates that he served the In-
fallibilist cause.   Himself devoted, and, no doubt,
honestly devoted, to Ultramontane principles, he
did not hesitate to do violence to history and join
in destroying what freedom the Church at large
had retained, in order to exalt the Chair of Peter
to a position unheard of even at Trent, not to say
in the Middle Ages.   His activity, his assiduity,
and his tireless powers of persuasion contributed largely to the satisfaction at that Council
of the wishes of Pius IX., who presently rewarded
him with the Cardinalate.   But the opponents of
the new dogma, who were as superior in learning
to the Infallibilists as they proved inferior in
numbers, carried back with them to Germany and
North America an undying distrust of the astute
Englishman who had shown more than a convert's proverbial eagerness for rushing to extremes
and forcing others to follow.   I remember to
have met some of the anti-Infallibilist prelates
returning to America in the autumn of 1870;
and in our many talks on shipboard they spoke of
the Archbishop in terms no more measured than
Nestorius may have used of St. Cyril after the
Council of Ephesus.

    But Manning's powers shone forth most fully
in the course he gave to his policy as Arch-

bishop of Westminster and head of the Roman hierarchy in Britain. He had two difficulties to confront. One was the suspicion of the old English Roman Catholic families, who distrusted him as a recent recruit from Protestantism, a man brought up in ideas unfamiliar to their conservative minds. The other was the aversion of the ruling classes in England, and indeed of Englishmen generally, to the pretensions of Rome, an aversion which, among the Tories, sprang from deep-seated historical associations, and among the Whigs drew further strength from dislike to the reactionary tendencies of the Popedom on the European continent, and especially its resistance to the freedom and unity of Italy. In 1850 the creation by the Pope of a Roman Catholic hierarchy in England, followed by Cardinal Wiseman's letter dated from the Flaminian Gate, had evoked a burst of anti-papal feeling which never quite subsided during Wiseman's lifetime. Both these enmities Manning overcame. The old Catholic families rallied to a prelate who supported with dignity and vigour the pretensions of their church; while the suspicions of Protestants were largely, if not universally, allayed when they noted the attitude of a patriotic Englishman, zealous for the greatness of his country, which the Archbishop assumed, as well as the heartiness with which he threw himself into moral and philanthropic causes. Loyalty to

s

Rome never betrayed him into any apparent disloyalty to England. Too prudent to avow sympathy with either political party, he seemed less opposed to Liberalism than his predecessor had been or than most of the English Catholics were. While, of course, at issue with the Liberal party upon educational questions, he was believed to lean to Home Rule, and maintained good relations with the Irish leaders. He joined those who worked for the better protection of children and the repression of vice, advocated total abstinence by precept and example, and did much to promote it among the poorer Roman Catholic population. Discerning the growing magnitude of what are called labour questions, he did not recoil from proposals to limit by legislation the hours of toil, and gladly exerted himself to settle differences between employers and workmen, showing his own sympathy with the needs and hardships of the latter. Thus he won a popularity with the London masses greater than any prelate of the Established Church had enjoyed, while the middle and upper classes noted with pleasure that, however Ultramontane in his theology, he always spoke and wrote as an Englishman upon non-theological subjects.

In this there was no playing of a part, for he sincerely cared about temperance, the welfare of children, the advancement of the labouring class, and the greatness of England. But there was

also a sage perception of the incidental service
which his attitude in these matters could render
to his church; and he relished opportunities of
proving that a Catholic prelate could be not only
a philanthropist but also a patriot. He saw the
value of the attitude, though he used it honestly,
and if he was not artful, he was full of art.
Truth, for its own sake, he neither loved nor
sought, but, having once adopted certain conclusions, doctrinal and practical, subordinated everything else to them. Power he loved, yet not wholly
for the pleasure which he found in exerting it, but
also because he knew that he was fit to use it,
and could use it, to promote the aims he cherished.
To his church he was devoted heart and soul; nor
could any one have better served it so far as
England was concerned. No one in our time,
hardly even Cardinal Newman, has done so much
to sap and remove the old Protestant fears and
jealousies of Rome, fears and jealousies which
had descended from days when they were less
unreasonable than the liberality or indifference
of our times will allow. Truly the Roman
Church is a wonderful institution, fertile beyond
any other, since in each succeeding age she has
given birth to new types of force suited to the
conditions she has to deal with. In Manning she
developed a figure full of a kind of charm and
strength which could hardly have found due
scope within a Protestant body: a man who never

obtruded a claim, yet never yielded one; who
was the loyal servant of a spiritual despotism,
yet apparently in sympathy with democratic ideas
and movements; equally welcome among the
poorest Irish of his diocese and at the gatherings
of the great; ready to join in every good work
with those most opposed to his own doctrines,
yet standing detached as the austere and unbending representative of a world-embracing power.

Since these pages were written there has appeared a Life of Cardinal Manning which, for the
variety and interest of its contents, and for the
flood of light which it throws upon its subject,
deserves to rank among the best biographies in
the English language. It reveals the inner life
of Manning, his high motives and his tortuous
methods, his piety and his aspirations, his occasional lapses from sincerity and rectitude, with a
fulness to which one can scarcely find a parallel.
As was remarked by Mr. Gladstone, who was so
keenly interested in the book that for months he
could talk of little else, it leaves nothing for the
Day of Judgment.

It would be idle to deny that Manning's
reputation did in some measure suffer. Yet it
must in fairness be remembered that an ordeal
such as that to which he has been thus subjected
is seldom applied, and might, if similarly applied,
have lowered many another reputation. Cicero

has suffered in like manner. We should have thought more highly of him, though I do not know that we should have liked him better, if his letters had not survived to reveal weaknesses which other men, or their biographers, were discreet enough to conceal.

I have not attempted to rewrite the preceding pages in the light of Mr. Purcell's biography, for to do so would have extended them beyond the limits of a sketch. I have, moreover, found that the disclosures contained in the biography do not oblige me to darken the colours of the sketch itself. Taken all in all, these intimate records of Manning's life tend to confirm the view that, along with his love of power and pre-eminence, along with his carelessness about historic truth, along with the questionable methods he sometimes allowed himself to use, there lay deep in his heart a genuine and unfailing sympathy with many good causes, such as the cause of temperance, and a real tenderness for the poor and for children. If he was far removed from a saint, still less was he the mere worldly ecclesiastic, crafty and ambitious, who has in all ages been a familiar and unlovely type of character.

EDWARD AUGUSTUS FREEMAN[1]

EDWARD FREEMAN was born at Harborne in South Staffordshire on 2nd August 1823, and died at Alicante on 16th March 1892, in the course of an archæological and historical journey to the east and south of Spain, whither he had gone to see the sites of the early Carthaginian settlements. His life was comparatively uneventful, as that of learned men in our time usually is. He was educated at home and at a private school till he went to Oxford at the age of eighteen. There he was elected a scholar of Trinity College in 1841, took his degree (second class in *literae humaniores*) in 1845, and was elected a fellow of Trinity shortly afterwards. Marrying in 1847, he lost his fellowship, and settled in 1848 in Gloucestershire, and at a later time went to live in Monmouthshire, whence he migrated in 1860 to Somerleaze, a pretty spot about a mile and a half to the north-

---

[1] An excellent Life of Freeman has been written by his friend Mr. W. R. W. Stephens, afterwards Dean of Winchester, whose death while these pages were passing through the press has caused the deepest regret to all who had the opportunity of knowing his literary gifts and his lovable character.

west of Wells in Somerset. Here he lived
till 1884, when he was appointed (on the recommendation of Mr. Gladstone) to the Regius
Professorship of Modern History at Oxford.
Thenceforth he spent the winter and spring in
the University, returning for the long vacation
to Somerleaze, a place he dearly loved, not only
in respect of the charm of the surrounding
scenery, but from its proximity to the beautiful
churches of Wells and to many places of historical interest. For the greater part of his manhood
his surroundings were those of a country gentleman, nor did he ever reconcile himself to town
life, for he loved the open sky, the fields and hills,
and all wild creatures, though he detested what
are called field sports, knew nothing of natural
history, and had neither taste nor talent for
farming. As he began life with an income sufficient to make a gainful profession unnecessary,
he did not prepare himself for any, but gave free
scope from the first to his taste for study and
research. Thus the record of his life is, with the
exception of one or two incursions into the field
of practical politics, a record of his historical work
and of the journeys he undertook in connection
with it.

History was the joy as well as the labour of
his life. But the conception he took of it was
peculiar enough to deserve some remark. The
keynote of his character was the extraordinary

warmth of his interest in the persons, things, and places which he cared for, and the scarcely less conspicuous indifference to matters which lay outside the well-defined boundary line of his sympathies. If any branch of inquiry seemed to him directly connected with history, he threw himself heartily into it, and drew from it all it could be made to yield for his purpose. About other subjects he would neither read nor talk, no matter how completely they might for the time be filling the minds of others. While an undergraduate, and influenced, like most of the abler men among his Oxford contemporaries, by the Tractarian opinions and sentiments then in their full force and freshness,[1] he became interested in church architecture, discerned the value which architecture has as a handmaid to historical research, set to work to study mediæval buildings, and soon acquired a wonderfully full and exact knowledge of the most remarkable churches and castles all over England. He taught himself to sketch, not artistically, but sufficiently well to record characteristic points, and by the end of his life he had

---

[1] The scholars of Trinity were then (1843) all High Churchmen, and never dined in hall on Fridays. Fourteen years later there was not a single High Churchman among them. Ten or fifteen years afterwards Anglo-Catholic sentiment was again strong. Freeman said that his revulsion against Tractarianism began from a conversation with one of his fellow-scholars, who had remarked that it was a pity there had been a flaw in the consecration of some Swedish bishops in the sixteenth century, for this had imperilled the salvation of all Swedes since that time. He was startled, and began to reconsider his position.

accumulated a collection of hundreds of drawings
made by himself of notable buildings in France,
Germany, Italy, and Dalmatia, as well as in the
British Isles. Architecture was always thenceforward to him the prime external record and
interpreter of history. But it was the only art in
which he took the slightest interest. He cared
nothing for pictures or statuary; was believed
to have once only, when his friend J. R. Green
dragged him thither, visited a picture-gallery in
the course of his numerous journeys; and did not
seem to perceive the significance which paintings
have as revealing the thoughts and social condition of the time which produced them. Another
branch of inquiry cognate to history which he
prized was comparative philology. With no
great turn for the refinements of classical
scholarship, and indeed with some contempt for
the practice of Latin and Greek verse making
which used to absorb much of the time and
labour of undergraduates and their tutors at
Oxford and Cambridge, he was extremely fond
of tracing words through different languages so
as to establish the relations of the peoples who
spoke them, and, indeed, used to argue that all
teaching of languages ought to begin with
Grimm's law, and to base his advocacy of the
retention of Greek as a *sine qua non* for an Arts
degree in the University on the importance of
that law. But with this love for philology as an

instrument in the historian's hands, he took little pleasure in languages simply as languages — that is to say, he did not care to master, and was not apt at mastering, the grammar and idioms of a tongue. French was the only foreign language he spoke with any approach to ease, though he could read freely German, Italian, and modern Greek, and on his tour in Greece made some vigorous speeches to the people in their own tongue. He had learnt to pronounce Greek in the modern fashion, which few Englishmen can do; but how much of his classically phrased discourses did the crowds that acclaimed the distinguished Philhellene understand? So too he was a keen and well-trained archæologist, but only because archæology was to him a priceless adjunct — one might almost say the most trustworthy source — of the study of early history. As evidence of his accomplishments as an antiquary I cannot do better than quote the words of a master of that subject, who was also one of his oldest friends. Mr. George T. Clark says: —

He was an accurate observer, not only of the broad features of a country but of its ancient roads and earthworks, its prehistoric monuments, and its earlier and especially its ecclesiastical buildings. No man was better versed in the distinctive styles of Christian architecture, or had a better general knowledge of the earthworks from the study of which he might hope to correct or corroborate any written records, and by the aid of which he often infused life and reality into otherwise obscure narrations. . . . He visited every spot upon

which the Conqueror is recorded to have set his foot, compared many of the strongholds of his followers with those
they left behind them in Normandy, and studied the evidence
of Domesday for their character and possessions. When
writing upon Rufus he spent some time in examining the
afforested district of the New Forest, and sought for traces of
the villages and churches said to have been depopulated or
destroyed. And for us archæologists he did more than this.
When he attended a provincial congress and had listened to
the description of some local antiquity, some mound, or
divisional earthbank, or semi-Saxon church, he at once strove
to show the general evidence to be deduced from them, and
how it bore upon the boundaries or formation of some Celtic
or Saxon province or diocese, if not upon the general history
of the kingdom itself. . . . He thus did much to elevate the
pursuits of the archæologist, and to show the relation they
bore to the far superior labours of the historian.

Freeman was always at his best when in the field. It was
then that the full force of his personality came into play : his
sturdy upright figure, sharp-cut features, flowing beard, well-
modulated voice, clear enunciation, and fluent and incisive
speech. None who have heard him hold forth from the steps
of some churchyard cross, or from the top stone of some half-
demolished cromlech, can ever cease to have a vivid recollection of both the orator and his theme.

Freeman took endless pains to master the to-
pography of any place he had to deal with. When
at work in his later years on Sicilian history he
visited, and he has minutely described, the site of
nearly every spot in that island where a battle
or a siege took place in ancient times, so that
his volumes have become an elaborate historical
guide-book for the student or tourist.

But while he thus delighted in whatever bore
upon history as he conceived it, his conception

was one which belonged to the eighteenth century
rather than to our own time.   It was to him not
only primarily but almost exclusively a record
of political events — that is to say, of events in
the sphere of war, diplomacy, and government.
He expressed this view with concise vigour in
the well-known dictum, " History is past politics,
and politics is present history"; and though his
friends remonstrated with him against this view
as far too narrow, excluding from the sphere
of history many of its deepest sources of interest, he would never give way.   That historians should care as much (or more) for the
religious or philosophical opinions of an age, or
for its ethical and social phenomena, or for the
study of its economic conditions, as for forms
of government or battles and sieges, seemed to
him strange.   He did not argue against the
friends who differed from him, for he was ready
to believe that there must be something true and
valuable in the views of a man whom he respected; but he could not be induced to devote
his own labours to the elucidation of these
matters.   He would say to Green, "You may
bring in all that social and religious kind of
thing, Johnny, but I can't."   So when he went
to deliver lectures in the United States, he delighted in making new acquaintances there, and
was interested in the Federal system and in all
institutions which he could trace to their English

originals, but did not care to see anything or
hear anything about the economic development
or social life of the country.

The same predominant liking for the political
element in history made him indifferent to many
kinds of literature. It may indeed be said that
literature, simply as literature, did not attract
him. In his later years, at any rate, he seldom
read a book except for the sake of the political or
historical information it contained. Among the
writers whom he most disliked were Plato, Carlyle, and Ruskin, in no one of whom could he see
any merit. Plato, he said, was the only author
he had ever thrown to the other end of the room.
Neither, although very fond of the Greek and
Roman classics generally, did he seem to enjoy
any of the Greek poets except Homer and Pindar
and, to some extent, Aristophanes. His liking
for Pindar used to surprise us, because Pindar is
peculiarly the favourite poet of poetical minds;
and I suspect it was not so much the splendour of
Pindar's style and the wealth of his imagination
that Freeman enjoyed, as rather the profusion of
historical and mythological references. He was
impatient with the Greek tragedians, and still
more impatient with Virgil, because (as he said)
"Virgil cannot or will not say a thing simply."
Among English poets his preference was for
the old heroic ballads, such as the songs of
Brunanburh and Maldon, and, among recent

writers, for Macaulay's *Lays*.   The first thing
he ever published (1850) was a volume of verse,
consisting mainly of ballads, some of them very
spirited, on events in Greek and Moorish history.
It may be doubted if he remembered a line of
Shelley, Keats, Wordsworth, or Tennyson.   He
blamed Walter Scott for misrepresenting history
in *Ivanhoe*, but constantly read the rest of his
stories, taking special pleasure in *Peveril of the
Peak*.   He bestowed warm praise upon *Romola*,
on one occasion reading it through twice in a
single journey.   Mrs. Gaskell's *Mary Barton*,
Marryatt's *Peter Simple*, Trollope's *The Warden*
and *Barchester Towers*, were amongst his
favourites.   Among the moderns, Macaulay was
his favourite prose author, and he was wont to
say that from Macaulay he had learned never
to be afraid of using the same word to describe
the same thing, and that no one was a better
model to follow in the choice of pure English.
Limitations of taste are not uncommon among
eminent men.   What was uncommon in Freeman was the perfect frankness with which he
avowed his aversions, and the absence of any
pretence of caring for things which he did not
really care for.   He was in this, as in all other
matters, a singularly simple and truthful man,
never seeking to appear different from what he
was, and finding it hard to understand why other
people should not be equally simple and direct.

This directness made him express himself with an absence of reserve which often gave offence. Positive and definite, with a strong broad logic which every one could follow, he was a formidable controversialist even on subjects outside history. A good specimen of his powers was given in the argument against the cruelty of field sports which he carried on against Anthony Trollope. His cause was not a popular one in England, but he stated it so well as to carry off the honours of the fray.[1]

The restriction of his interest to a few topics — wide ones, to be sure — seemed to increase the intensity of his devotion to those few; and thus even the two chief practical interests he had in life connected themselves with his conception of

---

[1] Having had about the same time a brush with George Anthony Denison (Archdeacon of Taunton) and a less friendly passage of arms with James Anthony Froude, he wrote to me in 1870 : " I am greater than Cicero, who was smiter of one Antonius. I venture to think that I have whopped the whole *Gens Antonia* — first Anthony pure and simple, which is Trollope; secondly, James Anthony, whom I believe myself to have smitten, as Cnut did Eadric swiðe rihtlice, in the matter of St. Hugh; thirdly, George Anthony, with whom I fought again last Tuesday, carrying at our Education Board a resolution in favour of Forster's bill." Trollope and he became warm friends. Froude he heartily disliked, not, I think, on any personal grounds, but because he thought Froude indifferent to truth, and was incensed by the defence of Henry VIII.'s crimes.

It may be added that Freeman, much as he detested Henry VIII., used to observe that Henry had a sort of legal conscience, because he always wished his murders to be done by Act of Parliament, and that the earlier and better part of Henry's reign ought not to be forgotten. He was fond of quoting the euphemism with which an old Oxford professor of ecclesiastical history concluded his account of the sovereign whom, in respect of his relation to the Church of England, it seemed proper to handle gently: " The later years of this great monarch were clouded by domestic troubles."

history. One was the discharge of his duties as a magistrate in the local government of his county. While he lived at Somerleaze he rarely missed Quarter Sessions, speaking seldom, but valuing the opportunity of taking part in the rule of the shire. The other was the politics of the time, foreign politics even more than domestic. He was from an early age a strong Liberal, throwing himself into every question which bore on the Constitution, either in state or in church, for (as has been said) topics of the social or economic kind lay rather out of his sphere. When Mr. Gladstone launched his Irish Home Rule scheme in 1886, Freeman espoused it warmly, and praised it for the very point which drew most censure even from Liberals, the removal of the Irish members from Parliament. He was intensely English and Teutonic, and wished the Gael to be left to settle, or fight over, their own affairs in their own island, as they had done eight centuries ago. Even the idea of separating Ireland altogether from the English Crown would not have alarmed him, for he did not thank Strongbow and Henry II. for having invaded it; while, on the other hand, the plan of turning the United Kingdom into a federation, giving to England, Scotland, Ireland, and Wales each a local parliament of its own, with an imperial parliament for common concerns, shocked all his historical instincts.

In 1859 he was on the point of coming forward as a parliamentary candidate for the borough of Newport in Monmouthshire, and again at the election of 1868 he actually did stand for one of the divisions of Somerset, and showed in his platform speeches a remarkable gift of eloquence, and occasionally, also, of humour, coupled with a want of those minor arts which usually contribute more than eloquence does to success in electioneering. I went round with him, along with his and my friend Mr. Albert Dicey, and few are the candidates who get so much pleasure out of a contest as Freeman did. He was a strenuous advocate of disestablishment in Ireland, the question chiefly at issue in the election of 1868, because he thought the Roman Catholic Church was of right, and ought by law to be, the national Church there; but no less decidedly opposed to disestablishment in England, where it would have pained him to see the up-rooting of a system entwined with the ideas and events of the Middle Ages. In his later years he told me that if the Liberal party took up the policy of disestablishment in Wales, he did not know whether he could adhere to them, much as he desired to do so.

Similarly he disliked all schemes for drawing the colonies into closer relations with the United Kingdom, and even seemed to wish that they should sever themselves from it, as the United

T

States had done.   This view sprang partly from his feeling that they were very recent acquisitions, with which the old historic England had nothing to do, partly also from the impression made on him by the analogy of the Greek colonies. He held that the precedent of the Greek settlements showed the true and proper relation between a "metropolis," or mother-city, and her colonies to be one not of political dependence or interdependence, but of cordial friendliness and a disposition to render help, nothing more.   These instances are worth citing because they illustrate a remarkable difference between his way of looking historically at institutions and Macaulay's way.   A friend of his (the late Mr. S. R. Gardiner), like Freeman a distinguished historian, and like him a strong Home Ruler, wrote to me upon this point as follows: —

Freeman and Macaulay are alike in the high value they set upon parliamentary institutions.   On the other hand, when Macaulay wants to make you understand a thing, he compares it with that which existed in his own day.   The standard of the present is always with him.   Freeman traces it to its origin, and testifies to its growth.   The strength of this mode of proceeding in an historian is obvious.   Its weakness is that it does not help him to appreciate statesmanship looking forward and trying to find a solution of difficult problems.   Freeman's attitude is that of the people who cried out for the good laws of King Edward, trying to revive the past.

Freeman was apt to go beyond his own dictum about history and politics, for he sometimes made history present politics as well as past.

By far the strongest political interest — indeed it rose to a passion — of his later years was his hatred of the Turk. In it his historical and religious sentiment, for there was a good deal of the Crusader about him, was blended with his abhorrence of despotism and cruelty. Ever since the beginning of the Crimean war he had been opposed to the traditional English policy of supporting the Sultan. Ever since he had thought about foreign politics at all he had sympathised with the Christians of the East. So when Lord Beaconsfield seemed on the point of carrying the country into a war with Russia in defence of the Turks, no voice rose louder or bolder than his in denouncing the policy then popular with the upper classes in England. On this occasion he gave substantial proof of his earnestness by breaking off his connection with the *Saturday Review* because it had espoused the Turkish cause. This cost him £600 a year ($3000), a sum he could ill spare, and took from him what had been the joy of his heart, opportunities of delivering himself upon all sorts of current questions. But his sense of duty forbade him to write for a journal which was supporting a misguided policy and a minister whom he thought unscrupulous.

His habit of speaking out his whole mind with little regard to the effect his words might produce, or to the way in which they might be twisted, sometimes landed him in difficulties. One utterance raised an outcry at the time, because it was made at a conference held in London in December 1876 to oppose Lord Beaconsfield's Eastern policy. The Duke of Westminster and Lord Shaftesbury presided at the forenoon and afternoon sessions, and the meeting, which told powerfully on the country, was wound up by Mr. Gladstone. Freeman's speech, only ten minutes long, but an oratorical success at the moment, contained the words, " Perish the interests of England, perish our dominion in India, rather than that we should strike one blow or speak one word on behalf of the wrong against the right." This flight of rhetoric was perverted by his opponents into " Perish India"; and though he indignantly repudiated the misrepresentation, it continued to be repeated against him for years thereafter, and to be cited as an instance of the irresponsible violence of the friends of the Eastern Christians.

The most conspicuous and characteristic merits of Freeman as an historian may be summed up in six points : love of truth, love of justice, industry, common sense, breadth of view, and power of vividly realising the political life of the past.

Every one knows the maxim, *pectus facit theologum*,[1] a maxim accountable, by the way,

---

[1] "The heart makes the theologian."

for a good deal of weak theology. More truly may it be said that the merits of a great historian are far from lying wholly in his intellectual powers. Among the highest of such merits, merits which the professional student has even more reason to appreciate than the general reader, because he more frequently discerns the disturbing causes, are two moral qualities. One is the zeal for truth, with the willingness to undertake, in a search for it, a toil by which no credit will ever be gained. The other is a clear view of, and loyal adherence to, the permanent moral standards. In both these points Freeman stood in the front rank. He was kindly and fair in his judgments, and ready to make all the allowances for any man's conduct which the conditions of his time suggested, but he hated cruelty, falsehood, oppression, whether in Syracuse twenty-four centuries ago or in the Ottoman empire to-day. That conscientious industry which spares no pains to get as near as possible to the facts never failed him. Though he talked less about facts and verities than Carlyle did, Carlyle was not so assiduous and so minutely careful in sifting every statement before he admitted it into his pages. That he was never betrayed by sentiment into partisanship it would be too much to say. Scottish critics have accused him, perhaps not without justice, of being led by his English patriotism to overstate the claims of the English

Crown to suzerainty over Scotland.   J. R. Green,
as well as the late Mr. C. H. Pearson, thought
that the same cause disposed him to overlook
the weak points in the character of Harold son
of Godwin, one of his favourite heroes.   But
there have been few writers who have so seldom
erred in this way; few who have striven so
earnestly to do full justice to every cause and
every person.   Even the race prejudices which
he allowed himself to indulge, in letters and talk,
against Irishmen, Frenchmen, and Jews, scarcely
ever appear in his books.   The characters he
has drawn of Lucius Cornelius Sulla, William
the Conqueror and William the Red, St. Thomas
of Canterbury (none of whom he liked), and, in
his *History of Sicily*, of Nicias, are models of the
fairness which historical portraiture requires.   It
is especially interesting to compare his picture
of the unfortunate Athenian with the equally
vigorous but harsher view of Grote.   Freeman,
whom many people thought fierce, was one of
the most soft-hearted of men, and tolerant of
everything but perfidy and cruelty.   Though
disposed to be positive in his opinions, he was
always willing to reconsider a point when any
new evidence was discovered or any new argument brought to his notice, and not unfrequently
modified his view in the light of such evidence
or arguments.   It was this passion for accuracy
and for that lucidity of statement which is the

necessary adjunct of real accuracy, that made him deal so sternly with confused thinkers and careless writers. Carelessness seemed to him a moral fault, because a fault which true conscientiousness excludes. So also clearness of conception and exact precision in the use of words were so natural to him, and appeared so essential to good work, that he would set down the want of them rather to indolence than to incapacity, and apply to them a proportionately severe censure. Mere ignorance he could pardon, but when it was, as often happens, even in persons of considerable pretensions, joined to presumption, his wrath was the hotter because he deemed it a wholly righteous wrath. Never touching any subject which he had not mastered, he thought it his duty as a critic to expose impostors, and rendered in this way, during the years when he wrote for the *Saturday Review*, services to English scholarship second only to those which were embodied in his own treatises. It must be confessed that he enjoyed the work, and, like Samuel Johnson, was not displeased to be told that he had " tossed and gored several persons."

His determination to get to the bottom of a question was the cause of the censure he so freely bestowed both on lawyers, who were wont to rest content with their technicalities, and not go back to the historical basis on which those technicalities rested, and on politicians who fell into the habit of using stock phrases which muddled or misrepresented the principles involved. The expression "national property," as applied to tithes, incensed him, and gave occasion for some of his most vigorous writing. So the common-place grumblings against the presence of bishops in the House of Lords, which may be heard from people who acquiesce in the presence of hereditary peers, led him to give the most clear and forcible statement of the origin and character of that House which our time has produced. Here he was on ground he knew thoroughly. But his habits of accuracy were not less fully illustrated by his atti-tude towards branches of history he had not ex-plored. With a profound and minute knowledge of English history down to the fourteenth century, so far as his aversion to the employment of manuscript authorities would allow, and a scarcely inferior knowledge of foreign European history during the same period, with a less full but very sound knowledge down to the middle of the sixteenth century, and with a thorough mastery of pretty nearly all ancient history, his familiarity with later European history, and with the history of such outlying regions as India or America, was not much beyond that of the average educated man. He used to say when questioned on these matters that "he had not come down to that yet." But when he had occasion to refer to those periods or countries, he hardly ever made a mistake. If he did not know, he did not refer; if he referred, he had seized, as if by instinct, something which was really important and serviceable for his purpose. The same remark applies (speaking generally) to Gibbon and to Macaulay, and I have heard Freeman make it of the writings of Mr. Goldwin Smith, for whom he had a warm admiration.

Freeman's abstention from the use of manuscript sources was virtually prescribed by his persistence in refusing to work out of his own library, or, as he used to say, out of a room which he could consider to be his library for the time being. As, however, the original authorities for the times with which he chiefly dealt are, with few or unimportant exceptions, all in print, this habit can hardly be considered a defect in his historical qualifications. In handling the sources he was a judicious critic and a sound scholar, thoroughly at home in Greek and Latin, and sufficiently equipped in Anglo-Saxon, or, as he called it, Old English. Of his breadth of view, of the command he had of the whole sweep of his knowledge, of his delight in bringing together things the most remote in place or time, it is superfluous to speak. These merits are perhaps most conspicuously seen in the plan of his treatise on Federal Government, as well as in the execution of that one volume which unfortunately was all he produced of what might

have been, if completed, a book of the utmost
value.   But one or two trifling illustrations
of this habit of living in an atmosphere in
which the past was no less real to him than
the present may be forgiven.   When careless
friends directed letters to him at "Somerleaze,
Wookey, Somerset," Wookey being a village a
quarter of a mile from his house, but on the other
side of the river Axe, he would write back com-
plaining that they were "confusing the England
and Wales of the seventh century."   When his
attention had been called to a discussion in the
weekly journals about Shelley's first wife he wrote
to me, "Why will they worry us with this
Harrietfrage? You and I have quite enough
to do with Helen, and Theodora, and Mary
Stuart."   So in addressing Somersetshire rustics
during his election campaign in 1868, he could
not help on one occasion referring to Ptolemy
Euergetes, and on another launching out into
an eloquent description of the Landesgemeinde
of Uri.

Industry came naturally to Freeman, because
he was fond of his own studies and did not
think of his work as task work.   The joy in
reading and writing about bygone times sprang
from the intensity with which he realised them.
He had no geographical imagination, finding
no more pleasure in books of travel than in
dramatic poetry.   But he loved to dwell in the

past, and seemed to see and feel and make himself a part of the events he described. Next
to their worth as statements of carefully investigated facts, the chief merit of his books lies in
the sense of reality which fills them. The politics
of Corinth or Sicyon, the contest of William the
Red with St. Anselm, interested him as keenly
as a general election in which he was himself a
candidate. Looking upon current events with
an historian's eye, he was fond, on the other
hand, of illustrating features of Roman history
from incidents he had witnessed when taking
part in local government as a magistrate; and
in describing the relations of Hermocrates and
Athenagoras at Syracuse he drew upon observa-
tions which he had made in watching the discussions of the Hebdomadal Council at Oxford.
This power of realising the politics of ancient
or mediæval times was especially useful to him
as a writer, because without it his minuteness
might have verged on prolixity, seeing that he
cared exclusively for the political part of history.
It was one of the points in which he rose superior
to most of those German students with whom it
is natural to compare him. Many of them have
equalled him in industry and diligence; some
have surpassed him in the ingenuity which they
bring to bear upon obscure problems; but few of
them have shown the same gift for understanding
what the political life of remote times really was.

Like Gibbon, Freeman was not a mere student, but also a man with opportunities of mixing in affairs, accustomed to bear his share in the world's work, and so better able than the mere student can be to comprehend how that work goes forward. Though he was too peculiar in his views and his way of stating them to have been adapted either to the House of Commons or to a local assembly, and would indeed have been wasted upon nine-teen-twentieths of the business there transacted, he loved politics and watched them with a shrewdly observant eye. Though he indulged his foibles in some directions, he could turn upon history a stream of clear common sense which sometimes made short work of German conjectures. And he was free from the craving to have at all hazards something new to advance, be it a trivial fact or an unsupported guess. He was accustomed of late years to complain that German scholarship seemed to be suffering from the passion for *etwas Neues*, and the consequent disposition to disparage work which did not abound with novelties, however empty or transient such novelties might be.

To think of the Germans is to think of industry. Freeman was a true Teuton in the mass of his production. Besides the seven thick volumes devoted to the Norman Conquest and William Rufus, the four thick volumes to Sicily, four large volumes of collected essays, and nine or ten smaller volumes on architectural subjects, on the English constitution, on the United States, on the Slavs and the Turks, he wrote an even greater quantity of matter which appeared in the *Saturday Review* during the twenty years from 1856 to 1876, and it was by these articles, not less than by his books, that he succeeded in dispelling many current errors and confusions, and in establishing some of his own doctrines so firmly that we now scarcely remember what iteration and reiteration, in season and out of season, and much to the impatience of those who remembered that they had heard these doctrines often before, were needed to make them accepted by the public. Freeman's swift facility was due to his power of concentration. He always knew what he meant an article to contain before he sat down to his desk; and in his historical researches he made each step so certain that he seldom required to reinvestigate a point or to change, in revising for the press, the substance of what he had written.

In his literary habits he was so methodical and precise that he could carry on three undertakings at the same time, keeping on different tables in his working rooms the books he needed for each, and passing at stated hours from one to the other. It is often remarked that the growth of journalism, forcing men to write hastily and profusely, tends to injure literature both in matter and in manner. In point of matter, Freeman, though for the best part of his life a very prolific journalist, did not seem to suffer. He was as exact, clear, and thorough at the end as he had been at the beginning. On his style, however, the results were unfortunate. It retained its force and its point, but it became diffuse, not that each particular sentence was weak, or vague, or wordy, but that what was substantially the same idea was apt to be reiterated, with slight differences of phrase, in several successive sentences or paragraphs. He was fond of the Psalter, great part of which he knew by heart, and we told him that he had caught too much of the manner of Psalm cxix. This tendency to repetition caused some of his books, and particularly the *Norman Conquest* and *William Rufus*, to swell to a portentous bulk. Those treatises, which constitute a history of England from A.D. 1042 to 1100, would be more widely read if they had been, as they ought to have been, reduced to three or four volumes; and as he came to perceive this, he resolved in the last year of his life to republish the *Norman Conquest* in a condensed form. To be obliged to compress was a wholesome, though unwelcome, discipline, and the result is seen in some of his smaller books, such as the historical essays, and the sketches of English towns, often wonderfully fresh and vigorous bits of work. Anxiety to be scrupulously accurate runs into prolixity, and Freeman so loved his subjects that it pained him to omit any characteristic detail a chronicler had preserved; as he once observed to a distinguished writer who was dealing with a much later period, "You know so much about your people that you have to leave out a great deal, I know so little that I must tell all I know." The tendency to repeat the same word too frequently sprang from his preference for words of Teutonic origin and his pride in what he deemed the purity of his English. His pages would have been livelier had he felt free to indulge in the humour with which his private letters sparkled; for he was full of fun, though it often turned on points too recondite for the public. But it was only in the notes to his histories, and seldom even there, that he gave play to one of the merits that most commended him to his friends.

So far of his books. He was, however, also Regius Professor of History at Oxford during the last eight years of his life, and thus the head of the historical faculty in his own University which he dearly loved. That he was less effective as a teacher than as a writer may be partly ascribed to his having come too late to a new kind of work, and one which demands the freshness of youth; partly also to the

cramping conditions under which professors
have to teach at Oxford, where everything is
governed by a system of examinations which
Freeman was never tired of denouncing as ruinous to study. His friends, however, doubted
whether the natural bent of his mind was
towards oral teaching. It was a peculiar mind,
which ran in a deep channel of its own, and
could not easily, if the metaphor be permissible,
be drawn off to irrigate the adjoining fields.
He was always better at putting his own
views in a clear and telling way than at
laying his intellect alongside of yours, apprehending your point of view, and setting himself to meet it. Or, to put the same thing
differently, you learned more by listening to
him than by conversing with him. He had
not the quick intellectual sympathy and effu-
sion which feels its way to the heart of an audience, and indeed derives inspiration from the
sight of an audience. In his election meetings
I noticed that the temper and sentiment of the
listeners did not in the least affect him; what
he said was what he himself cared to say, not
what he felt they would wish to hear. So also
in his lecturing he pleased himself, and chose
the topics he liked best rather than those which
the examination scheme prescribed to the students. Perhaps he was right, for he was of those
whose excellence in performance depends upon

the enjoyment they find in the exercise of their powers. But even on the topics he selected, he did not take hold of and guide the mind of the students, realising their particular difficulties and needs, but simply delivered his own message in his own way. Admitting this deficiency, the fact remains that he was not only an ornament to the University by the example he set of unflagging zeal, conscientious industry, loyalty to truth, and love of freedom, but also a stimulating influence upon those who were occupied with history. He delighted to surround himself with the most studious of the younger workers, gave them abundant encouragement and recognition, and never grudged the time to help them by his knowledge or his counsel.

Much the same might be said of his lifelong friend and illustrious predecessor in the chair of history (Dr. Stubbs), whom Freeman had been generously extolling for many years before the merits of that admirable scholar became known to the public. Stubbs disliked lecturing; and though once a year he delivered a " public lecture " full of wisdom, and sometimes full of wit also, he was not effective as a teacher, not so effective, for instance, as Bishop Creighton, who won his reputation at Merton College long before he became Professor of Ecclesiastical History at Cambridge. But Stubbs, by his mere presence in the University, and by the inexhaustible kindness with

U

which he answered questions and gave advice, rendered great services to the studies of the place. It may be doubted whether, when he was raised to the episcopal bench, history did not lose more than the Church of England gained.   Other men of far less ability could have discharged five-sixths of a bishop's duties equally well, but there was no one else in England, if indeed in Europe, capable of carrying on his historical researches.   So Dr. Lightfoot was, as Professor at Cambridge, doing work for Christian learning even more precious than the work which is still affectionately re-membered in his diocese of Durham.

Few men have had a genius for friendship equal to Freeman's.   The names of those he cared for were continually on his lips, and their lives in his thoughts; their misfortunes touched him like his own; he was always ready to defend them, always ready to give any aid they needed.   No differences of opinion affected his regard.   Sensitive as he was to criticism, he received their censure on any part of his work without offence.   The need he felt for knowing how they fared and for sharing his thoughts with them expressed itself in the enormous correspond-ence, not of business, but of pure affection, which he kept up with his many friends, and which forms, for his letters were so racy that many of them were preserved, the fullest record of his life.

This warmth of feeling deserves to be dwelt on, because it explains the tendency to vehemence in controversy which brought some enmities upon him. There was an odd contrast between his fondness for describing wars and battles and that extreme aversion to militarism which made him appear to dislike the very existence of a British army and navy. So his combativeness, and the zest with which he bestowed shrewd blows on those who encountered him, though due to his wholesome scorn for pretenders, and his hatred of falsehood and injustice, seemed inconsistent with the real kindliness of his nature. The kindliness, however, no one who knew him could doubt; it showed itself not only in his care for dumb creatures and for children, but in the depth and tenderness of his affections. Of religion he spoke little, and only to his most intimate friends. In opinion he had drifted a long way from the Anglo-Catholic position of his early manhood; but he remained a sincerely pious Christian.

Though his health had been infirm for some years before his death, his literary activity did not slacken, nor did his powers show signs of decline. There is nothing in his writings, nor in any writings of our time, more broad, clear, and forcible than many chapters of the *History of Sicily*. Much of his work has effected its purpose, and will, by degrees, lose its place in the public eye. But much will live on into a yet distant future, because it has been done so thoroughly, and contains so much sound and vigorous thinking, that coming generations of historical students will need it and value it almost as our own has done.

ROBERT LOWE
VISCOUNT SHERBROOKE[1]

HAD Robert Lowe died in 1868, when he became a Cabinet Minister, his death would have been a political event of the first magnitude; but when he died in 1892 (in his eighty-second year) hardly anybody under forty years of age knew who Lord Sherbrooke was, and the new generation wondered why their seniors should feel any interest in the disappearance of a superannuated peer whose name had long since ceased to be heard in either the literary or the political world. It requires an effort to believe that he was at one time held the equal in oratory and the superior in intellect of Mr. Bright and Mr. Gladstone. There are few instances in our annals of men who have been equally famous and whose fame has been bounded by so short a span out of a long life.

No one who knew Lowe ever doubted his abilities. He made a brilliant reputation, first at Winchester (where, as his autobiography tells us,

[1] A carefully written Life of Lord Sherbrooke (in two volumes) by Mr. Patchett Martin was published in 1896. The most interesting part of it is the short fragment of autobiography with which it begins, and which carries the story down to Lowe's arrival in Australia.

he was miserable) and then at Oxford, where he was the contemporary and fully the peer of Roundell Palmer (afterwards Lord Chancellor Selborne) and of Archibald Tait (afterwards Archbishop of Canterbury).   He was much sought after and wonderfully effective as a private tutor or "coach" in classical subjects, being not only an excellent scholar but extremely clear and stimulating as a teacher.   He retained his love of literature all through life, and made himself, *inter alia permulta*, a good Icelandic scholar and a fair Sanskrit scholar.   For mathématics he had no turn at all. Active sports, he tells us, he enjoyed, characteristically adding, "they open to dulness also its road to fame."   When he left the University, where anecdotes of his caustic wit were long current, he tried his fortune at the Bar, but with such scant success that he presently emigrated to New South Wales, soon rose to prominence and unpopularity there, returned in ten years with a tolerable fortune and a detestation of democracy, became a leading-article writer on the *Times*, entered Parliament, but was little heard of till Lord Palmerston gave him (in 1859) the place of Vice-President of the Committee of Council on Education.   His function in that office was to administer the grants made from the national treasury to elementary schools, and as he found the methods of inspection rather lax, and noted a tendency to superficiality and a neglect of back-

ward children, he introduced new rules for the
distribution of the grant (the so-called "Revised
Code") which provoked violent opposition. The
motive was good, but the rules were too mechani-
cal and rigid and often worked harshly; so he
was presently driven from office by an attack led
by Lord Robert Cecil (now Lord Salisbury).

Though Lowe became known by this struggle,
his conspicuous fame dates from 1865, when he
appeared as the trenchant critic of a measure for
extending the parliamentary franchise in boroughs,
introduced by a private member. Next year
his powers shone forth in their full lustre. The
Liberal Ministry of Lord Russell, led in the
House of Commons by Mr. Gladstone, had
brought in a Franchise Extension Bill (applying
to boroughs only) which excited the dislike
of the more conservative or more timid among
their supporters. This dislike might not have gone
beyond many mutterings and a few desertions
but for the vehemence with which Lowe opposed
the measure. He fought against it in a series of
speeches which produced a greater impression in
the House of Commons, and roused stronger
feelings of admiration and hostility in the
country, than any political addresses had done
since 1832. The new luminary rose so suddenly to the zenith, and cast so unexpected a
light that everybody was dazzled; and though
many dissented, and some attacked him bitterly,

few ventured to meet him in argument on the ground he had selected. The effect of these speeches of 1866 can hardly be understood by any one who reads them to-day unless he knows how commonplace and "practical," that is to say, averse to general reasonings and historical illustrations, the character of parliamentary debating was becoming even in Lowe's time. It is still more practical and still less ornate in our own day.

The House of Commons then contained, and has indeed usually contained (though some Houses are much better than others), many capable lawyers, capable men of business, capable country gentlemen; many men able to express themselves with clearness, fluency, and that sort of temperate good sense which Englishmen especially value. Few, however, were able to produce finished rhetoric; still fewer had a range of thought and knowledge extending much beyond the ordinary education of a gentleman and the ordinary ideas of a politician; and the assembly was one so intolerant of rhetoric, and so much inclined to treat, as unpractical, facts and arguments drawn from recondite sources, that even those who possessed out-of-the-way learning were disposed, and rightly so, to use it sparingly. In Robert Lowe, however, a remarkable rhetorical and dialectical power was combined with a command of branches of historical, literary, and economic knowledge so unfamiliar to the average member as to have for him all the charm of novelty. The rhetoric was sometimes too elaborate. The political philosophy was not always sound. But the rhetoric was so polished that none could fail to enjoy it; and the political philosophy was put in so terse, bright, and pointed a form that it made the ordinary country gentleman fancy himself a philosopher while he listened to it in the House or repeated it to his friends at the club. The speeches, which, though directed against a particular measure, constituted an indictment of democratic government in general, had the advantages of expressing what many felt but few had ventured to say, and of being delivered from one side of the House and cheered by the other side. No position gives a debater in the House of Commons such a vantage ground for securing attention. Its rarity makes it remarkable. If the speaker who attacks his own party is supposed to do so from personal motives, the personal element gives piquancy. If he may be credited with conscientious conviction, his shafts strike with added weight, for how strong must conviction be when it turns a man against his former friends. Accordingly, nothing so much annoys a party and gratifies its antagonists as when one of its own recalcitrant members attacks it in flank. When one looks back now at the contents of these speeches —

there were only five or six of them — and finds
one's self surprised at their success, this favouring circumstance and the whole temper of the
so-called "upper classes" need to be remembered.   The bulk of the wealthier commercial
class and a large section of the landed class had
theretofore belonged to the Liberal party.   Most
of them, however, were then already beginning to
pass through what was called Whiggism into
habits of thought that were practically Tory.
They did not know how far they had gone till
Lowe's speeches told them, and they welcomed
his ideas as justifying their own tendencies.

In themselves, as pieces either of rhetoric or
of "civil wisdom," the speeches are not first-rate.
No one would dream of comparing them to
Burke's, in originality, or in richness of diction,
or in weight of thought.   But for the moment
they were far more appreciated than Burke's
were by the House of his time, which thought of
dining while he thought of convincing.   Robert
Lowe was for some months the idol of a large
part of the educated class, and indeed of that
part chiefly which plumed itself upon its culture.
I recollect to have been in those days at a
breakfast party given by an eminent politician
and nominal supporter of the Liberal Ministry,
and to have heard Mr. G. S. Venables, the leader
of the *Saturday Review* set, an able and copious
writer who was a sort of literary and political

oracle among his friends, deliver, amid general applause, including that of the host, the opinion that Lowe was an intellectual giant compared to Mr. Gladstone, and that the reputation of the latter had been extinguished for ever.

This period of glory, which was enhanced by the fall of Lord Russell and Mr. Gladstone from power in June 1866 — the defeat came on a minor point, but was largely due to Lowe's speeches — lasted till Lowe, who had now become a force to be counted with, obtained office as Chancellor of the Exchequer in the Liberal Ministry which Mr. Gladstone formed in the end of 1868. From that moment his position declined. He lost popularity and influence both with the country and in the House of Commons. His speeches were always able, but they did not seem to tell when delivered from the ministerial bench. His financial proposals, though ingenious, were thought too ingenious, and showed a deficient perception of the tendencies of the English mind. No section likes being taxed, but Lowe's budgets met with a more than usually angry opposition. His economies and retrenchments, so far from bringing him the credit he deserved, exposed him to the charge of cheese-paring parsimony, and did much to render the Ministry unpopular. Before that Ministry fell in 1874, Lowe, who had in 1873 exchanged the Exchequer for the Home Office, had almost ceased to be a personage in politics. He did nothing to retrieve his fame during the six years of opposition that followed, seldom spoke, took little part in the denunciation of Lord Beaconsfield's Eastern and Afghan policy, which went on from 1876 till 1880, and once at least gave slight signs of declining mental power. So in 1880 he was relegated to the House of Lords, because the new Liberal Government of that year could not make room for him. Very soon thereafter his memory began to fail, and for the last ten years of his life he had been practically forgotten, though sometimes seen, a pathetic figure, at evening parties. There is hardly a parallel in our parliamentary annals to so complete an eclipse of so brilliant a luminary.

This rapid obscuration of a reputation which was genuine, for Lowe's powers had been amply proved, was due to no accident, and was apparent long before mental decay set in. The causes lay in himself. One cause was purely physical. He was excessively short-sighted, so much so that when he was writing a letter, his nose was apt to rub out the words his pen had traced; and this defect shut him out from all that knowledge of individual men and of audiences which is to be obtained by watching their faces. Mr. Gladstone, who never seemed to resent Lowe's attacks, and greatly admired his gifts — it was not so clear that Lowe reciprocated the admiration — used to relate that on one occasion when a foreign potentate met the Minister in St. James's Park and put out his hand in friendly greeting, Lowe repelled his advances, and when the King said, " But, Mr. Lowe, you know me quite well," he answered, " Yes, indeed, I know you far too well, and I don't want to have anything more to do with you." He had mistaken the monarch for a prominent politician with whom he had had a sharp encounter on a deputation a few days before! For social purposes Lowe might almost as well have been blind; yet he did not receive that kind of indulgence which is extended to the blind. In the interesting fragment of autobiography which he left, he attributes his unpopularity entirely to this cause, declaring that he was really of a kindly nature, liking his fellow-men just as well as most of them like one another.[1] But in truth his own character had something to answer for. Without being ill-natured, he was deemed a hard-natured man, who did not appear to consider the feelings of others. He had indeed a love of mischief, and gleefully tells in his autobiography how, when travelling in his youth through the Scottish Highlands, he drove the too self-conscious Wordsworth wild by his incessant praise of Walter Scott.[2]

[1] In his autobiography he writes, " With a quiet temper and a real wish to please, I have been obliged all my life to submit to an amount of unpopularity which I really did not deserve, and to feel myself condemned for what were really physical rather than moral deficiencies."

[2] There was an anecdote current in the University of Oxford down to my time that when Lowe was examining in the examination which the statutes call " Responsions," the dons " Little-go," and the undergraduates

He had not in political life more than his fair
share of personal enmities. One of them was
Disraeli's. They were not unequally matched.
Lowe was intellectually in some respects stronger,
but he wanted Disraeli's skill in managing men
and assemblies. Disraeli resented Lowe's sarcasms, and on one occasion, when the latter
had made an indiscreet speech, went out of his
way to inflict on him a personal humiliation.

Nor was this Lowe's only defect. Powerful
in attack, he was feeble in defence. Terrible as
a critic, he had, as his official career showed, little
constructive talent, little tact in shaping or recommending his measures. Unsteady or inconstant
in purpose, he was at one moment headstrong,
at another timid or vacillating. These faults,
scarcely noticed when he was in opposition,
sensibly reduced his value as a minister and as a
Cabinet colleague.

In private Lowe was good company, bright,
alert, and not unkindly. He certainly did not,
as was alleged of another famous contemporary,

"Smalls," a friend coming in while the *viva voce* was in progress, asked
him how he was getting on. "Excellently," said Lowe, "five men
plucked already, and the sixth very shaky." Another tale, not likely to
have been invented, relates that when he and several members of the
then Liberal Ministry were staying in Dublin with the Lord Lieutenant,
and had taken an excursion into the Wicklow hills, they found themselves
one afternoon obliged to wait for half an hour at a railway station. To
pass the time, Lowe forthwith engaged in a dispute about the charge with
the car-drivers who had brought them, a dispute which soon became hot
and noisy, to the delight of Lowe, but to the horror of the old Lord
Chancellor, who was one of the party.

Lord Westbury, positively enjoy the giving of pain. But he had a most unchristian scorn for the slow and the dull and the unenlightened, and never restrained his scorching wit merely for the sake of sparing those who came in his way. If the distinction be permissible, he was not cruel but he was merciless, that is to say, unrestrained by compassion. Instances are not wanting of men who have maintained great influence in spite of their rough tongues and the enmities which rough tongues provoke. But such men have usually also possessed some of the arts of popularity, and have been able to retain the adherence of their party at large, even when they had alienated many who came into personal contact with them. This was not Lowe's case. He did not conceal his contempt for the multitude, and had not the tact needed for humouring it, any more than for managing the House of Commons. The very force and keenness of his intellect kept him aloof from other people and prevented him from understanding their sentiments. He saw things so clearly that he could not tolerate mental confusion, and was apt to reach conclusions so fast that he missed perceiving some of the things which are gradually borne in upon slower minds. There are also instances of strong men who, though they do not revile their opponents, incur hatred because their strength and activity make them feared. Hostility concentrates itself on the

opponents deemed most formidable, and a political leader who is spared while his fellows are
attacked cannot safely assume that this immunity
is a tribute to his virtues.   Incessant abuse fell to
the lot of Mr. Bright, who was not often, and of
Mr. Gladstone, who was hardly ever, personally
bitter in invective.   But in compensation Mr.
Bright and Mr. Gladstone received enthusiastic
loyalty from their followers.   For Lowe there was
no such compensation.   Even his own side did
not love him.   There was also a certain harshness,
perhaps a certain narrowness, about his views.
Even in those days of rigid economics, he took an
exceptionally rigid view of all economic problems,
refusing to make allowance for any motives
except those of bare self-interest.   Though he
did not belong by education or by social
ties to the Utilitarian group, and gave an un-
gracious reception to J. S. Mill's first speeches
in the House of Commons, he was a far more
stringent and consistent exponent of the harder
kind of Benthamism than was Mill himself.   He
professed, and doubtless to some extent felt, a
contempt for appeals to historical or literary
sentiment, and relished nothing more than derid-
ing his own classical training as belonging to an
effete and absurd scheme of education.   He left
his mark on our elementary school system by
establishing the system of payment by results,
but nearly every change made in that system

since his day has tended to destroy the alterations
he made and to bring back the older condition
of things, though no doubt in an amended form.
His ideas of University reform were crude and
barren, limited, indeed, to the substitution of what
the Germans call " bread studies " for mental cultivation, and to the extension of the plan of com-
petitive examinations for honours and money
prizes, a plan which more and more displeases
the most enlightened University teachers, and
is felt to have done more harm than good to
Oxford and Cambridge, where it has had the
fullest play.   He had also, and could give good
reasons for his opinion, a hearty dislike to endowments of all kinds ; and once, when asked by
a Royal Commission to suggest a mode of im-
proving their application, answered in his trenchant
way, " Get rid of them.   Throw them into the sea."

It would not be fair to blame Lowe for the
results which followed his vigorous action against
the extension of the suffrage in 1866, for no one
could then have predicted that in the following
year the Tories, beguiled by Mr. Disraeli, would
reverse their former attitude and carry a suffrage
bill far wider than that which they had rejected a
year before.   But the sequel of the successful
resistance of 1866 may stand as a warning to
those who think that the course of thoroughgoing
opposition to a measure they dislike is, because
it seems courageous, likely to be the right and

x

wise course for patriotic men. Had the moderate
bill of 1866 been suffered to pass, the question of
further extending the suffrage might possibly have
slept for another thirty years, for there was no
very general or urgent cry for it among the working people, and England would have continued
to be ruled in the main by voters belonging to
the middle class and the upper section of the
working class. The consequence of the heated
contest of 1866 was not only to bring about
a larger immediate change in 1867, but to
create an interest in the question which soon
prompted the demand for the extension of household suffrage to the counties, and completed in
1884-85 the process by which England has become virtually a democracy, though a plutocratic
democracy, still affected by the habits and notions
of oligarchic days. Thus Robert Lowe, as much
as Disraeli and Gladstone, may in a sense be
called an author of the tremendous change which
has passed upon the British Constitution since
1866, and the extent of which was not for a
long while realised. Lowe himself never re-
canted his views, but never repeated his declaration of them, feeling that he had incurred
unpopularity enough, and probably feeling also
that the case was hopeless.

People who disliked his lugubrious forecasts
used to call him a Cassandra, perhaps forgetting
that, besides the distinctive feature of Cassandra's

prophecies that nobody believed them, there was
another distinctive feature, viz. that they came
true. Did Lowe's? It is often profitable and
sometimes amusing to turn back to the predictions through which eminent men relieved their
perturbed souls, and see how far these superior
minds were able to discern the tendencies, already
at work in their time, which were beginning to
gain strength, and were destined to determine
the future. Whoever reads Lowe's speeches of
1865-67 may do worse than glance at the same
time at a book,[1] long since forgotten, which contains the efforts of a group of young University
Liberals to refute the arguments used by him
and by Lord Cairns, the strongest of his allies,
in their opposition to schemes of parliamentary
reform.

To compare the optimism of these young
writers and Lowe's pessimism with what has
actually come to pass is a not uninstructive
task. True it is that England has had only
thirty-five years' experience of the Reform Act
of 1867, and only seventeen years' experience
of that even greater step towards pure democracy which was effected by the Franchise and
Redistribution Acts of 1884-85. We are still
far from knowing what sorts of Parliaments and
policies the enlarged suffrage will end by giving.
But some at least of the mischiefs Lowe foretold

---

[1] *Essays on Reform*, published in 1867.

have not arrived. He expected first of all a rapid increase in corruption and intimidation at parliamentary elections. The quality of the House of Commons would decline, because money would rule, and small boroughs would no longer open the path by which talent could enter. Members would be either millionaires or demagogues, and they would also become far more subservient to their constituents. Universal suffrage would soon arrive, because no halting place between the £10 franchise [1] and universal suffrage could be found. Placed on a democratic basis, the House of Commons would not be able to retain its authority over the Executive. The House of Lords, the Established Church, the judicial bench (in that dignity and that independence which are essential to its usefulness), would be overthrown as England passed into "the bare and level plain of democracy where every ant-hill is a mountain and every thistle a forest tree." These and the other features characteristic of popular government on which Lowe savagely descanted were pieced together out of Plato and Tocqueville, coupled with his own disagreeable experiences of Australian politics. None of the predicted evils can be said to have as yet become features of the polity and government of England,[2]

---

[1] The then borough qualification, which Mr. Gladstone's Bill proposed to reduce to £7.

[2] Mr. Gladstone said to me in 1897 that the extension of the suffrage had, in his judgment, improved the quality of legislation, making it more

though the power of the House relatively to the Cabinet does seem to be declining. Yet some of Lowe's incidental remarks are true, and not least true is his prediction that democracies will be found just as prone to war, just as apt to be swept away by passion, as other kinds of government have been. Few signs herald the approach of that millennium of peace and enlightenment which Cobden foretold and for which Gladstone did not cease to hope.

No one since Lowe has taken up the part of *Advocatus diaboli* against democracy which he played in 1866.[1] Since Disraeli passed the Household Suffrage in Boroughs Bill in 1867, a nullification of Lowe's triumph which incensed him more than ever against Disraeli, no one has ever come forward in England as the avowed enemy of changes designed to popularise our government. Parties have quarrelled over the time and the manner of extensions of the franchise, but the issue of principle raised in 1866 has not been

regardful of the interests of the body of the people, but had not improved the quality of the House of Commons.

[1] Sir H. S. Maine's *Quarterly Review* articles, published in a volume under the title of *Popular Government*, come nearest to being a literary presentation of the case against democracy, but they are, with all their ingenuity and grace of style, so provokingly vague and loosely expressed that there can seldom be found in them a proposition with which one can agree, or from which one can differ. E. de Laveleye's well-known book is not much more substantial, but instruction may (as respects France) be found in the late Edmond Schérer's *De la Démocratie*, and (as respects England and the United States) in M. Ostrogorski's recent book, *Democracy and the Organisation of Political Parties.*

raised again.   Even in 1884, when Mr. Gladstone
carried his bill for assimilating the county franchise
to that existing in boroughs, the Tory party did
not oppose the measure in principle, but confined
themselves to insisting that it should be accom-
panied by a scheme for the redistribution of seats.
The secret, first unveiled by Disraeli, that the
masses will as readily vote for the Tory party as
for the Liberal, is now common property, and
universal suffrage, when it comes to be offered, is
as likely to be offered by the former party as by
the latter.   This gives a touch of historical interest to Lowe's speeches of 1866.   They are the
swan-song of the old constitutionalism.   The
changes which came in 1867 and 1884 must have
come sooner or later, for they were in the natural
line of development as we see it all over the
world; but they might have come much later
had not Lowe's opposition wrecked the moderate
scheme of 1866.   Apart from that episode Lowe's
career would now be scarcely remembered, or
would be remembered by those who knew his
splendid gifts as an illustration of the maxim that
mere intellectual power does not stand first among
the elements of character that go to the winning
of a foremost place.

WILLIAM ROBERTSON SMITH

ROBERTSON SMITH,[1] the most widely learned and one of the most powerful teachers that either Cambridge or Oxford could show during the years of his residence in England, died at the age of forty-seven on the 31st of March 1894. To the English public generally his name was little known, or was remembered only in connection with the theological controversy and ecclesiastical trial of which he had been the central figure in Scotland fifteen years before. But on the Continent of Europe and by Orientalists generally he was regarded as the foremost Semitic scholar of Britain, and by those who knew him as one of the most remarkable men of his time.

He was born in 1846 in the quiet pastoral valley of the Don, in Aberdeenshire. His father,

[1] No Life of Robertson Smith has yet been written, but it is hoped that one may be prepared by his intimate friend, Mr. J. Sutherland Black. A portrait of him (by his friend Sir George Reid, late President of the Royal Scottish Academy) hangs in the library of Christ's College, Cambridge, to which Smith's collection of Oriental books was presented by his friends, and another has been placed in the Divinity College of the United Free Presbyterian Church at Aberdeen. A memorial window has been set up in the chapel of the University of Aberdeen, where he won his first distinctions. I have to thank my friend Mr. Black for some suggestions he has kindly made after perusing this sketch.

who was a minister of the Scottish Free Church
in the parish of Keig, possessed high mathematical
talent, and his mother, who survived him six years,
was a woman of great force of character, who
retained till her death, at seventy-six years of
age, the full exercise of her keen intelligence.
Smith went straight from his father's teaching to
the University of Aberdeen, and after graduating
there, continued his studies first at Bonn in 1865,
and afterwards at Göttingen (1869). When only
twenty-four he became Professor of Oriental
Languages in the College or Divinity School of
the Free Church at Aberdeen, and two years
later was chosen one of the revisers of the Old
Testament, a striking honour for so young a
man. In 1881 he became first assistant-editor
and then editor-in-chief of the ninth edition of the
Encyclopædia Britannica. He was exceptionally
qualified for the post by the variety of his attain-
ments and by the extreme quickness of his mind,
which rapidly acquired knowledge on almost any
kind of subject. Those who knew him are agreed
that among all the eminent men who have been
connected with this great *Encyclopædia* from its
first beginning a century and a half ago until now
he was surpassed by none, if equalled by any, in
the range of his learning and in the capacity to
bring learning to bear upon editorial work. He
took infinite pains to find the most competent
writers, and was able to exercise effective per-

sonal supervision over a very large proportion of the articles. The ninth edition was much fuller and more thorough than any of its predecessors; and good as the first twelve volumes were, a still higher level of excellence was attained in the latter half, a result due to his industry and discernment. Not a few of the articles on subjects connected with the Old Testament were from his own pen; and they were among the best in the work.

The appearance of one of them, that entitled " Bible," which contained a general view of the history of the canonical books of Scripture, their dates, authorship, and reception by the Christian Church, became a turning-point in his life. The propositions he stated regarding the origin of parts of the Old Testament, particularly the Pentateuch, excited alarm and displeasure in Scotland, where few persons had become aware of the conclusions reached by recent Biblical scholars in Continental Europe. The article was able, clear, and fearless, plainly the work of a master hand. The views it advanced were not for the most part due to Smith's own investigations, but were to be found in the writings of other learned men. Neither would they now be thought extreme; they are in fact accepted to-day by many writers of unquestioned orthodoxy in Britain and a (perhaps smaller) number in the United States. In 1876, however, these views were new and startling to those who had not studied in Germany or followed the researches of such men as Ewald, Kuenen, and Wellhausen. The Scottish Free Church had theretofore prided itself upon the rigidity of its orthodoxy; and while among the younger ministers there were a good many able and learned scholars holding what used to be called "advanced views," the mass of the elder and middle-aged clergy had gone on in the old-fashioned traditions of verbal inspiration, and took every word in the Five Books (except the last chapter of Deuteronomy) to have been written down by Moses.   It was only natural that their anger should be kindled against the young pro-fessor, whose theories seemed to cut away the ground from under their feet.   Proceedings were (1876) taken against him before the Presbytery of Aberdeen, and the case found its way thence to the Synod of Aberdeen, and ultimately to the General Assembly of the Free Church.   In one form or another (for the flame was lit anew by other articles published by him in the *Encyclo-pædia*) it lingered on for five years.   So far from yielding to the storm, Robertson Smith defied it, maintaining not only the truth of his views, but their compatibility with the Presbyterian standards as contained in the Confession of Faith and the Longer and Shorter Catechisms.   In this latter contention he was successful, proving that the divines of the sixteenth and seventeenth centuries had not committed themselves to any specific

doctrine of inspiration, still less to any dogmatic
deliverance as to the authorship of particular
books of Scripture. The standards simply declared that the Word of God was contained in the
canonical books, and as there had been little or
no controversy between Protestants and Roman
Catholics regarding the date or the authorship or
the divine authority of those books (apart of
course from disputes regarding the Apocrypha),
had not dealt specifically with those last mentioned matters. As it was by reference to the
Confession of Faith that the offence alleged had
to be established, Smith made good his defence;
so in the end, finding it impossible to convict him
of deviation from the standards, and thereby to
deal with him as an ordained minister of the
Church, his adversaries fell back on the plan of
depriving him, by an executive rather than judicial
vote, not indeed of his clerical status, but of his
professorship, on the ground of the alleged "un-
settling character" of his teaching.

Meanwhile, however, there had been an immense rally to him of the younger clergy and
of the less conservative among the laity. The
main current of Scottish popular thought and
life had ever since the Reformation flowed in
an ecclesiastical channel; and even nowadays,
when Scotland is rapidly becoming Anglicised,
a theological or ecclesiastical question excites a
wider and keener interest there than a similar

question would do in England. So in Scotland
for four years "the Robertson Smith case" was
the chief topic of discussion outside as well as
inside the Free Church. The sympathy felt for
the accused was heightened by the ingenuity,
energy, and courage with which he defended his
position, showing a power of argument and
repartee which made it plain that he would
have held a distinguished place in any assembly
whatever. If his debating had a fault, it was
that of being almost too dialectically cogent, so
that his antagonists felt that they were being
foiled on the form of the argument before they
could get to the issues they sought to raise.
But while he was an accomplished lawyer in
matters of form, he was no less an accomplished
theologian in matters of substance. Although the
party of repression triumphed so far as to deprive
him of his chair, the victory virtually remained
with him, not only because he had shown that the
Scottish Presbyterian standards did not condemn
the views he held, but also because his defence
and the discussions which it occasioned had, in
bringing those views to the knowledge of a great
number of thoughtful laymen, led such persons
to reconsider their own position. Some of them
found themselves forced to agree with Smith.
Others, who distrusted their capacity for arriving
at a conclusion, came at least to think that the
questions involved did not affect the essentials of

faith, and must be settled by the ordinary canons of historical and philological criticism. Thus the trial proved to be a turning-point for the Scottish Churches, much as the *Essays and Reviews* case had been for the Church of England eighteen years earlier. Opinions formerly proscribed were thereafter freely expressed. Nearly all the doctrinal prosecutions subsequently attempted in the Scottish Presbyterian Churches have failed. Much feeling has been excited, but the result has been to secure a greater latitude than was dreamt of forty years ago. At first the rigidly orthodox section of the Free Church, now almost confined to the Highlands, thought of seceding from the main body on the ground that tolerance was passing into indifference or unbelief. But the new ideas continued to grow, and the sentiment in favour of letting clergymen as well as lay church members put a lax construction on the doctrinal standards drawn up in the sixteenth and seventeenth centuries, has spread as widely in Scotland as in England. The Presbyterian Churches in America and the Roman Catholic Church now stand almost alone among the larger Christian bodies in retaining something of the ancient rigidity. Even the Roman Church begins to feel the solvent power of these researches. It may be conjectured that as the process of adjusting the letter of Scripture to the conclusions of science which Galileo was not permitted to apply in the field of astronomy has now been generally applied in the fields of geology and biology, so all the churches will presently reconcile themselves to the conclusions of historical and linguistic criticism, now that such criticism has become truly scientific in its methods.

Having no longer any tie to Scotland, as he had never desired a pastoral charge there, since he felt his vocation to lie in study and teaching, Smith was hesitating which way to turn, when the offer of the Lord Almoner's Readership in Arabic, which had become vacant in 1883, determined him to settle in Cambridge. He had travelled in Arabia a few years earlier, thereby adding a colloquial familiarity to his grammatical mastery of the language. He was an ardent student of Arabic literature, and indeed devoted more time to it than to Hebrew. Though he had felt deeply the attacks made upon him, and was indignant at the mode of his dismissal, he was not in the least dispirited; and his self-control was shown by the way in which he resisted the temptation, to which controversialists are prone, of going further than they originally meant and thereby damaging the position of their supporters. Still, he was weary of controversy, and pleased to see before him a prospect of learned quiet and labour, although the salary of the Readership was less than £100 a year. Fortunately he had come to a place where gifts like his were

appreciated. The Master and Fellows of Christ's
College elected him to a fellowship with no
duties of tuition attached to it — a wise and graceful recognition of his merits which did them the
more credit because they had very little personal
knowledge of him, while he had possessed no
prior tie with the University. Christ's is one of
the smaller colleges, but has almost always had
men of distinction among its fellows, and has maintained a high standard of teaching. In the list of
its alumni stand the names of John Milton, Isaac
Barrow, Ralph Cudworth, and Charles Darwin.
Robertson Smith dwelt in it for the rest of his
days, entering into the life of hall and common-
room with great zest, for he was of an extremely
sociable turn, and the College became proud of
him. When a vacancy occurred in the office of
University Librarian, he was chosen to fill it.
His knowledge of and fondness for books fitted
him excellently for the place, but the details of
administration worried him, and it was a change
for the better when (in 1889), on the death
of his friend, William Wright, he became Professor of Arabic.[1] His efforts to build up a

[1] There was an aged Jewish scholar who came now and then to
Cambridge in those days, and who, as sometimes happens, disliked
other scholars labouring in the same field. He was (so it used to be said)
one of the few who knew exactly how the word which we write Jehovah
or Iahve ought to be pronounced, and it was believed that he had
solemnly cursed Wright, Smith, and a third Semitic scholar in the Sacred
Name. All three died soon afterwards.

What would have been thought of this in the Middle Ages!

school of Oriental studies on the foundations laid
by Wright, and with the help of an eminent
Syriac scholar, Bensley, were proving successful,
and a considerable number of able young men
were gathering round him, when (in 1890) the
hand of disease fell upon him, obliging him first
to curtail and afterwards to intermit his lectures.
The last year of his life was a year of suffering,
borne with uncomplaining fortitude.

What with work on the *Encyclopædia Britannica*, with the distractions of his prolonged trial,
with the time spent in oral teaching, and with
the physical weakness of his latest years, Smith's
leisure available for literary production was not
large, and the books he has left do not adequately
represent either his accumulated knowledge or
his faculty of investigation. The earlier books —
The Old Testament in the Jewish Church and
The Prophets of Israel (the latter a series of
lectures delivered at Glasgow)— are comparatively
popular in handling. The two later — *Kinship
and Marriage in Early Arabia* and *The Religion
of the Semites* — are more abstruse and technical,
and also more original, dealing with topics in
which their author was a pioneer, though he
had been influenced by, and acknowledged in
the amplest way his obligations to, his friend
John F. Maclennan, the author of *Primitive
Marriage*. *The Religion of the Semites*, though
masterly in plan and execution, and though it

has excited the admiration of the few Oriental scholars competent to appraise its substantial merit, suffers from its incompleteness. Only the first volume was published, for death overtook the author before he could put into final shape the materials he had collected for the full development of his theories. As the second volume would have traced the connection between the primitive religion of the Arab branches of the Semitic stock (including Israel) and the Hebrew religion as we have it in the earlier books of the Old Testament, the absence of this finished statement is a loss to science. Changes had passed upon his views since he wrote the incriminated articles, and he said to me (I think about 1888) that he would no longer undertake any clerical duties. He had a sensitive conscience, and held that no clergyman ought to use language in the pulpit which did not express his personal convictions.

What struck one most in Robertson Smith's writings was the easy command wherewith he handled his materials. His generalisations were based on an endlessly patient and careful study of details, a study in which he never lost sight of guiding principles. With perfect lucidity and an unstrained natural vigour, there was a sense of abounding and overflowing knowledge which inspired confidence in the reader, making him feel he was in the hands of a master. On all that pertained to the languages and literature of the

Y

Arabic branch of the Semitic races, ancient and modern (for he did not claim to be an Assyriologist), his knowledge was accurate no less than comprehensive. Full of deference to the great scholars — no one spoke with a warmer admiration of Nöldeke, Wellhausen, and Lagarde than he did — he was a stringent critic of unscientific work in the sphere of history and physics as well as in that of philology, quick to expose the uncritical assumptions or loose hypotheses of less careful though more pretentious students. He used to say that when he had disposed of the *Encyclopædia Britannica*, he might undertake a " Dictionary of European Impostors." Oriental lore was only one of many subjects in which he might have achieved distinction. His mathematical talents were remarkable, and during two sessions he taught with conspicuous success the class of Natural Philosophy in the University of Edinburgh as assistant professor. He had a competent acquaintance with not a few other practical arts, including navigation, and once, when the compasses of the vessel on which he was sailing in the Red Sea got out of order, he proved to be the person on board most competent to set them right. In metaphysics and theology, in ancient history and many departments of modern history, he was thoroughly at home. Few, indeed, were the subjects that came up in the course of conversation on which he was not able to throw

light, for the range of his acquirements was not
more striking than the swiftness and precision
with which he brought knowledge to bear wherever it was wanted.

There was hardly a line of practical life in
which he might not have attained a brilliant
success. But the passion for knowledge made
him prefer the life of a scholar, and seemed to
have quenched any desire even for literary fame.

Learning is commonly thought of as a weight
to be carried, which makes men dull, heavy, or
pedantic. With Robertson Smith the effect seemed
to be exactly the opposite. Because he knew so
much, he was interested in everything, and threw
himself with a joyous freshness and keenness into
talk alike upon the most serious and the lightest
topics. He was combative, apt to traverse a proposition when first advanced, even though he might
come round to it afterwards; and a discussion
with him taxed the defensive acumen of his
companions. Having once spent five weeks
alone with him in a villa at Alassio on the
Riviera, I observed to him when we parted
that we had had (as the Americans say) " a
lovely time " together, and that there was not
an observation I had made during those weeks
which he had not contested. He laughed
and did not contest that observation. Yet this
tendency, while it made his society more stimulating, did not make it less agreeable, because

he never seemed to seek to overthrow an adversary, but only to get at the truth of the case, and his manner, though positive, had about it nothing either acrid or conceited. One could imagine no keener intellectual pleasure than his company afforded, for there was, along with an exuberant wealth of thought and knowledge, an intensity and ardour which lit up every subject which it touched. I once invited him and John Richard Green (the historian) to meet at dinner. They took to one another at once, nor was it easy to say which lamp burned the brighter. Smith had wider and more accurate learning, and stronger logical power, but Green was just as swift, just as fertile, just as ingenious. In stature Smith, like Green, was small, almost diminutive; his dark brown eyes bright and keen; his speech rapid; his laugh ready and merry, for he had a quick sense of humour and a power of enjoying things as they came. The type of intellect suggested a Teutonic Scot of the Lowlands, but in appearance and temperament he was rather a Scottish Celt of the Highlands, with a fire and a gaiety, an abounding vivacity and vitality, which made him a conspicuous figure wherever he lived, in Aberdeen, in Edinburgh, in Cambridge. Even by his walk, with its quick, irregular roll, one could single him out at a distance in the street.

When a man is attractive personally, he is all the more attractive for being unlike other

men, and he often becomes the centre of a
group. This was the case with Smith. His
numerous friends were so much interested by
him that when they met their talk was largely
of him, and many friendships were based on
a common knowledge of this one person. Indeed, the geniality, elevation, and simplicity of
his character gave him a quite unusual hold on
those who had come to know him well. Few
men, leading an equally quiet and studious life,
have inspired so much regard and affection in so
large a number of persons; few teachers have had
an equal power of stimulating and attracting their
pupils. He loved teaching hardly less than he
loved the investigation of truth, and he was the
most faithful and sympathetic of friends, one who
was felt to be unique while he lived and irreplace-
able when he had departed.

I have spoken of the courage he had shown
in confronting his antagonists in the ecclesiastical
courts. That courage did not fail him in the
severer trials of his last illness. The nature of
the disease of which he died was disclosed to
him by his physician in September 1892, while
an international Congress of Orientalists, in which
he presided over the Semitic section, was holding
its meetings. A festival dinner was being given
in honour of the Congress the same afternoon.
When the physician had spoken, Smith simply
remarked, " This means the death my brother

died " (one of his brothers had been struck by the same malady a few years before). He went straight to the dinner, and was throughout the evening the gayest and brightest of the guests.

Fancy sometimes indulges herself in imagining what part the eminent men one has known would have played had their lot been cast in some other age. So I have fancied that Archbishop Tait (described in an earlier chapter) ought to have been Primate of England under Edward the Sixth or Elizabeth. He would have guided the course of reform more prudently and more firmly than Cranmer did ; he would have shown a broader spirit than did Parker or Whitgift. So Cardinal Manning, had he lived in the seventeenth century, might haply have become General of the Jesuit Order, and enjoyed the secret control of the politics of the Catholic world. So Robertson Smith, had he been born in the great age of the mediæval universities, might, like the bold dialectician of whom Dante speaks, have " syllogised invidious truths "[1] in the University of Paris ; or had Fortune placed him two centuries later among the scholars of the Italian Renaissance in its glorious prime, the fame of his learning might have filled half Europe.

[1] *Parad.* x. 136, of Sigier, " Sillogizzó invidiosi veri."

HENRY SIDGWICK

Henry Sidgwick was born at Skipton, in York-shire, where his father was head-master of the ancient grammar school of the town, on 31st May 1838.[1] The family belonged to Yorkshire. He was a precocious boy, and used to delight his brothers and sister by the fertility of his imagination in inventing games and stories. Educated at Rugby School under Goulburn (afterwards Dean of Norwich), he was sent at an unusually early age to Trinity College, Cambridge. His brilliant University career was crowned by the first place in the classical tripos, and by a first class in the mathematical tripos, and he was speedily elected a Fellow of Trinity. Intellectual curiosity and an interest in the problems of theology presently drew him to Germany, where he worked at Hebrew and Arabic under Ewald at Göttingen, as well as with other eminent teachers. After hesitating for a time whether to devote himself to Oriental studies or to classical scholarship, he was drawn back to

[1] It is hoped that a Life of Sidgwick, together with a selection from his letters, may before long be published.

philosophy by his desire to investigate questions bearing on natural theology, and finally settled down to the pursuit of what are called in Cambridge the moral sciences — metaphysics, ethics, and psychology; becoming first a College Lecturer and then (in 1875) a University Prælector in these subjects. In 1869 he resigned his Fellowship, feeling that he could no longer consider himself a "*bona fide* member of the Church of England," that being the condition then attached by law to the holding of fellowships in the Colleges at Cambridge. This step caused surprise, for the test was deemed a very vague and light one, having been recently substituted for a more stringent requirement, and there had been many holders of fellowships who were at least as little entitled to call themselves *bona fide* members of the Established Church as he was. But, as was afterwards said of him by Mrs. Cross (George Eliot), Sidgwick was expected by his intimate friends to conform to standards higher than average men prescribe for their own conduct. Taken in conjunction with the fact that several English Dissenters and Scottish Presbyterians had won the distinction of a Senior Wranglership and been debarred from fellowships, though they were in theological opinion more orthodox than some nominal members of the Established Church who were holding fellowships, Sidgwick's conscientious act made a great im-

pression in Cambridge and did much to hasten
that total abolition of tests in the Universities,
which was effected by statute in 1871; for in
England concrete instances of hardship and injustice are more powerful incitements to reform
than the strongest abstract arguments, and Sidgwick was already so eminent and so respected
a figure that all Cambridge felt the absurdity of
excluding such a man from its honours and emolu-
ments. In 1883 he was appointed Professor of
Moral Philosophy, and continued to hold that post
till three months before his death in 1900, when
failing health determined him to resign it.

His life was the still and tranquil life of the
thinker, teacher, and writer, varied by no events
more exciting than those controversies over
reforms in the studies and organisation of the
University in which his sense of public duty
frequently led him to bear a part.

These I pass over, but there is one branch of
his active work to which special reference ought
to be made, viz. the part he took in promoting the
University education of women. In or about the
year 1868 he joined with the late Miss Anne
Jane Clough (sister of the poet Arthur Clough)
and a few other friends in establishing a course
of lectures and a hall of residence for women
at Cambridge, which grew into the institution
called Newnham College. It and Girton College,
founded by other friends of the same cause

about the same time, were the two first institutions in England which provided for women,
together with residential accommodation, a complete University training equivalent and similar
to that provided by the two ancient English
universities for men. The teaching was mainly
given by the University professors and lecturers,
the curriculum was the same as the University
prescribed, and the women students, though not
legally admitted to the University, were examined by the University examiners at the same
time as the other students. Henry Sidgwick
was, from the foundation of Newnham onwards,
the moving spirit and the guiding hand among
its University friends, the spirit which inspired
the policy and the hand which piloted the
fortunes of the College. Its growth to its present
dimensions, and its usefulness, not only directly,
but through the example it has set, have been
largely due to his assiduous care and temperate
wisdom. He had married (in 1876) Miss Eleanor
Mildred Balfour, and when she accepted the princi-
palship of Newnham after Miss Clough's death, in
1889, he and she transferred their residence to
the College, and lived thenceforward at it. The
England of our time has seen no movement of
opinion more remarkable or more beneficial than
that which has recognised the claims of women
to the highest kind of education, and secured a
substantial, if still incomplete, provision therefor.

The change has come so quietly and unob-
trusively that few people realise how great it
is. Few, indeed, remember what things were
forty years ago, as few realise when waste lands
have been stubbed and drained and tilled what
they were like in their former state. No one did
more than Sidgwick to bring about this change.
Besides his work for Newnham, he took a lead
in all the movements that have been made to
obtain for women a fuller admission to University
privileges, and well deserved the gratitude of
Englishwomen for his unceasing efforts on their
behalf.

The obscure problems of psychology had a
great attraction for him, and he spent much time
in investigating them, being one of the founders,
and remaining all through his later life a leading
and guiding member, of the Society for Psychical
Research, which has for the last twenty years
cultivated this field with an industry and ability
which have deserved larger harvests than have
yet been reaped. Two remarkable men, both
devoted friends of his, worked with him, Edmund
Gurney and Frederic Myers the poet, the latter
of whom survived him a few months only. It
was characteristic of Sidgwick that he never committed himself to any of the bold and possibly
oversanguine anticipations formed by some of
the other members of the Society, while yet he
never was deterred by failure, or by the discovery

of deceptions, sometimes elaborate and long sustained, from pursuing inquiries which seemed to him to have an ultimate promise of valuable results. The phenomena, he would say, may be true or false; anyhow they deserve investigation. The mere fact that so many persons believe them to be genuine is a problem fit to be investigated. If they are false, it will be a service to have proved them so. If they contain some truth, it is truth of a kind so absolutely new as to be worth much effort and long effort to reach it. In any case, science ought to take the subject out of the hands of charlatans.

The main business of his life, however, was teaching and writing. Three books stand out as those by which he will be best remembered — his *Methods of Ethics*, his *Principles of Political Economy*, and his *Elements of Politics*. All three have won the admiration of those who are experts in the subjects to which they respectively relate, and they continue to be widely read in universities both in Britain and in America. All three bear alike the peculiar impress of his mind.

It was a mind of singular subtlety, fertility, and ingenuity, which applied to every topic an extremely minute and patient analysis. Never satisfied with the obvious view of a question, it seemed unable to acquiesce in any broad and sweeping statement. It discovered objections to every accepted doctrine, exceptions to every rule.

It perceived minute distinctions and qualifications which had escaped the notice of previous writers. These qualities made Sidgwick's books somewhat difficult reading for a beginner, who was apt to ask what, after all, was the conclusion to which he had been led by an author who showed him the subject in various lights, and added not a few minor propositions to that which had seemed to be the governing one.   But the student who had already some knowledge of the topic, who, though he apprehended its main principles, had not followed them out in detail or perceived the difficulties in applying them, gained immensely by having so many fresh points presented to him, so many fallacies lurking in currently accepted notions detected, so many conditions indicated which might qualify the amplitude of a general proposition.   The method of discussion was stimulating.   Sometimes it reminded one of the Socratic method as it appears in Plato, but more frequently it was the method of Aristotle, who discusses a subject first from one side, then from another, throws out a number of remarks, not always reconcilable, but always suggestive, regarding it, and finally arrives at a view which he delivers as being probably the best, but one which must be taken subject to the remarks previously made.   The reader often feels in Sidgwick's treatment of a subject as he often feels in Aristotle's, that he would like to be left

with something more definite and positive, something that can be easily delivered to learners as
an established truth. He desires a bolder and
broader sweep of the brush. But he also feels
how much he is benefited by the process of
sifting and analysing to which every conception
or dogma is subjected, and he perceives that
he is more able to handle it afterwards in his
own way when his attention has been called to
all these distinctions and qualifications or anti-
nomies which would have escaped any vision less
keen than his author's. For those who, in an age
prone to hasty reading and careless thinking, are
disposed to underrate the difficulties of economic
and political questions, and to walk in a vain
conceit of knowledge because they have picked
up some large generalisations, no better discipline
can be prescribed than to follow patiently such
a treatment as Sidgwick gives; nor can any
reader fail to profit from the candour and the
love of truth which illumine his discussion of a
subject.

The love of truth and the sense of duty guided
his life as well as his pen. Though always
warmly interested in politics, he was of all the
persons I have known the least disposed to be
warped by partisanship, for he examined each
political issue as it arose on its own merits, apart
from predilections for either party or for the
views of his nearest friends. We used to wonder

how such splendid impartiality would have stood a
practical test such as that of the House of Commons. His loyalty to civic duty was so strong as
on one occasion to bring him, in the middle of
his vacation, all the way from Davos, in the
easternmost corner of Switzerland, to Cambridge,
solely that he might record his vote at a parliamentary election, although the result of the election
was already virtually certain.

Sidgwick's attitude toward the Benthamite
system of Utilitarianism illustrates the cautiously
discriminative habit of mind I have sought to
describe. If he had been required to call himself by any name, he would not have refused that
of Utilitarian, just as in mental philosophy he
leaned to the type of thought represented by the
two Mills rather than to the Kantian idealism of
his friend and school contemporary, the Oxford
professor T. H. Green. But the system of
Utility takes in his hands a form so much more
refined and delicate than was given to it by
Bentham and James Mill, and is expounded with
so many qualifications unknown to them, that it
has become a very different thing, and is scarcely,
if at all, assailable by the arguments which moral-
ists of the idealistic type have brought against
the older doctrine. Something similar may be
said of his treatment of bimetallism in his book
on political economy. While assenting to some of
the general propositions on which the bimetallic

theory rests, he points out so many difficulties in
the application of that theory to the actual conditions of currency that his assent cannot be cited
as a deliverance in favour of trying to turn theory
into practice.   He told me in 1896 that he held
the political and other practical objections to an
attempt to establish a bimetallic system to be virtually insuperable.   When he treats of free trade, he
is no less guarded and discriminating.   He points
out various circumstances or conditions under
which a protective tariff may become, at least
for a time, justifiable, but never abandons the
free trade principle as being generally true and
sound, a principle not to be departed from
save for strong reasons of a local or temporary
kind.   His general economic position is equally
removed from the "high and dry" school of
Ricardo on the one hand, and from the "Katheder-
Sozialisten" and the modern "sentimental" school
on the other.   In all his books one notes a tendency to discover what can be said for the view
which is in popular disfavour, even often for
that which he does not himself adopt, and to
set forth all the objections to the view which
is to receive his ultimate adhesion.   There is a
danger with such a method of losing breadth and
force of effect.   One is ready to cry, "Do lapse
for a moment into dogmatism."   Yet it ought to be
added that Sidgwick's subtlety is always restrained
by practical good sense, as well as by the desire to

reconcile opposite views. His arguments, though they often turn on minute distinctions, are not bits of fine-drawn ingenuity, but have weight and substance in them.[1]

One book of his which has not yet (December 1902) been published, but which I have had the privilege of reading in proof, displays his constructive power in another light. It is a course of lectures on the development of political institutions in Europe from early times down to our own. Here, as he is dealing with concrete matter, the treatment is more broad, and the line of exposition and argument more easy to follow, than in the treatises already referred to. It is a masterly piece of work, and reveals a wider range of historical knowledge and a more complete mastery of historical method than had been shown in his earlier books, or indeed than some of his friends had known him to possess.

The tendency to analysis rather than to construction, the abstention from the deliverance of doctrines easy to comprehend and repeat, which belong to his writings on ethics and economics, do not impair the worth of his literary criticisms. In this field his fine perception and discriminative

[1] It was his aim to avoid as much as possible technical terms or phrases whose meaning was not plain to the average reader. An anecdote was current that once when, in conducting a university examination, he was perusing the papers of a candidate who had darkened the subject by the use of extreme Hegelian phraseology, he turned to his co-examiner and said, "I can see that this is nonsense, but is it the right kind of nonsense ? "

z

taste had full scope. He was an incessant reader, especially of poetry and novels, with a retentive memory for poetry, as well as a finely modulated and expressive voice in reciting it. His literary judgments had less of a creative quality, if the expression be permissible, than Matthew Arnold's, but are not otherwise inferior to those of that brilliant though sometimes slightly prejudiced critic. No one of his contemporaries has sur- passed Sidgwick in catholicity and reasonableness, in the power of delicate appreciation, or in an exquisite precision of expression. His essay on Arthur Hugh Clough, prefixed to the latest edition of Clough's collected poems, is a good specimen of this side of his talent. Clough was one of his favourites, and has indeed been called the pet poet of University men. Sidgwick's literary essays, which appeared occasionally in magazines, were few, but they well deserve to be collected and republished, for this age of ours, though largely occupied in talking about literature, has produced comparatively little criticism of the first order.

Sidgwick did not write swiftly or easily, be- cause he weighed carefully everything he wrote. But his mind was alert and nimble in the highest degree. Thus he was an admirable talker, seeing in a moment the point of an argument, seizing on distinctions which others had failed to perceive, suggesting new aspects from which a question might be regarded, and enlivening every topic by a keen yet sweet and kindly wit. Wit, seldom allowed to have play in his books, was one of the characteristics which made his company charming. Its effect was heightened by a hesitation in his speech which often forced him to pause before the critical word or phrase of the sentence had been reached. When that word or phrase came, it was sure to be the right one. Though fond of arguing, he was so candid and fair, admitting all that there was in his opponent's case, and obviously trying to see the point from his opponent's side, that nobody felt annoyed at having come off second best, while everybody who cared for good talk went away feeling not only that he knew more about the matter than he did before, but that he had enjoyed an intellectual pleasure of a rare and high kind. The keenness of his penetration was not formidable, because it was joined to an indulgent judgment: the ceaseless activity of his intellect was softened rather than reduced by the gaiety of his manner. His talk was conversation, not discourse, for though he naturally became the centre of nearly every company in which he found himself, he took no more than his share. It was like the sparkling of a brook whose ripples seem to give out sunshine.

Though Sidgwick's writings are a mine of careful and suggestive thinking, he was even more remarkable than his books. Though his

conversation was delightful, the impression of its
fertility and its wit were the least part of the
impression which his personality produced. An
eminent man is known to the world at large by
what he gives them in the way of instruction or
of pleasure. A man is prized and remembered
by his friends for what he was in the intercourse
of life. Few men of our time have influenced
so wide or so devoted a circle of friends as did
Henry Sidgwick; few could respond to the calls
of friendship with a like sympathy or wisdom.
His advice was frequently asked in delicate
questions of conduct, and he was humorously
reminded that, by his own capacity as well as
by the title of his chair, he was a professor of
casuistry. His stores of knowledge and helpful
criticism were always at the service of his pupils
or his fellow-workers.

From his earliest college days he had been
just, well balanced, conscientious alike in the pursuit of truth and in the regulation of his own life,
appearing to have neither prejudices nor enmities,
and when he had to convey censure, choosing the
least cutting words in which to convey it. Yet
in earlier years there had been in him a touch
of austerity, a certain remoteness or air of detachment, which confined to a very few persons
the knowledge of his highest qualities. As he
grew older his purity lost its coldness, his keenness of discernment mellowed into a sweet and

persuasive wisdom. A life excellently conducted, a life which is the expression of fine qualities, and in which the acts done are in harmony with the thoughts and words of the man, is itself a beautiful product, whether of untutored nature or of thought and experience turning every faculty to the best account. In the modern world the two types of excellence which we are chiefly bidden to admire are that of the active philanthropist and that of the saint. The ancient world produced and admired another type, to which some of its noblest characters conformed, and which, in its softer and more benignant aspect, Sidgwick presented. In his indifference to wealth and fame and the other familiar objects of human desire, in the almost ascetic simplicity of his daily life, in his pursuit of none but the purest pleasures, in his habit of subjecting all impulses to the law of reason, the will braced to patience, the soul brought into harmony with the divinely appointed order, he seemed to reproduce one of those philosophers of antiquity who formed a lofty conception of Nature and sought to live in conformity with her precepts. But the gravity of a Stoic was relieved by the humour and vivacity which belonged to his nature, and the severity of a Stoic was softened by the tenderness and sympathy which seemed to grow and expand with every year. In Cambridge, where, though the society is a large one, all the teachers become personally known to one another, and the students have opportunities of familiar intercourse with the teachers, affection as well as admiration gathered round him. His thoughts quickened and his example inspired generation after generation of young men passing through the University out into the life of England, as a light set high upon the bank beams on the waves of a river gliding swiftly to the sea.

It was a life of single-minded devotion to truth and friendship, a life serene and gentle, free alike from vanity and from ambition, bearing without complaint the ill-health which sometimes checked his labours, viewing with calm fortitude those problems of man's life on which his mind was always fixed, untroubled in the presence of death.

> Felix qui potuit rerum cognoscere causas
> Quique metus omnes et inexorabile fatum
> Subiecit pedibus strepitumque Acherontis avari.

When his friends heard of his departure there rose to mind the words in which the closing scene of the life of Socrates is described by the greatest of his disciples, and we thought that among all those we had known there was none of whom we could more truly say that in him the spirit of philosophy had its perfect work in justice, in goodness, and in wisdom.

EDWARD ERNEST BOWEN [1]

EVER since the publication of Stanley's Life of Dr. Arnold that eminent head-master has been taken as the model of a great teacher and ruler of boys, the man who, while stimulating the intelligence of his pupils, was even more concerned to discipline and mould their moral natures. Arnold has become the type of what Carlyle might have called " The Hero as Schoolmaster." Though there have been many able men at the head of large schools since his time, including three who afterwards rose to be Archbishops of Canterbury, as well as a good many who have become bishops, his fame remains unrivalled, and the type created by his career, or rather perhaps by his biographer's account of it, still holds the field. Moreover, during the sixty years that have passed since Arnold's death scarcely a word has been said regarding any other masters than the head. During those years the English universities have sent into the great schools a large proportion of

[1] Since this sketch was written a very interesting *Life of Edward Bowen* by his nephew (the Hon. and Rev. W. E. Bowen) has appeared. Some of his (too few) essays and a collection of his school-songs are appended to it.

343

their most capable graduates as assistant teachers;
and some of the strongest men among these
graduates have never, from various causes, and
often because they preferred to remain laymen,
been raised to the headships of the schools.
Every one knows that a school depends for its
wellbeing and success more largely on the assist-
ants taken together than it does on the head-
master.   Most people also know that individual
assistant masters are not unfrequently better
scholars, better teachers, and more influential
with the boys than is their official superior.   Yet
the assistant masters have remained unhonoured
and unsung in the general chorus of praise of
the great schools which has been resounding
over England for nearly two generations.

Edward Bowen was all his life an assistant master, and never cared to be anything else.   As he
had determined not to take orders in the Church
of England, he was virtually debarred from many
of the chief head-masterships, which are, some
few of them by law, many more by custom, confined to Anglican clergymen.   But even when other
headships to which this condition was not attached
were known to be practically open to his acceptance, were, indeed, in one or two instances almost
tendered to him, he refused to become a candidate,
preferring his own simple and easy way of life
to the pomp and circumstance which convention
requires a head-master to maintain.   This ab-

stention, however, did not prevent his eminence
from becoming known to those who had opportunities of judging. In his later years he would,
I think, have been generally recognised by the
teaching profession as the most brilliant, and in
his own peculiar line the most successful, man
among the schoolmasters of Britain.

He was born on March 30, 1836, of an Irish
family (originally from Wales) holding property
in the county of Mayo. His father was a clergyman of the Church of England; his mother,
who survived him a few months (dying at the
age of ninety-four) and whom he tended with
watchful care during her years of widowhood,
was partly of Irish, partly of French extraction.
Like his more famous but perhaps not more
remarkable elder brother, Charles Bowen, who
became Lord Bowen, and is remembered as
one of the most acute and subtle judges as
well as one of the most winning personalities
of our time, he had a gaiety, wit, and versatility
which suggested the presence of Celtic blood.
He was educated at Blackheath School, and
afterwards at King's College in London, whence
he proceeded to Trinity College, Cambridge.
In 1860, after a career at the University, distinguished both in the way of honours and in
respect of the reputation he won among his
contemporaries, he became a master at Harrow,
and thenceforth remained there, leading an

uneventful and externally a monotonous life, but one full of unceasing and untiring activity in play and work. He died on Easter Monday 1901.

Nothing could be less like the traditional Arnoldine methods of teaching and ruling boys than Bowen's method was. The note of those methods was what used to be called moral earnestness. Arnold was grave and serious, distant and awe-inspiring, except perhaps to a few specially favoured pupils. Bowen was light, cheerful, vivacious, humorous, familiar, and, above all things, ingenious and full of variety. His leading principles were two — that the boy must at all hazards be interested in the lessons and that he should be at ease with the teacher.

A Harrow boy once said to his master, "I don't know how it is, sir, but if Mr. Bowen takes a lesson he makes you work twice as hard as other masters, but you like it twice as much and you learn far more." He was the most unexpected man in conversation that could be imagined, always giving a new turn to talk by saying something that seemed remote from the matter in hand until he presently showed the connection. So his teaching kept the boys alert, because its variety was inexhaustible. He seemed to think that it did not greatly matter what the lesson was so long as the pupil could be got to enjoy it. The rules of the school and the

requirements of the examinations for which boys
had to be prepared would not have permitted
him to try to any great extent the experiment
of varying subjects to suit individual tastes; but
he was fond of giving lessons in topics outside
the regular course, on astronomy for instance, of
which he had acquired a fair knowledge, and on
recent military history, which he knew wonderfully
well, better probably than any man in England outside the military profession. When the so-called
" modern side " was established at Harrow, in 1869,
he became head of it, having taken this post, not
from any want of classical taste and learning,
for he was an admirable scholar, and to the
end of his life wrote charming Latin verses, but
because he felt that this line of teaching needed
to be developed in a school which had been formerly almost wholly classical. For grammatical
minutiæ, for learning rules by heart, and indeed
for the old style of grammar-teaching generally,
he had an unconcealed contempt. He thought it
unkind and wasteful to let a boy go on puzzling
over difficulties of language in an author, and
permitted, under restrictions, the use of English
translations, or (as boys call them) " cribs."
Teaching was in his view a special gift of
the individual, which depended on the aptitude
for getting hold of the pupil's mind, and
enlisting his interest in the subject. He
had accordingly no faith in the doctrine that

teaching is a science which can be systematically studied, or an art in which the apprentice ought to be systematically trained.   When he was summoned as a witness before the Secondary Education Commission in 1894 he adhered, under cross-examination, to this view (so far as it affected schools like Harrow or Eton), refusing to be moved by the arguments of those among the Commissioners who cited the practice of Germany, where Pädagogik, as they call it, is elaborately taught in the universities. " I am unable," he said, " to conceive any machinery by which the art of teaching can be given practically to masters. That art is so much a matter of personal power and experience, and of various social and moral gifts, that I cannot conceive a good person made a good master by merely seeing a class of boys taught, unless he was allowed to take a real and serious part in it himself, unless he became a teacher himself. I can understand that at a primary school you can learn by going in and hearing a good teacher at work; but the teaching of a class of older boys is so different, and has so much of the social element in it, and it may vary so much that I should despair of teaching a young man how to take a class unless he was a long time with me. . . .   A master at a large public school is chiefly a moral and social force; a master is this to a much less extent at a primary school or in the ordinary day-schools, the grammar-schools of the country.   To

deal with boys when you have them completely
under your control for the whole of every day is
an altogether different thing, and requires different
virtues in the teacher from those that are required
in the case of day-schools."

Bowen may possibly have been mistaken, even
as regards the teachers in the great public board-
ing schools. His view seems to overlook or
disregard that large class of persons who have no
marked natural aptitude for teaching, but are capable of being, by special instruction and supervised
practice, kneaded and moulded into better teachers
than they would otherwise have grown to be. He
felt so strongly that no one ought to teach without
having a real gift and fondness for teaching that
he thought such difference as training could make
insignificant in comparison with the inborn talent.
Perhaps he generalised too boldly from himself,
for he had an enjoyment of his work, and a conscientiousness in always putting the very best of
himself into it — how much was conscientiousness
and how much was enjoyment, no one could tell
— as well as a quickness and vivacity which no
study of methods could have improved. As one
of his most eminent colleagues,[1] who was also his
life-long friend, observes: "The humdrum and
routine which must form so large a part of a
teacher's life were never humdrum or routine to
him, for he put the whole of his abounding

[1] Mr. R. Bosworth Smith.

energies into his work, and round its dryest details there played and flickered, as with a lambent flame, his joyous spirit, finding expression now perhaps in a striking parallel, now in a startling paradox, now in a touch of humour, and once again in a note of pathos."

The personal influence he exerted on the boys who lived in his House was quite as remarkable as his " form-teaching." Stoicism and honour were the qualities it was mainly directed to form. Every boy was expected to show manliness and endurance, and to utter no complaint. Where physical health was concerned he was indulgent; his House was the first which gave the boys meat at breakfast in addition to tea with bread and butter. But otherwise the discipline was Spartan, though not more Spartan than that he prescribed to himself, and the House was trained to scorn the slightest approach to luxury. Arm-chairs were forbidden except to sixth form boys. A pupil relates that when Bowen found he was in the habit of taking two hot baths a week the transgression was reproved with the words : " Oh boy, that's like the later Romans, boy." His maxims were : " Take sweet and bitter as sweet and bitter come." and " Always play the game." He never preached to the boys or lectured them ; and if he had to convey a reproof, conveyed it in a single sentence. But he dwelt upon honour as the foundation of character, and made every boy feel that he was expected to reach the highest standard of truth-fulness, courage, and duty to the little community of the House, or the cricket eleven, or the foot-ball team.

Some have begun to think that in English schools and universities too much time is given to athletic sports, and that they absorb too largely the thoughts and interests of the English youth. Bowen, however, attached the utmost value to games as a training in character. He used to descant upon the qualities of discipline, good fellowship, good-humour, mutual help, and post-ponement of self which they are calculated to foster. Though some of his friends thought that his own intense and unabated fondness for these games — for he played cricket and football up to the end of his life — might have biassed his judg-ment, they could not deny that the games ought to develop the qualities aforesaid.

"Consider the habit of being in public, the for-bearance, the subordination of the one to the many, the exercise of judgment, the sense of personal dig-nity. Think again of the organising faculty that our games develop. Where can you get command and obedience, choice with responsibility, criticism with discipline, in any degree remotely approach-ing that in which our social games supply them? Think of the partly moral, partly physical side of it, temper, of course, dignity, courtesy. . . . When the match has really begun, there is education, there is enlargement of horizon, self sinks, the common good is the only good, the bodily faculties exhilarate in functional development, and the make-believe ambition is glorified into a sort of ideality. Here is boyhood at its best, or very nearly at its best. *Sursum crura!* . . . When you have a lot of human beings, in highest social union and perfect organic action, developing the law of their race and falling in unconsciously with its best inherited traditions of brotherhood and common action, you are not far from getting a glimpse of one side of the highest good. There lives more soul in honest play, believe me, than in half the hymn-books."

These words, taken from a half-serious essay on Games written for a private society, give some part of Bowen's views. The whole essay is well worth reading.[1] Its arguments do not, however, quite settle the matter. The playing of games may have, and indeed ought to have, the excellent results Bowen claimed for it, and yet it may be doubted whether the experience of life shows that boys so brought up do in fact turn out substantially more good-humoured, unselfish, and fit for the commerce of the world than others who have lacked this training. And the further question remains whether the games are worth their costly candle. That they occupy a good deal of time at school and at college is not necessarily an evil, seeing that the time left

[1] It is printed in the *Life*.

for lessons or study is sufficient if well spent. The real drawback incident to the excessive devotion games inspire in our days is that they leave little room in the boy's or collegian's mind either for interest in his studies or for the love of nature. They fill his thoughts, they divert his ambition into channels of no permanent value to his mind or life; they continue to absorb his interest and form a large part of his reading long after he has left school or college. Nevertheless, be these things as they may, the opinion of a man so able and so experienced as Bowen was deserves to be recorded; and his success in endearing himself to and guiding his boys was doubtless partly due to the use he made of their liking for games.

He was never married, so the school became the sole devotion of his life, and he bequeathed to it the bulk of his property, directing an area of land which he had purchased on the top of the Hill to be always kept as an open space for the benefit of boys and masters.

It need hardly be said that he loved boys as he loved teaching. He took them with him in the holidays on walking tours. He kept up correspondence with many of his pupils after they left Harrow, and advised them as occasion rose. To many of them he remained through life the model whom they desired to imitate. But he was very chary of the exercise of influence. " A

2 A

boy's character," he once wrote, "grows like the Temple of old, without sound of mallet and trowel. What we can do is to arrange matters so as to give Virtue her best chance. We can make the right choice sometimes a little easier, we can prevent tendencies from blossoming into acts, and render pitfalls visible. How much indirectly and unconsciously we can do, none but the recording angel knows. 'You can and you should,' said Chiffers,[1] 'go straight to the heart of every individual boy.' Well, a fellow-creature's mind is a sacred thing. You may enter into that arcanum once a year, shoeless. And in the effort to control the spirit of a pupil, to make one's own approval his test and mould him by the stress of our own presence, in the ambition to do this, the craving for moral power and visible guiding, the subtle pride of effective agency, lie some of the chief temptations of a schoolmaster's work."

Such ways and methods as I have endeavoured to describe are less easy to imitate than those which belong to the Arnoldine type of schoolmaster. In Bowen's gaiety, in his vivacity, in the humour which interpenetrated everything he said or did, there was something individual. Teachers who do not possess a like vivacity, versatility, and humour cannot hope to apply with like success the method of familiarity and sympathy. Not indeed that Bowen stood altogether alone in his

---

[1] "Chiffers" is the typical would-be imitator of Arnold.

use of that method. There were others among his contemporaries who shared his view, and whose practice was not dissimilar. He was, however, the earliest and most brilliant exponent of the view, so his career may be said to open a new line, and to mark a new departure in the teacher's art.

I have mentioned his walking tours. He was a pedestrian of extraordinary force, rather tall, but spare and light, swift of foot, and tireless in his activity. As an undergraduate he had walked from Cambridge to Oxford, nearly ninety miles, in twenty-four hours, scarcely halting. At one time or another he had traversed on foot all the coast-line and great part of the inland regions of England. He was an accomplished Alpine climber. His passion for exercise of body as well as of mind was so salient a feature in his character that his friends wondered how he would be able to support old age. He was spared the trial, for he was gay and joyous as ever on the last morning of his life, and he died in a moment, while mounting his bicycle after a long ascent, among the lonely forests of Burgundy, then bursting into leaf under an April sun.

His interest in politics provided him with a short and strenuous interlude of public action, which varied the even tenor of his life at Harrow. At the general election of 1880 he stood as a candidate for the little borough of Hertford (which has since been merged in the county) against Mr.

Arthur Balfour, now (1902) First Lord of the Treasury in England. The pro-Turkish policy of Lord Beaconsfield, followed by the Afghan War of 1878, had roused many Liberals who usually took little part in political action. Bowen felt the impulse to denounce the conduct of the Ministry, and went into the contest with his usual airy suddenness. He had little prospect of success at such a place, for, like many of the so-called Academic Liberals of those days, he made the mistake of standing for a small semi-rural constituency, overshadowed by a neighbouring magnate, instead of for a large town, where both his opinions and his oratory would have been better appreciated. However, he enjoyed the contest thoroughly, amusing himself as well as the electors by his lively and sometimes impassioned speeches, and he looked back to it as a pleasant episode in his usually smooth and placid life. He was all his life a strong Liberal *vieille roche*, a lover of freedom and equality as well as of economy in public finance, a Free Trader, an individualist, an enemy of all wars and all aggressions, and in later years growingly indignant at the rapid increase of military and naval expenditure. He was also, like the Liberals of 1850-60 in general, a sympathiser with oppressed nationalities, though this feeling did not carry him the length of accepting the policy of Home Rule for Ireland, as to which he had grave doubts, yet doubts not

quite so serious as to involve his separation from
the Liberal party. Twice after 1880 he was on
the point of becoming a candidate for a seat in the
House of Commons, but whether his love for Harrow would have suffered him to remain in Parliament had he entered it may be doubted. One
could not even tell whether he was really disappointed that his political aspirations remained un-
fulfilled. Had he given himself to parliamentary
life, his readiness, ingenuity, and wit would have
soon made him valued by his own side, while his
sincerity and engaging manners would have commended him to both sides alike. His delivery was
always too rapid, and his voice not powerful, yet
these defects would have been forgotten in the interest which so peculiar a figure must have aroused.

His peace principles contrasted oddly with
his passion for military history, a passion which
prompted many vacation journeys to battle-fields
all over Europe, from Salamanca to Austerlitz.
He had followed the campaigns of Napoleon
through Piedmont and Lombardy, through Germany and Austria, as well as those of Wellington
in Spain and Southern France.[1] This taste is
not uncommon in men of peace. Freeman had
it; J. R. Green and S. R. Gardiner had it; and
the historical works of Sir George Trevelyan
and Dr. Thomas Hodgkin prove that it lives
in those genial breasts also. It was a pleasure

[1] He remarked once that he had so nearly exhausted the battle-fields of
the past that he must begin to devote himself to the battle-fields of the future.

to be led over a battle-field by Bowen, for he had
a good eye for ground, he knew the movements
of the armies down to the smallest detail, and he
could explain with perfect lucidity the positions
of the combatants and the tactical moves in the
game.

Twice only did he come across actual fighting,
once at Düppel in 1864, during the Schleswig-
Holstein war, and again in Paris during the siege
of the Communards by the forces that obeyed
Thiers and the Assembly sitting at Versailles.
He maintained that the Commune had been unfairly judged by Englishmen, and wrote a singularly interesting description of what he saw while
risking his life in the beleaguered city. There
was in him a great spirit of adventure, though the
circumstances of his life gave it little scope.

Travel was one of his chief pleasures, but it
was, if possible, a still greater pleasure to his
fellow-travellers, for he was the most agreeable
of companions, fertile in suggestion, candid in
discussion, swift in decision. He cared nothing
for luxury and very little for comfort; he was
absolutely unselfish and imperturbably good-
humoured; he could get enjoyment out of the
smallest incidents of travel, and his curiosity to
see the surface of the earth as well as the cities
of men was inexhaustible. He loved the unexpected, and if one had written proposing an
expedition to explore Tibet, he would have

telegraphed back, " Start to-night: do we meet
Charing Cross or Victoria ? "

I have dwelt on Bowen's gifts and methods
as a teacher, because teaching was the joy and
the business of his life, and because he showed
a new way in which boys might be stimulated
and guided. But he was a great deal besides
a teacher, just as his brother Charles was a
great deal besides a lawyer. Both had talents
for literature of a very high order. Charles
published a verse translation of Virgil's *Eclogues*
and the first six books of the *Æneid*, full of
ingenuity and refinement, as well as of fine poetic
taste. Edward's vein expressed itself in the
writing of songs. His school songs, composed
for the Harrow boys, became immensely popular with them, and their use at school celebra-
tions of various kinds has passed from Harrow
to the other great schools of England, even
to some of the larger girls' schools. The
songs are unique in their fanciful ingenuity and
humorous extravagance, full of a boyish joy in
life, in the exertion of physical strength, in the
mimic strife of games, yet with an occasional
touch of sadness, like the shadow of a passing
cloud as it falls on the cricket field over which
the shouts of the players are ringing. The metres
are various: all show rhythmical skill, and in all
the verse has a swing which makes it singularly
effective when sung by a mass of voices. Most

of the songs are dedicated to cricket or football, but a few are serious, and two or three of these have a beauty of thought and perfection of form which make the reader ask why a poetic gift so true and so delicate should have been rarely used. These songs were the work of his middle or later years, and he never wrote except when the impulse came upon him. The stream ran pure but it ran seldom. In early days he had been for a while, like many other brilliant young University men of his time, a contributor to the *Saturday Review*. (There surely never was a journal which enlisted so much and such varied literary talent as the *Saturday* did between 1855 and 1863.) Bowen's articles were, like his elder brother's, extremely witty. In later life he could seldom be induced to write, having fallen out of the habit, and being, indeed, too busy to carry on any large piece of work; but the occasional papers on educational subjects he produced showed no decline in his vivacity or in the abundance of his humour. Those who knew the range and the resources of his mind sometimes regretted that he would do nothing to let the world know them. But he was, to a degree most unusual among men of real power, absolutely indifferent, not only to fame, but to opportunities for exercising power or influence.

The stoicism which he sought to form in his pupils was inculcated by his own example. It

was a genial and cheerful stoicism, which checked
neither his affection for them nor his brightness
in society, and which permitted him to draw as
much enjoyment from small things as most
people can from great ones.   But if he had
the gaiety of an Irishman, he had a double portion
of English reserve.   He never gave expression
in words to his emotions.   He never seemed
either elated or depressed.   He never lost his
temper and never seemed to be curbing it.   His
tastes and way of life were simple to the verge of
austerity; nor did he appear to desire anything
more than what he had obtained.

It is natural — possibly foolish, yet almost
inevitable — that those who perceive in a friend
the presence of rare and brilliant gifts should
desire that his gifts should not only be turned
to full account for the world's benefit, but
should become so known and appreciated as
to make others admire and value what they
admire and value.   When such a man prefers to
live his life in his own way, and do the plain
duties that lie near him, with no thought of
anything further, they feel, though they may try
to repress, a kind of disappointment, as though
greatness or virtue had missed its mark because
known to few besides themselves.   Yet there is
a sense in which that friend is most our own who
has least belonged to the world, who has least
cared for what the world has to offer, who has

chosen the simplest and purest pleasures, who has rendered the service that his way of life required with no longing for any wider theatre or any applause to be there won. Is there indeed anything more beautiful than a life of quiet self-sufficing yet beneficent serenity, such as the ancient philosophers inculcated, a life which is now more rarely than ever led by men of shining gifts, because the inducements to bring such gifts into the dusty thoroughfares of the world have grown more numerous?   Bowen had the best equipment for a philosopher. He knew the things that gave him pleasure, and sought no others. He knew what he could do well. He followed his own bent. His desires were few, and he could gratify them all. He had made life exactly what he wished it to be. Intensely as he enjoyed travel, he never uttered a note of regret when the beginning of a Harrow school term stopped a journey at its most interesting point, so dearly did he love his boys. What more can we desire for our friends than this — that in remembering them there should be nothing to regret, that all who came under their influence should feel them-selves for ever thereafter the better for that in-fluence, that a happy and peaceful life should be crowned by a sudden and painless death?

EDWIN LAWRENCE GODKIN

As with the progress of science new arts emerge
and new occupations and trades are created, so
with the progress of society professions previously unknown arise, evolve new types of
intellectual excellence, and supply a new theatre
for the display of peculiar and exceptional gifts.
Such a profession, such a type, and the type
which is perhaps most specially characteristic of
our times, is that of the Editor. It scarcely
existed before the French Revolution, and is, as
now fully developed, a product of the last eighty
years. Various are its forms. There is the
Business Editor, who runs his newspaper as a
great commercial undertaking, and may neither
care for politics nor attach himself to any political
party. America still recollects the familiar
example set by James Gordon Bennett, the
founder of the *New York Herald*. There is the
Selective Editor, who may never pen a line,
but shows his skill in gathering an able staff
round him, and in allotting to each of them
the work he can do best. Such an one was
John Douglas Cook, a man of slender culti-

vation and few intellectual interests, but still remembered in England by those who forty years ago knew the staff of the *Saturday Review*, then in its brilliant prime, as possessed of an extraordinary instinct for the topics which caught the public taste, and for the persons capable of handling those topics.   John T. Delane, of the *Times*, had the same gift, with talents and knowledge far surpassing Cook's.   A third and usually more interesting form is found in the Editor who is himself an able writer, and who imparts his own individuality to the journal he directs.   Such an one was Horace Greeley, who, in the days before the War of Secession, made the *New York Tribune* a power in America.   Such another, of finer natural quality, was Michael Katkoff, who in his short career did much to create and to develop the spirit of nationality and imperialism in Russia thirty years ago.

It was to this third form of the editorial profession that Mr. Godkin belonged.   He is the most remarkable example of it that has appeared in our time — perhaps, indeed, in any time since the profession rose to importance; and all the more remarkable because he was never, like Greeley or Katkoff, the exponent of any widespread sentiment or potent movement, but was frequently in opposition to the feeling for the moment dominant.

Edwin Lawrence Godkin, the son of a Protestant clergyman and author, was born in the
county of Wicklow, in Ireland, in 1831. He
was educated at Queen's College, Belfast, read
for a short time for the English bar, but drifted
into journalism by accepting the post of corre-
spondent to the London *Daily News* during the
Crimean War in 1853-54. The horror of war which
he retained through his life was due to the glimpse
of it he had in the Crimea. Soon afterwards he
went to America, was admitted to the bar in New
York, but never practised, spent some months in
travelling through the Southern States on horse-
back, learning thereby what slavery was, and
what its economic and social consequences, was
for two or three years a writer on the *New York
Times*, and ultimately, in 1865, established in
New York a weekly journal called the *Nation*.
This he continued to edit, writing most of it
himself, till 1881, when he accepted the editor-
ship of the *New York Evening Post*, an old and
respectable paper, but with no very large circulation. The *Nation* continued to appear, but became practically a weekly edition of the *Evening
Post*, or rather, as some one said, the *Evening
Post* became a daily edition of the *Nation*, for
the tone and spirit that had characterised the
Nation now pervaded the *Post*. In 1900 failing
health compelled him to retire from active work,
and in May 1902 he died in England. Journalism

left him little leisure for any other kind of literary production; but he wrote in early life a short history of Hungary; and a number of articles which he had in later years contributed to the *Nation* or to magazines were collected and published in three volumes between 1895 and 1900. They are clear and wise articles, specially instructive where they deal with the most recent aspects of democracy.   But as they convey a less than adequate impression of the peculiar qualities which established his fame, I pass on to the work by which he will be remembered, his work as a weekly and daily public writer.

He was well equipped for this career by considerable experience of the world, by large reading, for though not a learned man, he had assimilated a great deal of knowledge on economical and historical subjects, and by a stock of positive principles which he saw clearly and held coherently.   In philosophy and economics he was a Utilitarian of the school of J. S. Mill, and in politics what used to be called a philosophical Radical, a Radical of the less extreme type, free from sentiment and from prejudices, but equally free from any desire to destroy for the sake of destroying. Like the other Utilitarians of those days, he was a moderate optimist, expecting the world to grow better steadily, though not swiftly; and he went to America in the belief that he should there find

more progress secured, and more of further progress in prospect, than any European country
could show. It was the land of promise, in
which all the forces making for good on which
the school of Mill relied were to be found at
work, hampered only by the presence of slavery.
I note this fact, because it shows that the pessimism of Mr. Godkin's later years was not due to a
naturally querulous or despondent temperament.

So too was his mind admirably fitted for the
career he had chosen. It was logical, penetrating, systematic, yet it was also quick and
nimble. His views were definite, not to say
dogmatic, and as they were confidently held,
so too they were confidently expressed. He
never struck a doubtful note. He never slurred
over a difficulty, nor sought, when he knew
himself ignorant, to cover up his ignorance.
Imagination was kept well in hand, for his constant aim was to get at and deal with the vital
facts of every case. If he was not original in the
way of thinking out doctrines distinctively his
own, nor in respect of any exuberance of ideas
bubbling up in the course of discussion, there was
fertility as well as freshness in his application of
principles to current questions, and in the illustrations by which he enforced his arguments.

As his thinking was exact, so his style was
clear-cut and trenchant. Even when he was
writing most swiftly, it never sank below a high

level of form and finish. Every word had its use and every sentence told. There was no doubt about his meaning, and just as little about the strength of his convictions. He had a gift for terse vivacious paragraphs commenting on some event of the day or summing up the effect of a speech or a debate. The touch was equally light and firm. But if the manner was brisk, the matter was solid: you admired the keenness of the insight and the weight of the judgment just as much as the brightness of the style. Much of the brightness lay in the humour. That is a plant which blossoms so much more profusely on Transatlantic soil that English readers of the *Nation* had usually a start of surprise when told that this most humorous of American journalists was not an American at all but a European, and indeed a European who never became thoroughly Americanised. It was humour of a pungent and sarcastic quality, usually directed to the detection of tricks or the exposure of shams, but it was eminently mirth-provoking and never malicious. Frequently it was ironical, and the irony sometimes so fine as to be mistaken for seriousness.

The *Nation* was from its very first numbers so full of force, keenness, and knowledge, and so unusually well written, that it made its way rapidly among the educated classes of the Eastern States. It soon became a power, but a power of a new

kind. Mr. Godkin wanted most of the talents
or interests of the ordinary journalist. He
gave no thought to the organisation of the
paper as a business undertaking. He scarcely
heeded circulation, either when his livelihood
depended upon the *Nation* of which he was the
chief owner, or when he was associated with
others in the ownership of the *Evening Post.*
He refused to allow any news he disapproved,
including all scandal and all society gossip, to
appear. He was prepared at any moment to
incur unpopularity from his subscribers, or even
to offend one half of his advertisers. He took
no pains to get news before other journals, and
cared nothing for those " beats " and " scoops " in
which the soul of the normal newspaper man
finds a legitimate source of pride. He was not
there, he would have said, to please either advertisers or subscribers, but to tell the American
people the truths they needed to hear, and if
those truths were distasteful, so much the more
needful was it to proclaim them. He was absolutely independent not only of all personal but
of all party ties. A public man was never
either praised or suffered to escape censure because he was a private acquaintance. He once
told me that the being obliged to censure those
with whom he stood in personal relations was
the least agreeable feature of his profession.
Whether an act was done by the Republicans

2 B

or by the Democrats made no difference to his judgment, or to the severity with which his judgment was expressed. His distrust of Mr. James G. Blaine had led him to support Mr. Cleveland at the election of 1884, and he continued to give a general approval to the latter statesman during both his presidential terms. But when Mr. Cleveland's Venezuelan message with its menaces to England appeared in December 1895, Mr. Godkin vehemently denounced it, as indeed he had frequently before blamed particular acts of the Cleveland administrations. He sometimes voted for the Republicans, sometimes for the Democrats, according to the merits of the transitory issue or the particular candidate, but after 1884 no one could have called him either a Republican or a Democrat.

Independence of party is less rare among American than among European newspapers; but courage such as Godkin's is rare everywhere. The editor of a century ago had in most countries to fear press censorship, or the law of political libel, or the frowns of the great. The modern editor, delivered from these risks, is exposed to the more insidious temptations of financial influence, of social pressure, of the fear of injuring the business interests of the paper, which are now sometimes enormous. Godkin's conscientiousness and pride made him equally indifferent to influence and to threats. As some one said, you might as well have tried to frighten the east wind. Clear, prompt, and self-confident, judging everything by a high standard of honour and public spirit, he distributed censure with no regard either to the official position or to the party affiliations of politicians. The "Weekly Day of Judgment" was the title bestowed upon the *Nation* by Charles Dudley Warner, who himself admired it. As Godkin expected — or at least demanded — righteousness from every one, he was more a terror to evil-doers than a praise to them that do well, and the fact that, having no private ends to serve, he thought only of truth and the public interest, made him all the more stringent. Because he was, and found it easy to be, fearless and in-dependent, he scarcely allowed enough for the timidity of others, and sometimes chastised the weak as sternly as the wicked. An editor who smites all the self-seekers and all the time-servers whom he thinks worth smiting, is sure to be-come a target for many arrows. But as Godkin was an equally caustic critic of the sentimental vagaries or economic heresies of well-meaning men or sections of opinion, he incurred hostility from quarters where the desire for honest adminis-tration and the purity of public life was hardly less strong than in the pages of the *Nation* itself. Though he took no personal part in politics, never appeared on platforms nor in any way put himself forward, his paper was so markedly himself that people talked of it as him. It was not "the *Nation* says" or "the *Post* says," but "Godkin says." Even his foreign birth was charged against him — a rare charge in a country so tolerant and catholic as the United States, where every office except that of President is open to newcomers as freely as to the native born.

He was called "un-American," and I have heard men who admired and read the *Nation* nevertheless complain that they did not want "to be taught by a European how to run this Republic." True it is that he did not see things or write about them quite as an American would have done. But was this altogether a misfortune? The Italian cities of the Middle Ages used to call in a man of character and mark from some other place and make him Podestá just because he stood outside the family ties and the factions of the city. Godkin's foreign education gave him detachment and perspective. It never reduced his ardour to see administration and public life in America made worthy of the greatness of the American people.

No journal could have maintained its circulation and extended its influence in the face of so much hostility except by commanding merits. The merits of the *Nation* were incontestable. It was the best weekly not only in America but in the world. The editorials were models

of style. The book reviews, many of them
in earlier days also written by Godkin himself,
were finished in point of form, and, when not
his own, came from the ablest specialist hands
in the country. The "current notes" of progress
in such subjects as geography, natural history,
and archæology were instructive and accurate.
So it was that people had to read the *Nation*
whether they liked it or not. It could not be
ignored. It was a necessity even where it was a
terror.

Yet neither the force of his reasoning nor
the brilliance of his style would have secured
Godkin's influence but for two other elements of
strength he possessed. One was the universal
belief in his disinterestedness and sincerity.
He was often charged with prejudice or bitterness, but never with any sinister motive; enemies
no less than friends respected him. The
other was his humour. An austere moralist
who is brimful of fun is rare in any country.
Relishing humour more than does any other
people, the Americans could not be seriously
angry with a man who gave them so abundant a
feast.

To trace the course he took in the politics of
the United States since 1860 would almost be
to outline the history of forty years, for there
was no great issue in the discussion of which
he did not bear a part. He was a strong sup-

porter of the Northern cause during the War of Secession, and by his letters to the London *Daily News* did something to enlighten English readers. When the problems of reconstruction emerged after the war, he suggested lines of action more moderate than those followed by the Republican leaders, and during many subsequent years denounced the "carpet-baggers," and advocated the policy of restoring self-government to the Southern States and withdrawing Federal troops. Incensed at the corruption of some of the men who surrounded President Grant during his first term, he opposed Grant's re-election, as did nearly all the reformers of those days. By this time he had begun to attack the "spoils system," and to demand a reform of the civil service, and he had also become engaged in that campaign against the Tammany organisation in New York City which he maintained with unabated energy till the end of his editorial career.[1] In 1884 he led the opposition to the candidacy of Mr. Blaine for President, and it was mainly the persistency with which the *Evening Post* set forth the accusations brought against that statesman that secured his defeat in New York State, and therewith his defeat in the election. It was on this occasion that the nick-

---

[1] The Tammany leaders had him repeatedly arrested, usually on Sunday mornings (that being the day on which it was least easy to find bail) for alleged criminal libels upon them. These prosecutions, threatened in the hope of intimidating him, never went further.

name of Mugwump[1] was first applied to Mr. Godkin by the ablest of his antagonists in the press, Mr. Dana of the *New York Sun*, a title before long extended to the Independents whom the *Post* led, and who constituted, during the next ten or twelve years, a section of opinion important, if not by its numbers, yet by the intellectual and moral weight of the men who composed it. When currency questions became prominent, Mr. Godkin was a strong opponent of bimetallism and of "silverism" in all its forms, and a not less strenuous opponent of all socialistic theories and movements. It need hardly be added that he had always been an upholder of the principles of Free Trade. Like a sound Cobdenite, he was an advocate of peace, and disliked territorial extension. He opposed President Grant's scheme for the acquisition of San Domingo, as he afterwards opposed the annexation of Hawaii. His close study of Irish history, and his old faith in the principle of nationality, had made him a strenuous advocate of Home Rule for Ireland. But no one was further than he from sharing the feelings of the American Irish towards England. He condemned the threats addressed in 1895 to Great Britain over the Venezuela question; and glad as he was to

---

[1] A Mugwump is in the Algonquin tongue an aged chief or wise man, and the name was meant to ridicule the *ex cathedra* manner ascribed to the *Evening Post*.

see that question settled by England's acceptance of an arbitration which she had previously
denied the right of the United States to
demand, he held that England must beware of
yielding too readily to pressure from the United
States, because such compliance would encourage
that aggressive spirit in the latter whose consequences for both countries he feared.   Never,
perhaps, did he incur so much obloquy as in
defending, almost single-handed, the British position in the Venezuelan affair.   The attacks made
all over the country on the *Evening Post* were,
he used to say, like storms of hail lashing against
his windows.   At the very end of his career, he
resisted the war with Spain and the annexation
of the Philippine Islands, deeming the acquisition of trans-Oceanic territories, inhabited by
inferior races, a dangerous new departure, opposed
to the traditions of the Fathers of the Republic,
and inconsistent with the principles on which the
Republic was founded.   No public writer has left
a more consistent record.

In private life Mr. Godkin was a faithful
friend and a charming companion, genial as well
as witty, considerate of others, and liked no less
than admired by his staff on the *Evening Post*,
free from cynicism, and more indulgent in his
views of human nature than might have been
gathered from his public utterances.   He never
despaired of democratic government, yet his

spirits had been damped by the faint fulfilment
of those hopes for the progress of free nations,
and especially of the United States, which had
illumined his youth. The slow advance of
economic truths, the evils produced by the increase of wealth, the growth of what he called
" chromo-civilisation," the indifference of the rich
and educated to politics, the want of nerve
among politicians, the excitability of the masses,
the tenacity with which corruption and misgovernment held their ground, in spite of repeated
exposures, in cities like New York, Philadel-
phia, and Chicago — all these things had so
sunk into his soul that it became hard to induce
him to look at the other side, and to appreciate the splendid recuperative forces which are
at work in America. Thus his friends were
driven to that melancholy form of comfort which
consists in pointing out that other countries are
no better. They argued that England in particular, to which he had continued to look as the
home of political morality and enlightened State
wisdom, was suffering from evils, not indeed the
same as those which in his judgment afflicted
America, but equally serious. They bade him
remember that moral progress is not continuous,
but subject to ebbs of reaction, and that America
is a country of which one should never despair,
because in it evils have often before worked out
their cure. He did regretfully own, after his

latest visits to Europe, that England had sadly
declined from the England of his earlier days,
and he admitted that the clouds under which his
own path had latterly lain might after a time be
scattered by a burst of sunshine ; but his hopes
for the near future of America were not brightened by these reflections.   Sometimes he seemed
to feel — though of his own work he never spoke
— as though he had laboured in vain for forty
years.

If he so thought, he did his work far less
than justice.   It had told powerfully upon the
United States, and that in more than one way.
Though the circulation of the *Nation* was never
large, it was read by the two classes which in
America have most to do with forming political
and economic opinion — I mean editors and University teachers.   (The Universities and Colleges,
be it remembered, are far more numerous, relatively to the population, in America than in England, and a more important factor in the thought
of the country.)   From the editors and the professors Mr. Godkin's views filtered down into the educated class generally, and affected its opinion.   He
instructed and stimulated the men who instructed
and stimulated the rest of the people.   To those
young men in particular who thought about
public affairs and were preparing themselves to
serve their country, his articles were an inspiration.   The great hope for American democracy

to-day lies in the growing zeal and the ripened intelligence with which the generation now come to manhood has begun to throw itself into public work. Many influences have contributed to this result, and Mr. Godkin's has been among the most potent.

Nor was his example less beneficial to the profession of journalism. There has always been a profusion of talent in the American press, talent more alert and versatile than is to be found in the press of any European country. But in 1865 there were three things which the United States lacked. Literary criticism did not maintain a high standard, nor duly distinguish thorough from flashy or superficial performances. Party spirit was so strong and so pervasive that journalists were content to denounce or to extol, and seldom subjected the character of men or measures to a searching and impartial examination. There was too much sentimentalism in politics, with too little reference of current questions to underlying principles, too little effort to get down to what Americans call the "hard pan" of facts. In all these respects the last forty years have witnessed prodigious advances; and, so far as the press is concerned — for much has been due to the Universities and to the growth of a literary class — Mr. Godkin's writings largely contributed to the progress made. His finished criticism, his exact method, his incisive handling of economic problems, his complete detachment from party, helped to form a new school of journalists, as the example he set of a serious and lofty conception of an editor's duties helped to add dignity to the position. He had not that disposition to enthrone the press which made a great English newspaper once claim for itself that it discharged in the modern world the functions of the mediæval Church. But he brought to his work as an anonymous writer a sense of responsibility and a zeal for the welfare of his country which no minister of State could have surpassed.

His friends may sometimes have wished that he had more fully recognised the worth of sentiment as a motive power in politics, that he had more frequently tried to persuade as well as to convince, that he had given more credit for partial instalments of honest service and for a virtue less than perfect, that he had dealt more leniently with the faults of the good and the follies of the wise. Defects in these respects were the almost inevitable defects of his admirable qualities, of his passion for truth, his hatred of wrong and injustice, his clear vision, his indomitable spirit.

The lesson of his editorial career is a lesson not for America only. Among the dangers that beset democratic communities, none are greater than the efforts of wealth to control, not only electors and legislators, but also the organs of public opinion, and the disposition of statesmen and journalists to defer to and flatter the majority, adopting the sentiment dominant at the moment, and telling the people that its voice is the voice of God. Mr. Godkin was not only inaccessible to the lures of wealth — the same may happily be still said of many of his craft-brethren — he was just as little accessible to the fear of popular displeasure. Nothing more incensed him than to see a statesman or an editor with his "ear to the ground" (to use an American phrase), seeking to catch the sound of the coming crowd. To him, the less popular a view was, so much the more did it need to be well weighed and, if approved, to be strenuously and incessantly preached. Democracies will always have demagogues ready to feed their vanity and stir their passions and exaggerate the feeling of the moment. What they need is men who will swim against the stream, will tell them their faults, will urge an argument all the more forcibly because it is unwelcome. Such an one was Edwin Godkin. Since the death of Abraham Lincoln, America has been generally more influenced by her writers, preachers, and thinkers than by her statesmen. In the list of those who have during the last forty years influenced her for good and helped by their pens to make her history, a list illustrated by such names as those of R. W. Emerson and Phillips Brooks and James Russell Lowell, his name will find its place and receive its well-earned meed of honour.

LORD ACTON

WHEN Lord Acton died on 19th June 1902, at
Tegern See in Bavaria, England lost the most truly
cosmopolitan of her children, and Europe lost one
who was, by universal consent, in the foremost rank
of her men of learning. He belonged to an old
Roman Catholic family of Shropshire, a branch
of which had gone to Southern Italy, where his
grandfather, General Acton, had been chief
minister of the King of Naples in the great
war, at the time when the Bourbon dynasty
maintained itself in Sicily by the help of
the British fleet, while all Italy lay under the
heel of Napoleon. His father, Sir Ferdinand
Acton, married a German lady, heiress of the
ancient and famous house of Dalberg, one of the
great families of the middle Rhineland; so John
Edward Emerich Dalberg-Acton was born half a
German, and connected by blood with the highest
aristocracy of Germany. He was educated at
Oscott, one of the two chief Roman Catholic
colleges of England, under Dr. Wiseman, afterwards Archbishop of Westminster and Cardinal;
but the most powerful influence on the develop-

ment of his mind and principles came from that glory of Catholic learning, a beautiful soul as well as a capacious intellect, Dr. von Döllinger, with whom Acton studied during some years at Munich. He sat for a short time in the House of Commons as member for Carlow (1859); and was afterwards elected for Bridgnorth (1865), but lost his seat (which he had gained by one vote only) on a scrutiny. In those days it was not easy for a Roman Catholic to find an English constituency, so in 1869 Mr. Gladstone procured his elevation to the peerage. He made a successful speech in the House of Lords in 1893, but took no prominent part in parliamentary life in either House, feeling himself too much of a student, and looking at current questions from a point of view unlike that of English politicians. Neither as a philosopher, nor as a historian, nor as a product of German training, could he find either Lords or Commons a congenial audience. When he was asked soon after he entered Parliament why he did not speak, he answered that he agreed with nobody and nobody agreed with him. But since he regarded politics as history in the course of making under his eyes, he continued to be all his life keenly interested in public affairs, watching and judging every move in the game. Mr. Gladstone, whose trusted friend he had been for many years, was believed to have on one occasion wished to place him in an important office; but political exigencies made this impossible, and the only public post he ever held was that of Lord-in-Waiting in the Ministry of 1892. In this capacity he was brought into frequent contact with Queen Victoria, who felt the warmest respect and admiration for him. He was one of the very few persons surrounding her who was familiar with most of the courts of Continental Europe, and could discuss with her from direct knowledge the men who figured in those courts. At Windsor he spent in the library of the Castle all the time during which he was not required to be in actual attendance on the Queen, a singular phenomenon among Lords-in-Waiting.

Unlike most English Roman Catholics, he was a strong Liberal, a Liberal of that orthodox type, individualist, free-trade, and peace-loving, which prevailed from 1846 till 1885. He was also a convinced Home Ruler, and had, indeed, adopted the principle of Home Rule for Ireland long before Mr. Gladstone himself was converted to it. His faith in that principle rested on the value he attached to self-government as a means of training and developing the political aptitudes of a people, and to the recognition of national sentiment, which he held to be, like other natural forces, useful when guided but formidable when repressed. So too his Liberalism was based on the love of freedom for its own sake, joined to the conviction that freedom is the best foundation for the stability of a constitution and the happiness of a people. Reliance on the power of freedom was, he used to say, one of the broadest of all the lessons he had learned from history. He applied it in ecclesiastical as well as in political affairs. At the time of the Vatican Council of 1870 he was, though a layman, prominent among those who constituted the opposition maintained by the Liberal section of the Roman Catholic Church to the affirmation of the dogma of papal infallibility. His full and accurate knowledge of ecclesiastical history was placed at the disposal of the prelates, such as Archbishop Dupanloup, Bishop Strossmayer, and Archbishop Conolly (of Halifax, Nova Scotia), who combated the Ultramontane party in the animated and protracted debates which illumined that Œcumenical Council. One, at least, of the treatises, and many of the letters in the press which the Council called forth were written either by him or from materials which he supplied, and he was recognised by the Ultramontanes, and in particular by Archbishop Manning, as being, along with Döllinger, the most formidable of their opponents behind the scenes. As every one knows, the Infallibilists triumphed, and the schism which led to the formation of the Old Catholic Church in Germany and Switzerland was the result. Döllinger was excommunicated; but against Lord Acton no action was taken, and he remained all his life a faithful member of the

2 C

Roman communion while adhering to the views he had advocated in 1870.

With this close hold upon practical life and this constant interest in the politics of the world, especially of England and the United States, no one could be less like that cloistered student who is commonly taken as the typical man of learning. But Lord Acton was a miracle of learning. Of the sciences of nature and their practical applications in the arts he had indeed no more knowledge than any cultivated man of the world is expected to possess. But of all the so-called "human subjects" his mastery was unequalled. Learning was the business of his life. He was gifted with a singularly tenacious memory. His industry was untiring. Wherever he was — in London, at Cannes in winter, at Tegern See in summer, at Windsor or Osborne with the Queen, latterly (till his health failed) at Cambridge during the University terms — he never worked less than eight hours a day. Yet, even after making every allowance for his memory and his industry, his friends stood amazed at the range and exactness of his knowledge. It was as various as it was profound, and much of it bore on recondite matters which few men study to-day. Though less minute where it touched the ancient and the early mediæval world than as respected more recent times, it might be said to cover the whole field of history, both civil and ecclesiastical, and became wonderfully

full and exact when it reached the Renaissance and
Reformation periods. It included not only the
older theology, but modern Biblical criticism.   It
included metaphysics; and not only metaphysics in
the more special sense, but the abstract side of
economics and that philosophy of law on which
the Germans set so much store. Most of the
prominent figures who have during the last half-
century led the march of inquiry in these subjects, men like Ranke and Fustel de Coulanges
in history, Wilhelm Roscher in economic science,
Adolf Harnack in theology, were his personal
friends, and he could meet them as an equal on
their own ground. On one occasion I had invited to meet him at dinner the late Dr. (afterwards Bishop) Creighton, who was then writing
his *History of the Popes*, and the late Professor
Robertson Smith, the most eminent Hebrew
and Arabic scholar in Britain. The conversation turned first upon the times of Pope Leo
the Tenth, and then upon recent controversies
regarding the dates of the books of the Old
Testament, and it soon appeared that Lord
Acton knew as much about the former as Dr.
Creighton, and as much about the latter as
Robertson Smith. The constitutional history of
the United States is a topic far removed from
those philosophical and ecclesiastical or theological lines of inquiry to which most of his time had
been given; yet he knew it more thoroughly than

any other living European, at least in England
and France, for of the Germans I will not venture
to speak, and he continued to read most of the
books of importance dealing with it which from
time to time were published. So, indeed, he
kept abreast of nearly all the literature of possible
utility bearing on history (especially ecclesiastical
history) and political theory that appeared in
Europe or America, reading much which his less
diligent or less eager friends thought scarcely
worthy of his perusal. And it need hardly be
said that his friends found him an invaluable guide
to the literature of any subject. In the sphere
of history more especially, one might safely
assume that a book which he did not know was
not worth knowing, while he was often able to
indicate, as being the right book to consult, some
work of which the person who consulted him
albeit not unversed in the subject, had never
heard. He had at one time four libraries, the
largest at his family seat, Aldenham in Shropshire, others at Tegern See, at Cannes, and in
London; and he could usually tell in which of
these the particular book he named was to be
found. Unlike most men who value their
libraries, he was fond of lending books, and
would sometimes put a friend to shame by asking
some weeks afterwards what the latter thought
of the volumes he had almost forced on the
borrower, and which the borrower had not found

time to read.   After saying this, I need scarcely
add that he was not a book collector in the usual
sense of the word.   He did not care for rare
editions, and still less did he care about bindings.

His Aldenham library was itself a monument
of learning and industry.[1]   In forming it he sought
to bring together the books needed for tracing
and elucidating the growth of formative ideas
and of institutions in the sphere of ecclesiastical
and civil polity, and to attain this he made it
include not only all the best treatises handling
these large and complex subjects, but a mass of
original records bearing as well on the local
histories of the cities and provinces of such
countries as Italy and France as on the general
history of the great European States and of the
Church.   This magnificent design he accomplished
by his own efforts before he was forty.   What was
still more surprising, he had found time to use the
books.   Nearly all of them show by notes pencilled
or marks placed in them that he had read some
part of them, and knew (so far as was needed for
his purpose) their contents.

Vast as his stores of knowledge were, they
were opened only to his few intimate friends.
It was not merely that he, as Tennyson said of
Edmund Lushington, "bore all that weight of
learning lightly, like a flower."   No one could

[1] This library, bought by Mr. Andrew Carnegie, was presented by him
to Mr. John Morley, and by the latter to the University of Cambridge.

have known in general society that he had any
weight of learning to bear. He seemed to be
merely a cultivated and agreeable man of the
world, interested in letters and politics, but disposed rather to listen than to talk. He was
sometimes enigmatic and "not incapable of cast-
ing a pearl of irony in the way of those who would
mistake it for pebbly fact."[1] A great capacity
for cynicism remained a capacity only, because
joined to a greater reverence for virtue. In a
large company he seldom put forth the fulness of his powers; it was in familiar converse
with persons whose tastes resembled his own
that the extraordinary finesse and polish of his
mind revealed themselves. His critical taste was
not only delicate, but exacting; his judgments
leaned to the side of severity. No one applied
a more stringent moral standard to the conduct
of men in public affairs, whether to-day or in
past ages. He insisted upon this, in his inaugural
lecture at Cambridge, as the historian's first duty.
" It is," said he, " the office of historical science to
maintain morality as the sole impartial criterion
of men and things." When he came to estimate
the value of literary work he seemed no less
hard to satisfy. His ideal, both as respected
thoroughness in substance and finish in form,
was impossibly high, and he noted every failure
to reach it. No one appreciated merit more

[1] The phrase is Professor Maitland's.

cordially. No one spoke with warmer admiration of such distinguished historians and theologians as the men whom I have just named. But the precision of his thinking and the fastidiousness of his taste gave more than a tinge of austerity to his judgment. His opinions were peculiarly instructive and illuminative to Englishmen, because he was only half an Englishman in blood, less than half an Englishman in his training and mental habits. He was as much at home in Paris or Berlin or Rome as he was in London, speaking the four great languages with almost equal facility, and knowing the men who in each of these capitals were best worth knowing. He viewed our insular literature and politics with the detachment not only of a Roman Catholic among Protestants, of a pupil of Döllinger and Roscher among Oxford and Cambridge men, but also of a citizen of the world, whose mastery of history and philosophy had given him an unusually wide outlook over mankind at large.

His interest in the great things, so far from turning him away from the small things, seemed to quicken his sense of their significance. It was a noteworthy feature of his view of history that he should have held that the explanation of most of what has passed in the light is to be found in what has passed in the dark. He was always hunting for the key to secret chambers, preferring to believe that the grand staircase is only for show, and meant to impose upon the multitude, while the real action goes on in hidden passages behind. No one knew so much of the gossip of the past; no one was more intensely curious about the gossip of the present, though in his hands it ceased to be gossip and became unwritten history. One was sometimes disposed to wonder whether he did not think too much about the backstairs. But he had seen a great deal of history in the making.

The passion for acquiring knowledge which his German education had fostered ended by becoming a snare to him, because it checked his productive powers. Not that learning burdened him, or clogged the soaring pinions of his mind. He was master of all he knew. But acquisition absorbed so much of his time that little was left for literary composition. (Döllinger saw the danger, for he observed that if Acton did not write a great book before he reached the age of forty, he would never do so.) It made him think that he could not write on a subject till he had read everything, or nearly everything, that others had written about it. It developed the habit of making extracts from the books he read, a habit which took the form of accumulating small slips of paper on which these extracts were written in his exquisitely neat and regular hand, the slips being arranged in cardboard boxes according to their subjects. He had hundreds of these boxes; and though much of their contents must no doubt be valuable, the time spent in distilling and bottling the essence of the books whence they came, might have been better spent in giving to the world the ideas which they had helped to evoke in his own mind. If one may take the quotations appended to his inaugural lecture as a sample of those he had collected, many of them were not exceptionally valuable, and did little more than show how the same idea, perhaps no recondite one, might be expressed in different words by different persons. When one read some article he had written, garnished and even overloaded with citations, one often felt that his own part was better, both in substance and in form, than the passages which he had culled from his predecessors. It becomes daily more than ever true that the secret of historical composition is to know what to neglect, since in our time it has become impossible to exhaust the literature of most subjects, and, as respects the last two centuries, to exhaust even the original authorities. Yet how shall one know what to neglect without at least a glance of inspection? Acton was unwilling to neglect anything; and his ardour for completeness drew him into a policy fit only for one who could expect to live three lives of mortal men.

The love of knowledge grew upon him till

it became a passion of the intellect, a thirst like the thirst for water in a parching desert. What he sought to know was not facts only, but facts in their relations to principles, facts so disposed and fitly joined together as to become the causeway over which the road to truth shall pass. For this purpose events were in his view not more important than the thoughts of men, because discursive and creative thought was to him the ruling factor in history. Hence books must be known — books of philosophic creation, books of philosophic reflection, no less than those which record what has happened. The danger of this conception is that everything men have said or written, as well as everything they have done, becomes a possibly significant fact ; and thus the search for truth becomes endless because the materials are inexhaustible.

He expressed in striking words, prefixed to a list of books suggested for a young man's perusal, his view of the aim of a course of historical reading. It is "to give force and fulness and clearness and sincerity and independence and elevation and generosity and serenity to his mind, that he may know the method and law of the process by which error is conquered and truth is won, discerning knowledge from probability and prejudice from belief, that he may learn to master what he rejects as fully as what he adopts, that he may understand the origin as well as the strength and vitality of systems and the better motive of men who are wrong . . . and to steel him against the charm of literary beauty and talent."[1]

Neither his passion for facts nor his appreciation of style and form made him decline to the right hand or to the left from the true position of a historian. He set little store upon what is called literary excellence, and would often reply, when questioned as to the merits of some book bearing an eminent name, "You need not read it; it adds nothing to what we knew." He valued facts only so far as they went to establish a principle or explained the course of events. It was really not so much in the range of his knowledge as in the profundity and precision of his thought that his greatness lay.

His somewhat overstrained conscientiousness, coupled with the practically unattainable ideal of finish and form which he set before himself, made him less and less disposed to literary production. No man of first-rate powers has in our time left so little by which posterity may judge those powers. In his early life, when for a time he edited the *Home and Foreign Review*, and when he was connected with the *Rambler* and the *North British Review*, he wrote frequently; and even between 1868 and 1890 he contributed to

---

[1] I owe this quotation to a letter of Sir M. E. Grant Duff's published soon after Lord Acton's death.

the press some few historical essays and a number of anonymous letters. But the aversion to
creative work seemed to grow on him. About
1890 he so far yielded to the urgency of a few
friends as to promise to reissue a number of his
essays in a volume, but, after rewriting and polish-
ing these essays during several years, he abandoned the scheme altogether. In 1882 he had
already drawn out a plan for a comprehensive
history of Liberty. But this plan also he
dropped, because the more he read with a view
to undertaking it the more he wished to read,
and the vaster did the enterprise seem to loom
up before him. With him, as with many men
who cherish high literary ideals, the Better proved
to be the enemy of the Good.

Twenty years ago, late at night, in his library
at Cannes, he expounded to me his view of how
such a history of Liberty might be written, and
in what wise it might be made the central thread
of all history. He spoke for six or seven minutes
only; but he spoke like a man inspired, seeming
as if, from some mountain summit high in air, he
saw beneath him the far winding path of human
progress from dim Cimmerian shores of prehistoric shadow into the fuller yet broken and
fitful light of the modern time. The eloquence
was splendid, but greater than the eloquence was
the penetrating vision which discerned through
all events and in all ages the play of those moral

forces, now creating, now destroying, always
transmuting, which had moulded and remoulded
institutions, and had given to the human spirit its
ceaselessly-changing forms of energy. It was as
if the whole landscape of history had been suddenly lit up by a burst of sunlight. I have never
heard from any other lips any discourse like this,
nor from his did I ever hear the like again.

His style suffered in his later days from
the abundance of the interspersed citations, and
from the overfulness and subtlety of the thought,
which occasionally led to obscurity. But when
he handled a topic in which learning was not required, his style was clear, pointed, and incisive,
sometimes epigrammatic. Several years ago he
wrote in a monthly magazine a short article upon
a biography of one of his contemporaries which
showed how admirable a master he was of polished
diction and penetrating analysis, and made one
wish that he had more frequently consented to
dash off light work in a quick unstudied way.

To the work of a University professor he came
too late to acquire the art of fluent and forcible
oral discourse, nor was the character of his mind,
with its striving after a flawless exactitude of
statement, altogether fitted for the function of
presenting broad summaries of facts to a youthful
audience. His predecessor in the Cambridge
chair of history, Sir John Seeley, with less knowledge, less subtlety, and less originality, had in

larger measure the gift of oral exposition and the power of putting points, whether by speech or by writing, in a clear and telling way.   No one, indeed, since Macaulay has been a better point-putter than Seeley was.   But Acton's lectures (read from MS.) were models of lucid and stately narrative informed by fulness of thought; and they were so delivered as to express the feeling which each event had evoked in his own mind. That sternness of character which revealed itself in his judgments of men and books never affected his relations to his pupils.   Precious as his time was, he gave it generously, encouraging them to come to him for help and counsel.   They were awed by the majesty of his learning.   Said one of them to me, "When Lord Acton answers a question put to him, I feel as if I were looking at a pyramid.   I see the point of it clear and sharp, but I see also the vast subjacent mass of solid knowledge."   They perceived, moreover, that to him History and Philosophy were not two things but one, and perceived that of History as well as of divine Philosophy it may be said that she too is "charming, and musical as is Apollo's lute."   Thus the impression produced in the University by the amplitude of Lord Acton's views, by the range of his learning, by the liberality of his spirit and his unfailing devotion to truth and to truth alone, was deep and fruitful.

When they wished that he had given to the world

more of his wisdom, his friends did not under-
value a life which was in itself a rare and exquisite
product of favouring nature and unwearied diligence.   They only regretted that the influence of
his ideas, of his methods, and of his spirit, had
not been more widely diffused in an enduring
form.   It was as when a plant unknown elsewhere
grows on some remote isle where ships seldom
touch.   Few see the beauty of the flower, and
here death came before the seed could be gathered
to be scattered in receptive soil.

To most men Lord Acton seemed reserved as
well as remote, presenting a smooth and shining
surface beneath which it was hard to penetrate.
He avoided publicity and popularity with the
tranquil dignity of one for whom the world of
knowledge and speculation was more than sufficient.   But he was a loyal friend, affectionate to
his intimates, gracious in his manners, blameless
in all the relations of life.   Comparatively few
of his countrymen knew his name, and those who
did thought of him chiefly as the confidant of Mr.
Gladstone, and as the most remarkable instance
of a sincere and steadfast Roman Catholic who
was a Liberal alike in politics and in theology.
But those who had been admitted to his friendship recognised him as one of the finest intelligences of his generation, an unsurpassed,
and indeed a scarcely rivalled, master of every
subject which he touched.

WILLIAM EWART GLADSTONE

OF no man who has lived in our times is it so hard to speak in a concise and summary fashion as of Mr. Gladstone. For fifty years he was so closely associated with the public affairs of his country that the record of his parliamentary life is virtually an outline of English political history during those years. His activity spread itself out over many fields. He was the author of several learned and thoughtful books, and of a multitude of articles upon all sorts of subjects. He showed himself as eagerly interested in matters of classical scholarship and Christian doctrine and ecclesiastical history as in questions of national finance and foreign policy. No account of him could be complete without reviewing his actions and estimating the results of his work in all these directions.

But the difficulty of describing and judging him goes deeper. His was a singularly complex nature, whose threads it was hard to unravel. His individuality was extremely strong. All that he said or did bore its impress. Yet it was an individuality so far from being self-consistent

as sometimes to seem a bundle of opposite
qualities capriciously united in a single person.
He might with equal truth have been called, and
he was in fact called, a conservative and a revolutionary. He was dangerously impulsive, and had
frequently to suffer for his impulsiveness; yet
he was also not merely prudent and cautious,
but so astute as to have been accused of craft
and dissimulation. So great was his respect
for tradition that he clung to views regarding the authorship of the Homeric poems and
the date of the books of the Old Testament which nearly all competent specialists
have now rejected. So bold was he in practical matters that he carried through sweeping
changes in the British constitution, changed the
course of English policy in the nearer East,
overthrew an established church in one part of
the United Kingdom, and committed himself
in principle to the overthrow of two other
established churches in other parts. He came
near to being a Roman Catholic in his religious
opinions, yet was for the last twenty years of
his life the trusted leader of the English Protestant Nonconformists and the Scottish Presbyterians. No one who knew him intimately
doubted his conscientious sincerity and earnestness, yet four-fifths of the English upper classes
were in his later years wont to regard him as a
self-interested schemer who would sacrifice his

2 D

country to his ambition. Though he loved general principles, and often soared out of the sight of his audience when discussing them, he generally ended by deciding upon points of detail the question at issue. He was at different times of his life the defender and the assailant of the same institutions, yet scarcely seemed inconsistent in doing opposite things, because his methods and his arguments preserved the same type and colour throughout. Those who had at the beginning of his career discerned in him the capacity for such diversities and contradictions would probably have predicted that they must wreck it by making his purposes fluctuating and his course erratic. Such a prediction might have proved true of any one with less firmness of will and less intensity of temper. It was the persistent heat and vehemence of his character, the sustained passion which he threw into the pursuit of the object on which he was for the moment bent, that fused these dissimilar qualities and made them appear to contribute to and increase the total force which he exerted.

The circumstances of Mr. Gladstone's political career help to explain, or, at any rate, will furnish occasion for the attempt to explain, this complexity and variety of character. But before I come to his manhood it is convenient to advert to three conditions whose influence on him was profound — the first his Scottish blood, the second

his Oxford education, the third his apprenticeship
to public life under Sir Robert Peel.

Theories of character based on race differences
are dangerous, because they are as hard to
test as they are easy to form.   Still, we all
know that there are specific qualities and tendencies usually found in the minds of men of
certain stocks, just as there are peculiarities in
their faces or in their speech.   Mr. Gladstone
was born and brought up in Liverpool, and
always retained a touch of Lancashire accent.
But, as he was fond of saying, every drop of
blood in his veins was Scotch.   His father's
family belonged to the Scottish Lowlands, and
came from the neighbourhood of Biggar, in the
Upper Ward of Lanarkshire, where the ruined
walls of Gledstanes [1] — "the kite's rock" — may
still be seen.   His mother was of Highland extraction, by name Robertson, from Dingwall, in
Ross-shire.   Thus he was not only a Scot, but a
Scot with a strong infusion of the Celtic element,
the element whence the Scotch derive most of
what distinguishes them from the northern English.   The Scot is more excitable, more easily
brought to a glow of passion, more apt to be
eagerly absorbed in one thing at a time.   He
is also more fond of exerting his intellect on
abstractions.   It is not merely that the taste for

---

[1] "Gled" is a kite or hawk.   The name was Gladstones till Mr. Gladstone's father dropped the final s.

metaphysical theology is commoner in Scotland
than in England, but that the Scotch have a
stronger relish for general principles. They
like to set out by ascertaining and defining such
principles, and then to pursue a series of logical
deductions from them.   They are, therefore,
bolder reasoners than the English, less content
to remain in the region of concrete facts, more
prone to throw themselves into the construction of a body of speculative doctrine.   The
Englishman is apt to plume himself on being
right in spite of logic; the Scotchman likes
to think that it is through logic he has reached
his results, and that he can by logic defend
them.   These are qualities which Mr. Gladstone
drew from his Scottish blood. He had a keen
enjoyment of the processes of dialectic.   He
loved to get hold of an abstract principle and to
derive all sorts of conclusions from it.   He was
wont to begin the discussion of a question by
laying down two or three sweeping propositions
covering the subject as a whole, and would then
proceed to draw from these others which he
could apply to the particular matter in hand.
His well-stored memory and boundless ingenuity
made the discovery of such general propositions
so easy a task that a method in itself agreeable
sometimes appeared to be carried to excess.   He
frequently arrived at conclusions which the judgment of the common-sense auditor did not

approve, because, although they seemed to have
been legitimately deduced from the general
principles just enunciated, they were somehow
at variance with the plain teaching of the facts.
At such moments one felt that the man who
was fascinating but perplexing Englishmen by
his subtlety was not himself an Englishman
in mental quality, but had the love for abstractions and refinements and dialectical analysis
which characterises the Scotch intellect. He
had also a large measure of that warmth and
vehemence, called in the sixteenth century the
perfervidum ingenium Scotorum, which belong to
the Scottish temperament, and particularly to
the Celtic Scot. He kindled quickly, and when
kindled, he shot forth a strong and brilliant flame.
To any one with less power of self-control such
intensity of emotion as he frequently showed
would have been dangerous; nor did this excitability fail, even with him, to prompt words
and acts which a cooler judgment would have
disapproved. But it gave that spontaneity which
was one of the charms of his nature; it produced
that impression of profound earnestness and of
resistless force which raised him out of the rank
of ordinary statesmen. The rush of emotion
swelling fast and full seemed to turn the whole
stream of intellectual effort into whatever channel
lay at the moment nearest.

With these Scottish qualities, Mr. Gladstone

was brought up at school and college (Eton
and Christ Church) among Englishmen, and received at Oxford, then lately awakened from a
long torpor, a bias and tendency which never
thereafter ceased to affect him. The so-called
"Oxford Movement," which afterwards obtained
the name of Tractarianism and carried Newman
and Manning, together with other less famous
leaders, on to Rome, had not yet, in 1831, when
Mr. Gladstone obtained his degree with double
first-class honours, taken visible shape, or become, so to speak, conscious of its own purposes.   But its doctrinal views, its peculiar vein
of religious sentiment, its respect for antiquity
and tradition, its proneness to casuistry, its taste
for symbolism, were already in the air as influences working on the more susceptible of the
younger minds.   On Mr. Gladstone they told
with full force.   He became, and never ceased
to be, not merely a High Churchman, but what
may be called an Anglo-Catholic, in his theology,
deferential not only to ecclesiastical tradition,
but to the living voice of the Visible Church,
revering the priesthood as the recipients (if
duly ordained) of a special grace and peculiar
powers, attaching great importance to the sacra-
ments, feeling himself nearer to the Church of
Rome, despite what he deemed her corruptions,
than to any of the non-Episcopal Protestant
churches.   Henceforth his interests in life were

as much ecclesiastical as political. For a time
he desired to be ordained a clergyman. Had
this wish, abandoned in deference to his father's
advice, been carried out, he must eventually have
become a leading figure in the Church of England and have sensibly affected her recent history.
The later stages in his career drew him away
from the main current of political opinion within
that church. He who had been the strongest
advocate of the principle of the State establishment of religion came to be the chief actor in
the disestablishment of the Protestant Episcopal
Church in Ireland, and a supporter of the policy
of disestablishment in Scotland and in Wales.
But the colour which these Oxford years gave
to his mind and thoughts was never effaced.
While they widened the range of his interests
and deepened his moral earnestness, they at the
same time confirmed his natural bent toward
over-subtle distinctions and fine-drawn reasonings,
and put him out of sympathy not only with the
attitude of the average Englishman, who is essen-
tially a Protestant — that is to say, averse to sacer-
dotalism, and suspicious of any other religious
authority than that of the Bible and the individual conscience — but also with two of the
strongest influences of our time, the influence
of the sciences of nature, and the influence of
historical criticism. Mr. Gladstone, though too
wise to rail at science, as many religious men

did till within the last few years, could never quite reconcile himself either to the conclusions of geology and zoology regarding the history of the physical world and the creatures which inhabit it, or to modern methods of critical inquiry as applied to Scripture and to ancient literature generally. The training which Oxford then gave, stimulating as it was, and free from the modern error of over-specialisation, was defective in omitting the experimental sciences, and in laying undue stress upon the study of language. A proneness to dwell on verbal distinctions and to trust overmuch to the analysis of terms as a means of reaching the truth of things is noticeable in many eminent Oxford writers of that and the next succeeding generation — some of them, like the illustrious F. D. Maurice, far removed from Cardinal Newman and Mr. Gladstone in theological opinion.

When, bringing with him a brilliant University reputation, he entered the House of Commons at the age of twenty-three, Sir Robert Peel was leading the Tory party with an authority and ability rarely surpassed in the annals of Parliament. Within two years the young man was admitted into the short-lived Tory ministry of 1834, and soon proved himself a promising lieutenant of the experienced chief. Peel was an eminently wary man, alive to the necessity of watching the signs of the times, of studying and interpreting the changeful phases of public opinion. Yet he always kept his own counsel. Even when he perceived that the policy he had hitherto followed would need to be modified, Peel continued to use guarded language and did not publicly commit himself to change till it was plain that the fitting moment had arrived. He was, moreover, a master of detail, slow to propound a plan until he had seen how its outlines were to be filled up by appropriate devices for carrying it out in practice. These qualities and habits of the minister profoundly affected his disciple. They became part of the texture of Mr. Gladstone's political character, and in his case, as in that of Peel, they sometimes brought censure upon him, as having locked up too long within his breast views or purposes which he thought it unwise to disclose till effect could be forthwith given to them. Such reserve, such a guarded attitude and tenderness for existing institutions, may have been not altogether natural to Mr. Gladstone's mind, but due partly to the influence of Peel, partly to the tendency to hold by tradition and the established order which reverence for Christian antiquity and faith in the dogmatic teachings of the Church had planted deep in his soul. The contrast between Mr. Gladstone's caution and respect for facts on the one hand, and his reforming fervour on the other, like the contrast which ultimately appeared between his sacerdotal tendencies and his political liberalism, contributed to make his character perplexing and to expose his conduct to the charge of inconsistency. Inconsistent, in the proper sense of the word, he was not, much less changeable. He was really, in his fundamental convictions and the main habits of his mind, one of the most tenacious and persistent of men. But there were always at work in him two tendencies. One was the speculative desire to probe everything to the bottom, to try it by the light of general principles and logic, and when it failed to stand this test, to reject it. The other was the sense of the complexity of existing social and political arrangements, and of the risk of disturbing any one part of them until the time had arrived for resettling other parts also. Every statesman feels both these sides to every concrete question of reform. No one has set them forth more cogently, and in particular no one has more earnestly dwelt on the necessity for the latter side, than the most profound thinker among British statesmen, Edmund Burke. When Mr. Gladstone stated either side with his incomparable force, people forgot that there was another side which would be no less vividly present to him at some other moment. He was not only, like all successful parliamentarians, necessarily something of an opportunist, though perhaps less so than his master, but was moved by emotion more than most statesmen, and certainly more than Peel. The relative strength with which the need for drastic reform or the need for watchful conservatism, as the case might be, presented itself to his mind depended largely upon the weight which his emotions cast into one or other scale, and this emotional element made it difficult to forecast his course. Thus his action in public life was the result of influences differing widely in their origin, influences, moreover, which could be duly appreciated only by those who knew him intimately.

Whoever has followed his political career has been struck by the sharp divergence of the views entertained by his fellow-countrymen about one who had been for so long a period under their observation. That he was possessed of boundless energy and brilliant eloquence all agreed. But agreement went no further. One section of the nation accused him of sophistry, of unwisdom, of a want of patriotism, of a lust for power. The other section not only repelled these charges, but admired in him a conscientiousness and a moral enthusiasm such as no political leader had shown for centuries. When the qualities of his mind and the aptitudes for politics which he showed have been briefly examined, it will be fitting to return to these divergent views of his character, and endeavour to discover which of them contains the larger measure of truth.

Meantime let it suffice to say that among the reasons that led men to misjudge him, this union in one person of opposite qualities was the chief. He was rather two men than one. Passionate and impulsive on the emotional side of his nature, he was cautious and conservative on the intellectual. Few understood the conjunction; still fewer saw how much of what was perplexing in his conduct it explained.

Mr. Gladstone sat for sixty-three years (1833-1895) in Parliament, was for twenty-eight years (1866-1894) the leader of his party, and was four times Prime Minister. He began as a high Tory, remained about fifteen years in that camp, was then led by the split between Peel and the Protectionists to take up an intermediate position, and finally was forced to cast in his lot with the Liberals, for in England, as in America, third parties seldom endure. No parliamentary career in English annals is comparable to his for its length and variety; and of those who saw its close in the House of Commons, there was only one man, Mr. Villiers (who died in January 1898), who could remember its beginning. Mr. Gladstone had been opposed in 1833 to men who might have been his grandfathers; he was opposed in 1894 to men who might have been his grandchildren. It is no part of my design to describe or comment on the events of such a life. All that can be done here is to indicate the more salient

characteristics which a study of his career as a
statesman and a parliamentarian sets before us.

The most remarkable of these characteristics
was the openness, freshness, and eagerness of
mind which he preserved down to the end of
his life. Most men form few new opinions
after thirty-five, just as they form few new
intimacies. Intellectual curiosity may remain
even after fifty, but its range narrows as a man
abandons the hope of attaining any thorough
knowledge of subjects other than those which
make the main business of his life. It is impossible to follow the progress of all the new ideas
that are set afloat in the world, impossible to
be always examining the foundations of one's
political or religious beliefs. Repeated disappointments and disillusionments make a man
expect less from changes the older he grows;
while indolence deters him from entering upon
new enterprises. None of these causes seemed
to affect Mr. Gladstone. He was as much
excited over a new book (such as Cardinal
Manning's Life) at eighty-four as when at
fourteen he insisted on compelling little Arthur
Stanley (afterwards Dean of Westminster, and
then aged nine) forthwith to procure and study
Gray's poems, which he had just perused himself.
His reading covered almost the whole field
of literature, except physical and mathematical
science. While frequently declaring that he

must confine his political thinking and leadership to a few subjects, he was so observant of
current events that the course of talk brought
up scarcely any topic in which he did not seem
to know what was the latest thing that had
been said or done. Neither the lassitude nor
the prejudices that usually accompany old age
prevented him from giving a fair consideration to
any new doctrines. But though his intellect was
restlessly at work, and though his curiosity disposed him to relish novelties, except in theology,
that bottom rock in his mind of caution and reserve, which has already been referred to, made
him refuse to part with old views even when he
was beginning to accept new ones. He allowed
both to " lie on the table " together, and while
declaring himself open to conviction, felt it
safer to speak and act on the old lines till the
process of conviction had been completed. It
took fourteen years, from 1846 to 1860, to carry
him from the Conservative into the Liberal camp.
It took five stormy years to bring him round to
Irish Home Rule, though his mind was constantly
occupied with the subject from 1880 to 1885,
and those who watched him closely saw that
the process had advanced a long way even in
1882. And as regards ecclesiastical establish-
ments, having written a book in 1838 as a warm
advocate of State churches, it was not till 1867
that he adopted the policy of disestablishment

for Ireland, not till 1890 that he declared himself ready to apply that policy in Wales and Scotland also.

Both these qualities — his disposition to revise his opinions in the light of new arguments and changing conditions, and the silence he maintained till the process of revision had been completed — exposed him to misconstruction. Commonplace men, unwont to give serious scrutiny to their opinions, ascribed his changes to self-interest, or at best regarded them as the index of an unstable purpose. Dull men could not understand why he should have forborne to set forth all that was passing in his mind, and saw little difference between reticence and dishonesty. In so far as they shook public confidence, these characteristics injured him in his statesman's work. Yet the loss was outweighed by the gain. In a country where opinion is active and changeful, where the economic conditions that legislation has to deal with are in a state of perpetual flux, where the balance of power between the upper, the middle, and the poorer classes has been swiftly altering during the last seventy years, no statesman can continue to serve the public if he adheres obstinately to the doctrines with which he started in life. He must — unless, of course, he stands aloof in permanent isolation — either subordinate his own views to the general sentiment of his party, and be driven to advocate courses he

secretly mislikes, or else, holding himself ready
to quit his party, if need be, must be willing
to learn from events, and to reconsider his
opinions in the light of emergent tendencies
and insistent facts. Mr. Gladstone's pride as
well as his conscience forbade the former alternative; it was fortunate that the tireless activity
of his intellect made the latter natural to him.
He was accustomed to say that the capital fault
of his earlier days had been his failure adequately
to recognise the worth and power of liberty, and
the tendency which things have to work out for
good when left to themselves. The application
of this principle gave room for many developments, and many developments there were. He
may have shown less than was needed of that
prescience which is, after integrity and courage,
the highest gift of a statesman, but which can
seldom be expected from an English minister,
too engrossed to find time for the patient reflection from which alone sound forecasts can
issue. But he had the next best quality, that
of remaining accessible to new ideas and learning
from the events which passed under his eyes.

With this openness and flexibility of mind
there went a not less remarkable ingenuity
and resourcefulness. Fertile in expedients, he
was still more fertile in reasonings by which
to recommend the expedients. The gift had
its dangers, for he was apt to be carried away

by the dexterity of his own dialectic, and to think that a scheme must be sound in whose support he could muster a formidable array of arguments. He never seemed at a loss, in public or in private, for a criticism, or for an answer to the criticisms of others. If his power of adapting his own mind to the minds of those whom he had to convince had been equal to the skill and swiftness with which he accumulated a mass of matter persuasive to those who looked at things in his own way, no one would have exercised so complete a control over the political opinion of his time. But his intellect lacked this power of adaptation. It moved on lines of its own, which were often misconceived, even by those who sought to follow him loyally. Thus, as already observed, he was blamed for two opposite faults. Some, pointing to the fact that he had frequently altered his views, denounced him as a demagogue profuse of promises, ready to propose whatever he thought likely to catch the people's ear. Others complained that there was no knowing where to have him; that he had an erratic mind, whose currents ran underground and came to the surface in unexpected places; that he did not consult his party, but followed his own impulses; that his guidance was unsafe because his decisions were unpredictable. Much of the suspicion with which he was regarded,

2 E

especially after 1885, arose from this view of his character.

It was an unfair view, yet nearer to the truth than that which charged him with seeking to flatter and follow the people. No great popular leader had in him less of the demagogue. He saw, of course, that a statesman cannot oppose the general will beyond a certain point, and may have to humour it in small things that he may direct it in great ones. He was obliged, as others have been, to take up and settle questions he deemed unimportant because they were troubling the body politic. Now and then, in his later days, he so far yielded to his party advisers as to express his approval of proposals in which his own interest was slight. But he was ever a leader, not a follower, and erred rather in not keeping his finger closely and constantly upon the pulse of public opinion. In this point, at least, one may discover in him a likeness to Disraeli. Slow as he was in maturing his opinions, Mr. Gladstone was liable to forget that the minds of his followers might not be moving along with his own, and hence his decisions sometimes took his party as well as the nation by surprise. But he was too self-absorbed, too eagerly interested in the ideas that suited his own cast of thought, to be able to watch and gauge the tendencies of the multitude. The three most remarkable instances in which

his new departures startled the world were his
declarations against the Irish Church establishment in 1867, against the Turks and the traditional English policy of supporting them in 1876,
and in favour of Irish Home Rule in 1886, and
in none of these did any popular demand suggest
his pronouncement. It was the masses who took
their view from him, not he who took a mandate
from the masses. In each of these cases he may,
perhaps, be blamed for not having sooner perceived,
or at any rate for not having sooner announced,
the need for a change of policy. But it was very
characteristic of him not to give the full strength
of his mind to a question till he felt that it pressed
for a solution. Those who listened to his private
talk were scarcely more struck by the range of
his vision than by his unwillingness to commit
himself on matters whose decision he could
postpone. Reticence and caution were sometimes carried too far, not merely because they
exposed him to misconstruction, but because
they withheld from his party the guidance it
needed. This was true in the three instances
just mentioned; and in the last of them it is
possible that earlier and fuller communications
might have averted the separation of some of
his former colleagues. Nor did he always
rightly divine the popular mind. His pro-
posal (in 1874) to extinguish the income-tax
fell completely flat, because the nation was

becoming indifferent to that economy in public expenditure which both parties had in the days of Peel and Lord John Russell vied in demanding. Cherishing his old financial ideals, Mr. Gladstone had not marked the change. So he failed to perceive how much the credit of his party was suffering (after 1871) from the belief of large sections of the people, that he was indifferent to the interests of England outside England. Perhaps, knowing the charge of indifference to be groundless, he underrated the effect which the iteration of it produced: perhaps his pride would not let him stoop to dissipate it.

Though the power of reading the signs of the times and swaying the mind of the nation may be now more essential to an English statesman than the skill which manages a legislature or holds together a cabinet, that skill counts for much, and must continue to do so while the House of Commons remains the governing authority of the country. A man can hardly reach high place, and certainly cannot retain high place, without possessing this kind of art. Mr. Gladstone was at one time thought to want it. In 1864, when Lord Palmerston's end was approaching, and Mr. Gladstone had shown himself the strongest man among the Liberal ministers in the House of Commons, people speculated about the succession to the headship of the party; and the wiseacres of the day were never tired of repeating that Mr. Gladstone could not possibly lead the House of Commons. He wanted tact, they said, he was too excitable, too impulsive, too much absorbed in his own ideas, too unversed in the arts by which individuals are conciliated. But when, after twenty-five years of his unquestioned reign, the time for his own departure drew nigh, men asked how the Liberal party in the House of Commons would ever hold together after it had lost a leader of such consummate capacity. The Whig critics of 1864 had grown so accustomed to Palmerston's way of handling the House as to forget that a man might succeed by quite different methods, and that defects, serious in themselves, may be outweighed by transcendent merits.

Mr. Gladstone had the defects ascribed to him. His impulsiveness sometimes betrayed him into declarations which a cooler reflection would have dissuaded. The second reading of the Irish Home Rule Bill of 1886 might possibly have been carried had he not been goaded by his opponents into words which were construed as recalling or modifying the concessions he had announced at a meeting of the Liberal party held just before. More than once precious time was wasted because antagonists, knowing his excitable temper, brought on discussions with the sole object of annoying

him and drawing from him some hasty deliverance.
Nor was he an adept, like Disraeli and Disraeli's famous Canadian imitator, Sir John A.
Macdonald, in the management of individuals.
His aversion for the meaner side of human
nature made him refuse to play upon it. Many
of the pursuits, and most of the pleasures,
which attract ordinary men had no interest for
him, so that much of the common ground on
which men meet was closed to him. He was,
moreover, too constantly engrossed by the subjects he loved, and by enterprises which specially
appealed to him, to have leisure for the lighter
but often vitally important devices of political
strategy. I remember hearing, soon after 1870,
how Mr. Delane, then editor of the *Times*, had
been invited to meet the Prime Minister at a
moment when the support of that newspaper
would have been specially valuable to the Liberal
government. Instead of using the opportunity
in the way that had been intended, Mr. Gladstone
dilated during the whole time of dinner upon
the approaching exhaustion of the English coal-
beds, to the surprise of the company and the unconcealed annoyance of the powerful guest. It
was the subject then uppermost in his mind, and
he either forgot, or disdained, to conciliate Mr.
Delane. Good nature as well as good sense
made him avoid giving offence by personal reflections in debate, and he usually suffered fools,

if not, like St. Paul's converts, gladly, yet patiently.[1] In the House of Commons he was entirely free from airs, and, indeed, from any assumption of superiority. The youngest member might accost him in the lobby and be listened to with perfect courtesy. But he had a bad memory for faces, seldom addressed any one outside the circle of his personal friends, and more than once made enemies by omitting to notice and show attention to recruits who, having been eminent in their own towns, expected to be made much of when they entered Parliament. Having himself plenty of pride and comparatively little vanity, he never realised the extent to which, and the cheapness with which, men can be captured and used through their vanity. Adherents were sometimes turned into dangerous foes because his preoccupation with graver matters dimmed his sense of what may be done to win support by the minor arts, such as an invitation to dinner or even a seasonable compliment. And his mind, flexible as it was in seizing new points of view and devising expedients to meet new circumstances, did not easily enter into the characters of other men. Ideas and causes interested him more than did

---

[1] One of his most intimate friends has, I think, said that " he never knew what it was to be bored." Fortunate, indeed, would he have been had this been so; but that one who had watched him long and closely should make the statement shows how gently bores fared at his hands.

I recollect his once remarking on the capacity for boring possessed by a gentleman who had been introduced and had talked for some fifteen minutes to him; but his own manner through the conversation had betrayed no impatience.

personal traits; his sympathy was keener and
stronger for the sufferings of nations or masses
of men than with the fortunes of an individual
man. With all his accessibility and kindliness, he was at bottom chary of real friendship,
while the circle of his intimates became constantly
smaller with advancing years. So it befell that
though his popularity among the general body
of his adherents went on increasing, and the admiration of his parliamentary followers remained
undiminished, he had in the House of Commons
few personal friends who linked him to the party
at large, and rendered to him those confidential
services which count for much in keeping all
sections in hearty accord and enabling the com-
mander to gauge the sentiment of his troops.

Of parliamentary strategy in that larger sense,
which covers familiarity with parliamentary forms
and usages, care and judgment in arranging the
business of the House, the power of seizing a
parliamentary situation and knowing how to
deal with it, the art of guiding a debate and
choosing the right moment for reserve and for
openness, for a dignified retreat, for a watchful defence, for a sudden rattling charge upon the
enemy — of all this no one had a fuller mastery.
His recollection of precedents was unrivalled, for
it began in 1833 with the first reformed Parliament, and it seemed as fresh for those remote
days as for last month. He enjoyed combat for

its own sake, not so much from inborn pugnacity, for he was not disputatious in ordinary
conversation, as because it called out his fighting
force and stimulated his whole nature. " I am
never nervous in reply," he once said, "though I
am sometimes nervous in opening a debate." No
one could be more tactful or adroit when a crisis
arrived whose gravity he had foreseen. In the
summer of 1881 the House of Lords made some
amendments to the Irish Land Bill which were
deemed ruinous to the working of the measure,
and therewith to the prospects of the pacification
of Ireland. A conflict was expected which might
have strained the fabric of the constitution. The
excitement which quickly arose in Parliament
spread to the nation. Mr. Gladstone alone
remained calm and confident. He devised a
series of compromises, which he advocated in conciliatory speeches. He so played his game that
by a few minor concessions he secured nearly all
the points he cared for, and, while sparing the
dignity of the Lords, steered his bill triumphantly
out of the breakers which had threatened to
engulf it. Very different was his ordinary demeanour in debate when he was off his guard.
His face and gestures while he sat in the House
of Commons listening to an opponent would
express all the emotions that crossed his mind.
He would follow every sentence as a hawk follows
the movements of a small bird, would some-

times contradict half aloud, sometimes turn to his next neighbour to vent his displeasure at the groundless allegations or fallacious arguments he was listening to, till at last, like a hunting leopard loosed from the leash, he would spring to his feet and deliver a passionate reply. His warmth would often be in excess of what the occasion required, and quite disproportioned to the importance of his antagonist. It was in fact the unimportance of the occasion that made him thus yield to his feeling. As soon as he saw that bad weather was coming, and careful seamanship wanted, his coolness returned, his language became measured, while passion, though it might increase the force of his oratory, never made him deviate a hand's breadth from the course he had chosen. The Celtic heat subsided, and the shrewd self-control of the Lowland Scot regained command.

It was by oratory that Mr. Gladstone rose to fame and power, as, indeed, by it most English statesmen have risen, save those to whom wealth and rank and family connections used to give a sort of presumptive claim to high office, like the Cavendishes and the Russells, the Bentincks and the Cecils. And for many years, during which Mr. Gladstone was suspected as a statesman because, while he had ceased to be a Tory, he had not fully become a Liberal, his eloquence was the main, one might almost say the sole, source of his influence

Oratory was a power in English politics even a century and a half ago, as the career of the elder Pitt shows. During the last seventy years, years which have seen the power of rank and family connections decline, it has, although less cultivated as a fine art, continued to be almost essential to the highest success, and it still brings a man quickly to the front, though it will not keep him there should he prove to want the other branches of statesmanlike capacity.

The permanent reputation of an orator depends upon two things, the witness of contemporaries to the impression produced upon them, and the written or printed record of his speeches. Few are the famous speakers who would be famous if they were tried by this latter test alone, and Mr. Gladstone was not one of them. It is only by a rare combination of gifts that one who speaks with so much force and brilliance as to charm his listeners is also able to deliver thoughts so valuable in words so choice that posterity will read them as literature. Some of the ancient orators did this; but we seldom know how far those of their speeches which have been preserved are the speeches which they actually delivered. Among moderns, a few French preachers, Edmund Burke, Macaulay, and Daniel Webster are perhaps the only speakers whose discourses have passed into classics and

find new generations of readers.[1]   Twenty years
hence Mr. Gladstone's will not be read, except, of
course, by historians.   Indeed, they ceased to be
read even in his lifetime.   They are too long,
too diffuse, too minute in their handling of details,
too elaborately qualified in their enunciation of
general principles.   They contain few epigrams
and few of those weighty thoughts put into telling
phrases which the Greeks called γνῶμαι.   The
style, in short, is not sufficiently rich or polished
to give an enduring interest to matter whose
practical importance has vanished.   The same
oblivion has overtaken all but a few of the
best speeches (or parts of speeches) of Grattan,
Sheridan, Pitt, Fox, Erskine, Canning, Plunket,
Brougham, Peel, Bright.   It may, indeed, be
said — and the examples of Burke and Macaulay
show that this is no paradox — that the speakers
whom posterity most enjoys are rarely those who
most affected the audiences that listened to them.[2]

If, on the other hand, Mr. Gladstone be judged
by the impression he made on his own time, his
place will be high in the front rank.   His speeches
were neither so concisely telling as Mr. Bright's
nor so finished in diction; but no other man

---

[1] Sermons belong to a somewhat different category, else I should have
to add the discourses of a few great preachers, such as Robert Hall, J. H.
Newman, Phillips Brooks.

[2] Though one of Macaulay's speeches (that against the exclusion of the
Master of the Rolls from the House of Commons) had the rare honour of
turning votes.

among his contemporaries — neither Lord Derby
nor Mr. Lowe, nor Lord Beaconsfield, nor Lord
Cairns, nor Bishop Wilberforce nor Bishop Magee
— taken all round, could be ranked beside him.
And he rose superior to Mr. Bright himself in
readiness, in variety of knowledge, in persuasive
ingenuity. Mr. Bright spoke seldom and required
time for preparation. Admirable in the breadth
and force with which he set forth his own position,
or denounced that of his adversaries, he was
not equally qualified for instructing nor equally
apt at persuading. Mr. Gladstone could both
instruct and persuade, could stimulate his friends
and demolish his opponents, and could do all
these things at an hour's notice, so vast and well
ordered was the arsenal of his mind. Pitt was
superb in an expository or argumentative speech,
but his stately periods lacked variety. Fox, incomparable in reply, was hesitating and confused
when he had to state his case in cold blood.
Mr. Gladstone showed as much fire in winding
up a debate as skill in opening it.

His oratory had, indeed, two faults. It wanted
concentration, and it wanted definition. There
were too many words, and the conclusion was
sometimes left vague because the arguments had
been too nicely balanced. I once heard Mr.
Cobden say: " I always listen to Mr. Gladstone
with pleasure and admiration, but I sometimes
have to ask myself, when he has sat down, ' What

after all was it that he meant, and what practical course does he recommend?'" These faults were balanced by conspicuous merits. There was a lively imagination, which enabled him to relieve even dull matter by pleasing figures, together with a large command of quotations and illustrations. There were powers of sarcasm, powers, however, which he rarely used, preferring the summer lightning of banter to the thunderbolts of invective. There was admirable lucidity and accuracy in exposition. There was art in the disposition and marshalling of his arguments, and finally — a gift now almost lost in England — there was a delightful variety and grace of appropriate gesture. But above and beyond everything else which enthralled the listener, there stood out four qualities. Two of them were merits of substance — inventiveness and elevation; two were merits of delivery — force in the manner, expressive modulation in the voice.

No one showed such swift resourcefulness in debate. His readiness, not only at catching a point, but at making the most of it on a moment's notice, was amazing. Some one would lean over the back of the bench he sat on and show a paper or whisper a sentence to him. Apprehending the bearings at a glance, he would take the bare fact and so shape and develop it, like a potter moulding a bowl on the wheel out of a lump of clay, that it grew into a cogent

argument or a happy illustration under the eye of
the audience, and seemed all the more telling
because it had not been originally a part of his
case. Even in the last three years of his parliamentary life, when his sight had so failed that he
read nothing, printed or written, except what it
was absolutely necessary to read, and when his
deafness had so increased that he did not hear
half of what was said in debate, it was sufficient
for a colleague to say into the better ear a few
words explaining how the matter at issue stood,
and he would rise to his feet and extemporise
a long and ingenious argument, or retreat with
dexterous grace from a position which the course
of the discussion or the private warning of the
Whips had shown to be untenable. Never was
he seen at a loss either to meet a new point
raised by an adversary or to make the best of
an unexpected incident. Sometimes he would
amuse himself by drawing a cheer or a contradiction from his opponents, and would then suddenly
turn round and use this hasty expression of their
opinion as the basis for a fresh argument of his
own. Loving conflict, he loved debate, and,
so far from being confused or worried by the
strain conflict put upon him, his physical health
was strengthened and his faculties were roused
to higher efficiency by having to prepare and
deliver a great speech. He had the rare faculty
of thinking ahead while he was speaking, and

could, while pouring forth a stream of glittering sentences, be at the same time (as one saw by watching his eye) composing an argument to be delivered five or ten minutes later. Once, at a very critical moment, when he was defending a great measure against the amendment — moved by a nominal supporter of his own — which proved fatal to it, a friend suddenly reminded him of an incident in the career of the mover which might be effectively used against him. When Mr. Gladstone sat down after delivering an impassioned speech, in the course of which he had several times approached and then sheered off from the incident, he turned round to the friend and said, " I was thinking all the time I was speaking whether I could properly use against —— what you told me, but concluded, on the whole, that it would be too hard on him."

The weakness of his eloquence sprang from its supersubtlety and superabundance. He was prone to fine distinctions. He multiplied arguments when it would have been better to rely upon two or three of the strongest. And he was sometimes so intent on refuting the particular adversaries opposed to him, and persuading the particular audience before him, that he forgot to address his reasonings to the public beyond the House, and make them equally applicable and equally convincing to the readers of next morning.

As dignity is one of the rarest qualities in

literature, so elevation is one of the rarest in oratory. It is a quality easier to feel than to analyse. One may call it a power of ennobling ordinary things by showing their relation to great things, by pouring high emotions round them, by bringing the worthier motives of human conduct to bear upon them, by touching them with the light of poetry. Ambitious writers and speakers strain after effects of this kind; but they are effects which study and straining cannot ensure. Vainly do most men flap their wings in the effort to soar; if they succeed in rising from the ground it is because some unusually strong burst of feeling makes them for the moment better than themselves. In Mr. Gladstone the capacity for feeling was at all times so strong, and the susceptibility of the imagination so keen, that he soared without effort. His vision seemed to take in the whole landscape. The points actually in question might be small, but the principles involved were to him far-reaching. The contests of to-day were ennobled by the effect they might have in a still distant future. There are rhetoricians skilful in playing by words and manner on every chord of human nature, rhetoricians who move you, and may even carry you away for the moment, but whose sincerity is doubted, because the sense of spontaneity is lacking. Mr. Gladstone was not of these. He never seemed to be

2 F

forcing an effect or assuming a sentiment. To listen to him was to feel convinced of his own conviction and to be warmed by the warmth with which he expressed it. Nor was this due to the perfection of his rhetorical art. He really did feel what he expressed. Sometimes, of course, like all statesmen, he had to maintain a cause whose weakness he perceived, as, for instance, when it became necessary to defend the blunder of a colleague, or a decision reached by some Cabinet compromise which his own judgment disapproved. But even in such cases he did not simulate feeling, but reserved his earnestness for those parts of the case on which it could be honestly expended. As this was generally true of the imaginative and emotional side of his eloquence, so was it especially true of his unequalled power of lifting a subject from the level on which other speakers had treated it into the purer air of permanent principle, perhaps even of moral sublimity.

The dignity and spontaneity which marked the substance of his speeches was no less conspicuous in their delivery. Nothing could be more easy and graceful than his manner on ordinary occasions, nothing more grave and stately than it became when he was making a ceremonial reference to some public event or bestowing a meed of praise on the departed. His expository discourses, such as those with which he introduced

a complicated bill or unfolded a financial statement, were models of their kind, not only for
lucidity, but for the pleasant smoothness, never
lapsing into monotony, with which the stream
of speech flowed from his lips. The task was
performed so well that people thought it an
easy task till they saw how inferior were the
performances of two subsequent chancellors of
the exchequer so able in their respective
ways as Sir Stafford Northcote and Mr. Lowe.
But when an occasion arrived which quickened
men's pulses in the House of Commons, a place
where feeling rises as suddenly as do the waves
of a Highland loch when a squall comes rushing down the glen, the vehemence of his feeling
found expression in the fire of his eye and the
resistless strength of his words. His utterance
did not grow swifter, nor did the key of his
voice rise, as passion raises and sharpens the
voice in most men. But the measured force with
which every sentence was launched, like a shell
hurtling through the air, the concentrated intensity of his look, as he defied antagonists in
front and swept his glance over the ranks of his
supporters around and behind him, had a startling and thrilling power which no other Englishman could exert, and which no Englishman had
exerted since the days of Pitt and Fox. The
whole proud, bold, ardent nature of the man
seemed to flash out, and one almost forgot what

the lips said in admiration of the towering personality.

People who read next day the report in the newspapers of a speech delivered on such an occasion could not comprehend the impression it had made on the listeners. "What was there in it so to stir you?" they asked. They had not seen the glance and the gestures; they had not heard the vibrating voice rise to an organ peal of triumph or sink to a whisper of entreaty. Mr. Gladstone's voice was naturally rich and resonant. It was a fine singing voice, and a pleasant voice to listen to in conversation, not the less pleasant for having a slight trace of Liverpool accent clinging to it. But what struck one in listening to his speeches was not so much the quality of the vocal chords as the skill with which they were managed. He had a gift of sympathetic expression, of throwing his feeling into his voice, and using its modulations to accompany and convey every shade of meaning, like that which a great composer exerts when he puts music to a poem, or a great executant when he renders at once the composer's and the poet's thought. And just as accomplished singers or violinists enjoy the practice of their art, so he rejoiced, perhaps unconsciously, yet intensely, in putting forth this faculty of expression; as appeared, indeed, from the fact that whenever his voice failed him (which sometimes befell in later years) his words came less easily, and even the chariot of his argument seemed to drive heavily. That the voice should so seldom have failed was wonderful. When he had passed his seventy-fifth year, it became sensibly inferior in volume and depth of tone. But its variety and delicacy remained. In April 1886, he being then seventy-seven, it held out during a speech of nearly four hours in length. In February 1890 it enabled him to deliver with extraordinary effect an eminently solemn and pathetic appeal. In March 1894 those who listened to it the last time it was heard in Parliament — they were comparatively few, for the secret of his impending resignation had been well kept — recognised in it all the old charm. The most striking instance I recall of the power it could exert is to be found in a speech made in 1883, during one of the tiresome debates occasioned by the refusal of the Opposition and of some timorous Liberals to allow Mr. Bradlaugh to be sworn as a member of the House of Commons. This speech produced on those who heard it an impression which its perusal to-day fails to explain. That impression was chiefly due to the grave and reverent tone in which he delivered some sentences stating the view that it is not our belief in the bare existence of a Deity, but the realising of him as being a Providence ruling the world, that has moral value and significance

for us. And it was due in particular to the solemn
dignity with which he declaimed six lines of
Lucretius, setting forth the Epicurean view that
the gods do not concern themselves with human
affairs. There were perhaps not twenty men
in the House of Commons who could follow the
sense of the lines so as to appreciate their bearing
on his argument. But these sonorous hexameters
— hexameters that seemed to have lived on
through nineteen centuries to find their application from the lips of an orator to-day — the
sense of remoteness in the strange language and
the far-off heathen origin, the deep and moving
note in the speaker's voice, thrilled the imagination of the audience and held it spellbound, lifting
for a moment the whole subject of debate into a
region far above party conflicts. Spoken by any
one else, the passage culminating in these Lucretian
lines might have produced little effect. It was the
voice and manner, above all the voice, with its mar-
vellous modulations, that made the speech majestic.

Yet one must not forget to add that with him,
as with some other famous statesmen, the impression made by a speech was in a measure due
to the admiring curiosity and wonder which his
personality inspired. He was so much the most
interesting human being in the House of Commons that, when he withdrew, many members
said that the place had lost half its attraction for
them, and that the chamber looked empty because

he was not in it. Plenty of able men remained.
But even the ablest seemed ordinary when compared with the figure that had vanished, a figure
in whom were combined, as in no other man of
his time, an unrivalled experience, an extraordinary
activity and versatility of intellect, a fervid imagination, and an indomitable will.

Though Mr. Gladstone's oratory was a main
source of his power, both in Parliament and over
the people, the effort of detractors to represent
him as a mere rhetorician will seem absurd to
the historian who reviews his whole career. The
rhetorician adorns and popularises the ideas
which have originated with others; he advocates
policies which others have devised; he follows
and expresses the sentiments which already prevail in his party. Mr. Gladstone was himself a
source of new ideas and new policies; he evoked
new sentiments or turned old sentiments into
new channels. Neither was he, as some alleged,
primarily a destroyer. His conservative instincts were strong; he cherished ancient custom.
When it became necessary to clear away an
institution he sought to put something else in
its place. He was a constructive statesman not
less conspicuously than were Pitt, Canning, and
Peel. Whether he was a philosophic statesman,
basing his action on large views obtained by
thought and study, philosophic in the sense in
which we apply the epithet to Pericles, Machia-

velli, Turgot, Burke, Jefferson, Hamilton, Stein
— if one class can be made to include persons
otherwise so dissimilar — may perhaps be doubted.
There are few instances in history of men who
have been great thinkers and also great legislators or administrators, because the two kinds of
capacity almost exclude one another.   As experts
declare that a man who should try to operate on
the Stock Exchange in reliance upon a profound
knowledge of the inner springs of European
politics and the financial resources of the great
States, would ruin himself before his perfectly
correct calculations had time to come true, so a
practical statesman, though he cannot know too
much, or look too far ahead, must beware of trust-
ing his own forecasts, must remember that he
has to deal with the next few months or years,
and to persuade persons who cannot be expected
to share or even to understand his views of the
future.   The habit of meditating on underlying
truths, the tendency to play the long game, are
almost certain to spoil a man for dealing effectively
with the present.   He will not be a sufficiently
vigilant observer; he will be out of sympathy
with the notions of the average man; his arguments will go over the head of his audience.   No
English prime minister has looked at politics
with the eye of a philosopher.   But Mr. Gladstone, if hardly to be called a thinker, showed
higher constructive power than any one else

has done since Peel. Were the memory of his oratorical triumphs to pass completely away, he would deserve to be remembered in respect of the mark he left upon the British statute-book and of the changes he wrought both in the constitution of his country and in her European policy.

Three groups of measures stand out as monuments of his skill and energy. The first of these three includes the financial reforms embodied in a series of fourteen budgets between the years 1853 and 1882, the most famous of which were the budgets of 1853 and 1860. In the former he continued the work begun by Peel by reducing and simplifying the customs duties. Deficiencies in revenue were supplied by the enactment of less oppressive imposts, and particularly by re-settling the income-tax, and by the introduction of a succession duty on real estate. The preparation and passing of this very technical and intricate Succession Duty Act was a most laborious enterprise, of which Mr. Gladstone used to speak as the severest mental strain he had ever undergone:

Καρτίστην δὴ τήν γε μάχην φάτο δύμεναι ἀνδρῶν.[1]

The budget of 1860, among other changes, abolished the paper duty, a boon to the press which was resisted by the House of Lords.

[1] "He said that this was the hardest battle of men he had entered" (*Iliad* vi. 185).

They threw out the measure, but in the following year Mr. Gladstone forced them to submit.
His achievements in the field of finance equal, if
they do not surpass, those of Peel, and are not
tarnished, as in the case of Pitt, by the recollection of a burden of debts incurred. To no
minister can be ascribed so large a share in
promoting the commercial and industrial prosperity of modern England, and in the reduction
of her national debt to the figure at which it
stood when it began to rise again in 1900.

The second group includes the parliamentary
reform bills of 1866 and 1884 and the Redistribution Bill of 1885. The first of these was defeated
in the House of Commons, but it led to the
passing next year, by Mr. Disraeli, of a more
sweeping measure. Taken together, these statutes
have turned Britain into a democratic country,
changing the character of her government almost
as profoundly as did the Reform Act of 1832.

The third group consists of a series of Irish
measures, beginning with the Church Disestablishment Act of 1869, and including the Land
Act of 1870, the University Education Bill of
1873 (defeated in the House of Commons), the
Land Act of 1881, and the Home Rule bills of
1886 and 1893. All these were in a special
manner Mr. Gladstone's handiwork, prepared as
well as brought in and advocated by him. All
were highly complicated, and of one, the Land

Act of 1881, which it took three months to carry
through the House of Commons, it was said
that so great was its intricacy that only three
men understood it — Mr. Gladstone himself, his
Attorney-General for Ireland, and Mr. T. M.
Healy. In preparing a bill no man could be
more painstaking. He settled and laid down the
principles himself; and when he came to work
them out with the draughtsman and the officials
who had special knowledge of the subject, he
insisted on knowing what their effect would be
in every particular. Indeed, he loved work for
its own sake, in this respect unlike Mr. Bright,
who once said to me with a smile, when asked
as to his methods of working, that he had never
done any work all his life. The value of this
mastery of details was seen when a bill came to
be debated in Committee. It was impossible to
catch Mr. Gladstone tripping on a point of fact,
or unprepared with a reply to the arguments
of an opponent. He seemed to revel in the
toil of mastering a tangle of technical details.

It is long since England, in this respect not
favoured by her parliamentary system, has produced a great foreign minister, nor has that title
been claimed for Mr. Gladstone. But he showed
on several occasions both his independence of
tradition and his faith in broad principles as fit
to be applied in international relations; and his
action in that field, though felt only at intervals,

has left abiding results in European history.   In
1851, he being then still a Tory, his pamphlet
denouncing the cruelties of the Bourbon government of Naples, and the sympathy he subsequently avowed with the national movement in
Italy, gave that movement a new standing in
Europe by powerfully recommending it to English
opinion. In 1870 the prompt action of his ministry
in arranging a treaty for the neutrality of Belgium
on the outbreak of the war between France and
Germany, averted the risk that Belgium might
be drawn into the strife.   In 1871, by concluding
the treaty of Washington, which provided for the
settlement by arbitration of the *Alabama* claims,
he not only set a precedent full of promise for
the future, but delivered England from what
would have been, in case of her being at war with
any European power, a danger fatal to her ocean
commerce.   And, in 1876, his onslaught upon the
Turks, after the Bulgarian massacres, roused an
intense feeling in England, turning the current of
opinion so decisively that Disraeli's ministry were
forced to leave the Sultan to his fate, and thus
became a cause of the ultimate deliverance of
Bulgaria, Eastern Rumelia, Bosnia, and Thessaly
from Mussulman tyranny.   Few English statesmen have equally earned the gratitude of the
oppressed.

Nothing lay nearer to his heart than the protection of the Christians of the East.   His sense of

personal duty to them was partly due to the feeling that the Crimean War had prolonged the rule of the Turk, and had thus imposed a special responsibility on Britain, and on the members of Lord Aberdeen's cabinet which drifted into that war. Twenty years after the agitation of 1876, and when he had finally retired from Parliament and political life, the massacres perpetrated by the Sultan on his Armenian subjects brought him once more into the field, and his last speech in public (delivered at Liverpool in the autumn of 1896) was a powerful argument in favour of British intervention to rescue the Eastern Christians. In the following spring he followed this up by a pamphlet on behalf of the freedom of Crete. In neither of these two cases did success crown his efforts, for the government, commanding a large majority in Parliament, pursued the course upon which it had already entered. Poignant regrets were expressed that Mr. Gladstone was no longer able to take effective action in the cause of humanity; yet it was a consolation to be assured that age and infirmity had not dulled his sympathies with that cause.

That he was right in 1876-78 in the view he took of the line of conduct England should adopt towards the Turks has been now virtually admitted even by his opponents. That he was also right in 1896, when urging action to protect the Eastern Christians, will probably be admitted ten years hence, when the facts of the case and the nature of the opportunity that existed for taking prompt action without the risk of a European war have become better known.   In both cases it was not merely religious sympathy, but also a far-sighted view of policy that governed his judgment.   He held that the faults of Turkish rule are incurable, and that the Powers of Western and Central Europe ought to aim at protecting the subject nationalities and by degrees extending self-government to them, so that they may grow into states, and in time be able to restore prosperity to regions ruined by long misgovernment, while constituting an effective barrier to the advance of Russia.   The jealousies of the Powers throw obstacles in the way of this policy, but it is a safe policy for England, and offers the best hope for the peoples of the East.

The facts just noted prove that he possessed and exerted a capacity for initiative in foreign as well as in domestic affairs.   In the Neapolitan case, in the *Alabama* case, in the Bulgarian case, he acted from his own convictions, with no previous suggestion of encouragement from his party; and in the last mentioned instance he took a course which did not at the moment promise any political gain, and which seemed to the English political world so novel and even startling that no ordinary statesman would have ventured on it.

His courage was indeed one of the most striking parts of the man.[1] It was not the rashness of an impetuous nature, for, impetuous as he was when stirred by some sudden excitement, he showed an Ulyssean caution whenever he took a deliberate survey of the conditions that surrounded him. It was the proud self-confidence of a strong character, which was willing to risk fame and fortune in pursuing a course it had once resolved upon; a character which had faith in its own conclusions, and in the success of a cause consecrated by principle; a character which obstacles did not affright, but rather roused to a higher combative energy. Few English statesmen have done anything so bold as was Mr. Gladstone's declaration for Irish Home Rule in 1886. He took not only his political power but the fame and credit of his whole past life in his hand when he set out on this new journey at seventy-seven years of age; for it was quite possible that the great bulk of his party might refuse to follow him, and he be left exposed to derision as the chief of an insignificant group. As it happened, the bulk of the party did follow him, though many of the most influential refused to do so.

---

[1] His physical courage was no less evident than his moral. For two or three years his life was threatened, and policemen were told off to guard him wherever he went. He disliked this protection so much (though the Home Office thought it necessary) that he used to escape from the House of Commons by a little frequented exit, give the policemen the slip, and stroll home to his residence along the Thames Embankment in the small hours of the morning. Fear was not in his nature.

But neither he nor any one else could have foretold this when his intentions were first announced.

We may now, before passing away from the
public side of Mr. Gladstone's career, return for
a moment to the opposite views of his character which were indicated some pages back.
He was accused of sophistry, of unwisdom, of
want of patriotism, of lust for power. Though it
is difficult to sift these charges without discussing
the conduct which gave rise to them, a task impossible here, each of them must be briefly examined.

The first charge is the most plausible. His ingenuity in discovering arguments and stating fine
verbal distinctions, his subtlety in discriminating
between views or courses apparently similar, were
excessive, and invited misconstruction. He had a
tendency to persuade himself, quite unconsciously,
that the course he desired to take was a course
which the public interest required. His acuteness
soon found reasons for that course; the warmth
of his emotions enforced the reasons. It was a
dangerous tendency, but it does not impeach his
honesty of purpose, the influence which his predilections unconsciously exerted upon his judgment
appeared also in his theological and literary
inquiries. I can recall no instance in which he
wilfully misstated a fact, or simulated a feeling, or
used an argument which he knew to be unsound.
He did not, as does the sophist, attempt "to make
the worse appear the better reason."

His wisdom will be differently judged by those who condemn or approve the chief acts of his policy. But it deserves to be noted that all the legislation he passed, even the measures which, like the Irish Church Disestablishment Bill, exposed him to angry attacks at the time, have now been approved by the all but unanimous judgment of Englishmen.[1] The same may be said of two acts which brought much invective upon him — his settlement of the *Alabama* claims, one of the wisest strokes of foreign policy ever accomplished by a British minister, and his protest against a support of the Turks in and after 1876. I pass by Irish Home Rule, because the wisdom of the course he took must be tested by results that are yet unborn, as I pass by his Egyptian policy in 1882-85, because it cannot be fairly judged till the facts have been fully made public. He may be open to blame for his participation in the Crimean War, for his mistaken view of the American Civil War, for his neglect of the Transvaal question when he took office in 1880, and for his omission during his earlier career to recognise the gravity of Irish disaffection and to study its causes. I have heard him lament that he had not twenty years earlier given the same attention to that abiding source of

---

[1] The late Protestant Episcopal Primate of Ireland said that Disestablishment had proved a blessing to his Church; and this would seem to be now the general view of Irish Protestants.

the difficulties of England which he gave from
1866 onwards. If in these instances he erred, it
must be remembered that he erred in company
with nine-tenths of British statesmen in both
political parties.

Their admiration did not prevent his friends
from noting tendencies which sometimes led him
to miscalculate the forces he had to deal with.
Being, like the younger Pitt, extremely sanguine,
he was prone to underrate difficulties. Hopeful-
ness is a splendid quality. It is both the child and
the parent of faith. Without it neither Mr. Pitt
nor Mr. Gladstone could have done what they did.
But it disposes its possessor to not sufficiently allow
for the dulness or the prejudice of others. So too
the intensity of Mr. Gladstone's own feeling made
him fail to realise how many of his fellow-country-
men did not know of, or were not shocked by, acts
of cruelty and injustice which had roused his indignation. If his hatred of ostentation suffered him to
perceive that a nation, however well assured of the
reality of its power and influence in the world, may
also desire that this power and influence should be
asserted and proclaimed to other nations, he refused
to humour that desire. He had a contempt for
what is called " playing to the gallery," with a deep
sense of the danger of stimulating the passions
which lead to aggression and war. To national
honour, as he conceived it, national righteousness
was vital. His spirit was that of Lowell's lines —

I love my country so as only they
Who love a mother fit to die for may.
I love her old renown, her ancient fame :
What better proof than that I loathe her shame?

It was this attitude that brought on him the charge of wanting patriotism, a charge first, I think, insinuated at the time of the *Alabama* arbitration, renewed when in 1876 he was accused of befriending Russia and neglecting " British interests," and sedulously repeated thereafter, although in those two instances the result had proved him right. There was this much to give a kind of colour to the charge, that he had scrupulously, perhaps too scrupulously, refrained from extolling the material power of England, preferring to insist upon her responsibilities; that he was known to regret the constant increase of naval and military expenditure, and that he had several times taken a course which honour and prudence seemed to him to recommend, but which had offended the patriots of the music-halls. But it was an unjust charge, for no man had a warmer pride in England, a higher sense of her greatness and her mission.

Was he too fond of power? Like other strong men, he enjoyed it.[1] That to secure it he ever either adopted or renounced an opinion,

[1] His abdication of leadership in 1875 was meant to be final, though when the urgency of Eastern affairs had drawn him back into strife, the old ardour revived, and he resumed the place of Prime Minister in 1880. It has been often said that he would have done better to retire from public life in 1880, or in 1885, yet the most striking proofs both of his courage and of his physical energy were given in the latest part of his career.

those who understood and watched the workings
of his mind could not believe.   He was not only
too conscientious, but too proud to forego any of
his convictions, and there were not a few occasions
when he took a course which considerations of
personal interest would have forbidden.   He did
not love office, feeling himself happier without its
cares, and when he accepted it did so, I think, in
the belief that there was work to be done which
it was laid upon him individually to do.   His
changes sprang naturally from the development of
his own ideas or (as in the case of his Irish policy)
from the teaching of facts.   He sometimes so far
yielded to his colleagues as to sanction steps which
he thought not the best, and may in this have
sometimes erred; yet compromises are unavoidable, for no Cabinet could be kept together if its
members did not now and then, in matters not
essential, yield to one another.   When all the facts
of his life come to be known, instances may be disclosed in which he was the victim of his own casuistry or of his deference to Peel's maxim that a
minister should not avow a change of view until
the time has come to give effect to it.   But it will
also be made clear that he strove to obey his conscience, that he acted with an ever-present sense
of his responsibility to the Almighty, and that he
was animated by an unselfish enthusiasm for
humanity, enlightenment, and freedom.

Whether he was a good judge of men was a

question much discussed among his friends. With all his astuteness, he was in some ways curiously simple; with all his caution, he was by nature unsuspicious, disposed to treat all men as honest till they gave him strong reasons for thinking otherwise. Those who professed sympathy with his views and aims sometimes succeeded in inspiring more confidence than they deserved. But where this perturbing influence was absent he showed plenty of insight, and would pass shrewd judgments on the politicians around him, permitting neither their behaviour towards himself nor his opinion of their moral character to affect his estimate of their talents. In making appointments in the Civil Service, or in the Established Church, he rose to a far higher standard of public duty than Palmerston or Disraeli had reached or cared to reach, taking great pains to find the fittest men, and giving little weight to political considerations.[1]

His public demeanour, and especially his excitability and vehemence of speech, made people attribute to him an overbearing disposition and an irritable temper. In private one did not find these faults. Masterful he certainly was, both in speech and in action. His ardent manner, the intensity of his look, the dialectical vigour with which he pressed an argument, were

[1] For instance, he recommended Dr. Stubbs for a bishopric and Sir John Holker for a lord justiceship, knowing both of them to be Tories.

apt to awe people who knew him but slightly, and make them abandon resistance. A gifted though somewhat erratic politician of long bygone days told me how he once fared when he had risen in the House of Commons to censure some act of his leader. " I had not gone on three minutes when Gladstone turned round and gazed at me so that I had to sit down in the middle of a sentence. I could not help it. There was no standing his eye." But he neither meant nor wished to beat down his opponents by mere authority. One who knew him as few people did observed to me, " When you are arguing with Mr. Gladstone, you must never let him think he has convinced you unless you are really convinced. Persist in repeating your view, and if you are unable to cope with him in skill of fence, say bluntly that for all his ingenuity and authority you think he is wrong, and you retain your own opinion. If he respects you as a man who knows something of the subject, he will be impressed by your opinion, and it will afterwards have due weight with him." In his own cabinet he was willing to listen patiently to everybody's views, and, indeed, in the judgment of some of his colleagues, was not, at least in his later years, sufficiently strenuous in asserting and holding to his own. It is no secret that some of the most important decisions of the ministry of 1880-85 were taken against his judgment, though, when they had been adopted, he was, of course, bound to defend them in Parliament as if they had received his individual approval. Nor, though tenacious, did he bear malice against those who had baffled him. He would exert his full force to get his own way, but if he could not get it, accepted the position with good temper.[1] He was too proud to be vindictive, too completely master of himself to be betrayed into angry words. Impatient he might sometimes be under a nervous strain, but never rude or rough. It was less easy to determine whether he was overmindful of injuries, but those who had watched him most closely held that mere opposition or even insult did not leave a permanent sting, and that the only thing he could not forget or forgive was faithlessness. Himself a model of loyalty to his colleagues, he followed his favourite poet in consigning the *traditori* to the lowest pit, although, like all statesmen, he often found himself obliged to work with those whom he distrusted.

He was less sensitive than Peel, as appeared from his attitude toward his two chief opponents. Disraeli's attacks did not seem to gall him, perhaps because, although he recognised the ability and admired the courage of his adversary,

---

[1] His respect and regard for Mr. Bright were entirely unaffected by the fact that Mr. Bright's opposition to the Home Rule Bill of 1886 had been the chief cause of its defeat.

he did not respect Disraeli's character, remembering his behaviour to Peel, and thinking him habitually untruthful.   Yet he never attacked Disraeli personally.   There was another of his opponents of whom he entertained a specially unfavourable opinion, but no one could have told from his speeches what that opinion was. Against Lord Salisbury, his chief antagonist from 1881 onwards, he showed no resentment, though Lord Salisbury had more than once spoken discourteously of him.   In 1890 he remarked to me *apropos* of some attack, "I have never felt angry at what Salisbury has said about me.   His mother was very kind to me when I was quite a young man, and I remember Salisbury as a little fellow in a red frock rolling about on the ottoman."

That his temper was naturally hot, no one who looked at him could doubt.   But he had it in such tight control, and it was so free from anything acrid or malignant, that it had become a good temper, worthy of a fine nature.   However vehement his expressions, they did not wound or humiliate, and those younger men who had to deal with him were not afraid of a sharp answer or an impatient repulse.   He was cast in too large a mould to have the pettiness of ruffled vanity or to abuse his predominance by treating any one as an inferior.   His manners were the manners of the old time, easy but stately.   Like his oratory, they were in what Matthew Arnold used to call the grand style; and the contrast in this respect between him and some of those who crossed swords with him in literary or theological controversy was apparent. His intellectual generosity was a part of the same largeness of nature. He cordially acknowledged his indebtedness to those who helped him in any piece of work, received their suggestions candidly, even when opposed to his own preconceived notions, did not hesitate to confess a mistake. Those who know the abundance of their resources, and have conquered fame, can doubtless afford to be generous. Julius Cæsar was, and George Washington, and so, in a different sphere, were Isaac Newton and Charles Darwin. But the instances to the contrary are so numerous that one may say of magnanimity that it is among the rarest as well as the finest ornaments of character.

The essential dignity of Mr. Gladstone's nature was never better seen than during the last few years of his life, after he had finally retired (in 1894) from public life. He indulged in no vain regrets, nor was there any foundation for the rumours, so often circulated, that he thought of re-entering the arena of strife. He spoke with no bitterness of those who had opposed, and sometimes foiled, him in the past. He gave vent to no criticisms of those who

from time to time filled the place that had been
his in the government of the country or the
leadership of his party.   Although his opinion
on current questions was frequently solicited, he
scarcely ever allowed it to be known, lest it
should embarrass his successors in the leadership
of the party, and never himself addressed the
nation, except (as already mentioned) on behalf
of what he deemed a sacred cause, altogether
above party — the discharge by Britain of her
duty to the victims of the Turk.   As soon as an
operation for cataract had enabled him to resume
his habit of working for seven hours a day, he
devoted himself with his old ardour to the preparation of an edition of Bishop Butler's works,
resumed his multifarious reading, planned (as he
told me in 1896) a treatise on the Olympian religion, and filled up the interstices of his working-
time with studies on Homer which he had been
previously unable to complete.   No trace of the
moroseness of old age appeared in his manners or
his conversation, nor did he, though profoundly
grieved at some of the events which he witnessed,
and owning himself disappointed at the slow advance made by a cause dear to him, appear less
hopeful than in earlier days of the general progress of the world, or less confident in the beneficent power of freedom to promote the happiness
of his country.   The stately simplicity which had
always charmed those who saw him in private,

seemed more beautiful than ever in this quiet evening of a long and sultry day. His intellectual powers were unimpaired, his thirst for knowledge undiminished. But a placid stillness had fallen upon him and his household; and in seeing the tide of his life begin slowly to ebb, one thought of the lines of his illustrious contemporary and friend : —

> Such a tide as moving seems asleep,
> Too full for sound or foam,
> When that which drew from out the boundless deep
> Turns again home.

Adding to his grace of manner a memory of extraordinary strength and quickness and an amazing vivacity and variety of mental force, any one can understand how fascinating Mr. Gladstone was in society. He enjoyed it to the last, talking as earnestly and joyously at eighty-seven as he had done at twenty on every topic that came up, and exerting himself with equal zest whether his interlocutor was an archbishop or a youthful curate. Though his party used to think that he overvalued the political influence of the great families, allotting them rather more than their share of honours and appointments, no one was personally more free from that taint of snobbishness which is frequently charged upon Englishmen. He gave the best he had to everybody alike, paying to men of learning and letters a respect which in England they seldom receive from the magnates who lead society. And although he was scrupulously observant of the rules of precedence and conventions of social life, it was easy to see that neither rank nor wealth had that importance in his eyes which the latter nowadays commands. Dispensing titles and decorations with a liberal hand, his pride always refused such so-called honours for himself.

It was often said of him that he lacked humour; but this was only so far true that he was apt to throw into small matters more force and moral earnestness than were needed, and to honour with a refutation opponents whom a little light sarcasm would have better reduced to their insignificance.[1] In private he was wont both to tell and to enjoy good stories; while in Parliament, though his tone was generally earnest, he could display such effective powers of banter and ridicule as to make people wonder why they were so rarely put forth. Much of what passes in London for humour is mere cynicism, and he hated cynicism so

[1] Usually overanxious to vindicate his own consistency, he showed on one occasion a capacity for recognising the humorous side of a position into which he had been brought. In a debate which arose in 1891 frequent references had been made to a former speech in which he had pronounced a highly-coloured panegyric upon the Church of England in Wales, the disestablishment of which he had subsequently become willing to support. He replied, " Many references have been made to a former speech of mine on this subject, and I am not prepared to deny that in that speech, when closely scrutinised, there may appear to be present some element of exaggeration." The House dissolved in laughter, and no further reference was made to the old speech.

heartily as to dislike even humour when it had
a cynical flavour. Wit he enjoyed, but did not
produce. The turn of his mind was not to
brevity, point, and condensation. He sometimes
struck off a telling phrase, but seldom polished
an epigram. His conversation was luminous
rather than sparkling; you were interested and
instructed while you listened, but it was not
so much the phrases as the general effect that
dwelt in your memory. An acute observer once
said to me that Mr. Gladstone showed in argument a knack of hitting the nail not quite on
the head. The criticism was so far just that
he was less certain to go straight to the vital
issue in a controversy than one expected from
his force and keenness.

After the death of Thomas Carlyle he was
probably the best talker in London, and a talker
in one respect more agreeable than either Carlyle
or Macaulay, inasmuch as he was no less ready
to listen than to speak, and never wearied the
dinner-table by a monologue. His simplicity,
his spontaneity, his geniality and courtesy, as well
as the fund of knowledge and of personal recollections at his command, made him so popular
in society that his opponents used to say it was
dangerous to meet him, because one might be
forced to leave off hating him. He was, perhaps, too prone to go on talking upon the
subject which filled his mind at the moment;

nor was it easy to divert his attention to something else which others might deem more important.[1] Those who stayed with him in the same country house sometimes complained that the perpetual display of force and eagerness tired them, as one tires of watching the rush of Niagara. His guests, however, did not feel this, for his own home life was quiet and smooth. He read and wrote a good many hours daily, but never sat up late, almost always slept soundly, never seemed oppressed or driven to strain his strength. With all his impetuosity, he was regular, systematic, and deliberate in his habits and ways of doing business. A swift reader and a surprisingly swift writer, he was always occupied, and was skilful in using even the scraps and fragments of his time. No pressure of work made him fussy, nor could any one remember to have seen him in a hurry.

The best proof of his swiftness, industry, and skill in economising time is supplied by the quantity of his literary work, which, considering the abstruse nature of the subjects to which much of it is related, would have been creditable to the diligence of a German professor

---

[1] His Oxford contemporary and friend, the late Mr. Milnes Gaskell, told me that when Mr. Gladstone was undergoing his *viva voce* examination for his degree, the examiner, satisfied with the candidate's answers on a particular matter, said, "And now, Mr. Gladstone, we will leave that part of the subject." "No," replied the examinee, "we will, if you please, not leave it yet." Whereupon he proceeded to pour forth a further flood of knowledge and disquisition.

sitting alone in his study. The merits of the work have been disputed. Mankind are slow to credit the same person with eminence in various fields. When they read the prose of a great poet, they try it by severer tests than would be applied to other writers. When a painter has won credit by his landscapes or his cattle pieces, he is seldom encouraged to venture into other lines. So Mr. Gladstone's reputation as an orator stood in his own light when he appeared as an author. He was read by thousands who would not have looked at the article or book had it borne some other name; but he was judged by the standard, not of his finest printed speeches, for his speeches were seldom models of composition, but rather by the impression which his finest speeches made on those who heard them. Since his warmest admirers could not claim for him as a writer of prose any such pre-eminence as belonged to him as a speaker, it followed that his written work was not duly appreciated. Had he been a writer and nothing else, he would have been eminent and powerful by his pen.

He might, however, have failed to secure a place in the front rank. His style was forcible, copious, rich with various knowledge, warm with the ardour of his temperament. But it suffered from an inborn tendency to exuberance which the long practice of oratory had confirmed. It was diffuse,

apt to pursue a topic into details, when these might
have been left to the reader's own reflection. It
was redundant, employing more words than were
needed to convey the substance. It was un-
chastened, indulging too freely in tropes and
metaphors, in quotations and adapted phrases
even when the quotation added nothing to the
sense but was suggested merely by some association in his own mind. Thus it seldom reached
a high level of purity and grace, and though one
might excuse the faults as natural to the work
of a swift and busy man, they were sufficient
to reduce the pleasure to be derived from the
form and dress of his thoughts. Nevertheless
there are not a few passages of rare merit,
both in the books and in the articles, among
which may be cited (not as exceptionally good,
but as typical of his strong points) the striking picture of his own youthful feeling toward
the Church of England contained in the *Chapter
of Autobiography*, and the refined criticism of
Robert Elsmere, published in 1888. Almost
the last thing he wrote, a pamphlet on the
Greek and Cretan question, published in the
spring of 1897, has the force and cogency of his
best days. Two things were never wanting to
him: vigour of expression and an admirable
command of appropriate words.

His writings fall into three classes: political,
theological, and literary — the last chiefly con-

sisting of his books and articles upon Homer
and the Homeric question. All the political
writings, except the books on *The State in its
Relations to the Church* and *Church Principles
considered in their Results*, belong to the class
of occasional literature, being pamphlets or
articles produced with a view to some current crisis or controversy. They are valuable
chiefly as proceeding from one who bore a
leading part in the affairs they relate to, and
as embodying vividly the opinions and aspirations of the moment, less frequently in respect
of permanent lessons of political wisdom, such
as one finds in Machiavelli or Tocqueville or
Edmund Burke. Like Pitt and Peel, Mr. Gladstone had a mind which, whatever its original
tendencies, had come to be rather practical than
meditative. He was fond of generalisations and
principles, but they were always directly related
to the questions that came before him in actual
politics; and the number of weighty maxims or
illuminative suggestions to be found in his writings and speeches is small in proportion to the
sustained vigour they display. Even Disraeli,
though his views were often fanciful and his
epigrams often forced, gives us more frequently
a brilliant (if only half true) historical *aperçu*, or
throws a flash of light into some corner of human
character. Of the theological essays, which are
mainly apologetic and concerned with the authen-

ticity and authority of Scripture, it is enough to say that they were the work of an accomplished amateur, who had been too busy to follow the progress of critical inquiry. His Homeric treatises, the most elaborate piece of work that proceeded from Mr. Gladstone's pen, are in one sense worthless, in another sense admirable. Those parts of them which deal with early Greek mythology, genealogy, and religion, and, in a less degree, the theories about Homeric geography and the use of Homeric epithets, have been condemned by the unanimous voice of scholars as fantastic. The premises are assumed without sufficient investigation, while the reasonings are fine-drawn and flimsy. Extraordinary ingenuity is shown in piling up a lofty fabric, but the foundation is of sand, and the edifice has hardly a solid wall or beam in it. A conjecture is treated as a fact; then an inference, possible but not certain, is drawn from this conjecture; a second possible inference is based upon the first; and we are made to forget that the probability of this second is at most only half the probability of the first. So the process goes on; and when the superstructure is complete, the reader is provoked to perceive how much dialectical skill has been wasted upon a series of hypotheses which a breath of common-sense criticism dissipates. If one is asked to explain the weakness in this particular department of a mind otherwise so strong, the answer would seem to be that the element of fancifulness in Mr. Gladstone's intellect, and his tendency to mistake mere argumentation for verification, were checked in practical politics by constant intercourse with friends and colleagues as well as by the need of convincing visible audiences, while in theological or historical inquiries his ingenuity roamed with fatal freedom over wide plains where no obstacles checked its course.   Something may also be due to the fact that his philosophical and historical education was received at a time when the modern critical spirit and the canons it recognises had scarcely begun to assert themselves at Oxford. Similar defects may be discerned in other eminent writers of his own and the preceding generation of Oxford men, defects from which persons of inferior power in later days might be free.   In some of these writers, and particularly in Cardinal Newman, the contrast between dialectical acumen, coupled with surpassing rhetorical skill, and the vitiation of the argument by a want of the critical faculty, is scarcely less striking; and the example of that illustrious man suggests that the dominance of the theological view of literary and historical problems, a dominance evident in Mr. Gladstone, counts for something in producing the phenomenon.

With these defects, Mr. Gladstone's Homeric work had the merit of being based on a full

and thorough knowledge of the Homeric text.
He had seen, at a time when few people in
England had seen it, that the Homeric poems
are an historical source of the highest value, a
treasure-house of data for the study of early
Greek life and thought, an authority all the more
trustworthy because an unconscious authority,
addressing not posterity but contemporaries.
This mastery of the matter contained in the
poems enabled him to present valuable pictures
of the political and social life of Homeric Greece,
while the interspersed literary criticisms are often
subtle and suggestive, erring, when they do err,
chiefly through the over-earnestness of his mind.
He often takes the poet too seriously; reading
an ethical purpose into descriptive or dramatic
touches which are merely descriptive or dramatic.
Passages whose moral tendency offends him are
reprobated as later insertions with a naïveté which
forgets the character of a primitive age.   But he
has for his author not only that sympathy which is
the best basis for criticism, but a justness of poetic
taste which the learned and painstaking German
commentator frequently wants.   That Mr. Gladstone was a sound scholar in that narrower sense of
the word which denotes a grammatical and literary
command of Greek and Latin, goes without saying.   Men of his generation kept a closer hold
upon the ancient classics than we do to-day; and
his habit of reading Greek for the sake of his

Homeric studies, and Latin for the sake of his theological, made this familiarity more than usually thorough. Like most Etonians, he loved and knew the poets by preference. Dante was his favourite poet, perhaps because Dante is the most theological and ethical of the great poets, and because the tongue and the memories of Italy had a peculiar attraction for him. He used to say that he found Dante's thought incomparably inspiring, but hard to follow, it was so high and so abstract. Theology claimed a place beside poetry; history came next, though he did not study it systematically. It seemed odd that he was sometimes at fault in the constitutional antiquities of England; but this subject was, until the day of Dr. Stubbs, pre-eminently a Whig subject, and Mr. Gladstone never was a Whig, never learned to think upon the lines of the great Whigs of former days. His historical knowledge was not exceptionally wide, but it was generally accurate in matters of fact, however fanciful he might be in reasoning from the facts, however wild his conjectures in the prehistoric region. In metaphysics strictly so called his reading did not go far beyond those companions of his youth, Aristotle and Bishop Butler; and philosophical speculation interested him only so far as it bore on Christian doctrine. Keen as was his interest in theology and in history, it is not certain that he would have produced work of permanent value in either sphere even had his life been wholly devoted to study. His mind seemed to need to be steadied, his ingenuity restrained, by having to deal with concrete matter for a practical end. Neither, in spite of his eminence as a financier and an advocate of free trade, did he show much taste for economic studies. On practical topics, such as the working of protective tariffs, the abuse of charitable endowments, the development of fruit-culture in England, the duty of liberal giving by the rich, the utility of thrift among the poor, his remarks were full of point, clearness, and good sense, but he seldom launched out into the wider sea of economic theory. He took a first-class in mathematics at Oxford, at the same time as his first in classics, but did not pursue the subject in later life. Regarding the sciences of experiment and observation, he seemed to feel as little curiosity as any educated man who notes the enormous part they play in the modern world can feel. Sayings of his have been quoted which show that he imperfectly comprehended the character of the evidence they rely upon and of the methods they employ. On one occasion he horrified a dinner-table of younger friends by refusing to accept some of the most certain conclusions of modern geology. No doubt he belonged, as Lord Derby (the Prime Minister) once said of himself, to a pre-scientific age. Perhaps he was unconsciously biassed by the notion that such sciences as geology and biology, for instance, were being used by some students to sap the foundations of revealed religion. But I can recall no sign of disposition to dissuade free inquiry either into those among the sciences of nature which have been supposed to touch theology, or into the date, authorship, and authority of the books of the Bible. He had faith not only in his creed, but in God as a God of truth, and in the power of research to elicit truth.

General propositions are dangerous, yet it seems safe to observe that great men have seldom been obscurantists or persecutors. Either the sympathy with intellectual effort which is natural to a powerful intellect, or the sense that free inquiry, though it may be checked by repression for a certain time or within a certain area, will ultimately have its course, dissuades them from that attempt to dam up the stream of thought which smaller minds regard as the obvious expedient for saving souls or institutions.

It ought to be added, for this was a remarkable feature of his character, that he had the deepest reverence for the great poets and philosophers, placing the career of the statesman on a far lower plane than that of those who rule the world by their thoughts enshrined in literature. He expressed in a striking letter to Tennyson's eldest son his sense of the immense superiority of the poet's life and work.   Once, in the lobby of the House of Commons, seeing his countenance saddened by the troubles of Ireland, I told him, in order to divert his thoughts, how some one had recently discovered that Dante had in his last years been appointed at Ravenna to a lectureship which raised him above the pinch of want.   Mr. Gladstone's face lit up at once, and he said, " How strange it is to think that these great souls whose words are a beacon-light to all the generations that have come after them, should have had cares and anxieties to vex them in their daily life, just like the rest of us common mortals."   The phrase reminded me that a few days before I had heard Mr. Darwin, in dwelling upon the pleasure a visit paid by Mr. Gladstone had given him, say, " And he talked just as if he had been an ordinary person like one of ourselves."   The two great men were alike unconscious of their greatness.

It was an unspeakable benefit to Mr. Gladstone that his love of letters and learning enabled him to find in the pursuit of knowledge a relief from anxieties and a solace under disappointments. Without some such relief his fiery and restless spirit would have worn itself out.   He lived two lives — the life of the statesman and the life of the student, and passed swiftly from the one to the other, dismissing when he sat down to his books all the cares of politics.   But he led a third life also, the secret life of the soul.   Religion was of

all things that which had the strongest hold upon
his thoughts and feelings. Nothing but his
father's opposition prevented him from becoming a clergyman when he quitted the University. Never thereafter did he cease to take
the warmest interest in everything that affected
the Christian Church. He lost his seat for Oxford
University by the votes of the country clergy,
who formed the bulk of the constituency. He incurred the displeasure of four-fifths of the Anglican communion by disestablishing the Protestant
Episcopal Church in Ireland, and from 1868 to the
end of his life found nearly all the clerical force
of the English establishment arrayed against him,
while his warmest support came from the Nonconformists of England and the Presbyterians of
Scotland. Yet nothing affected his devotion to
the Church in which he had been brought up, nor
to the body of Anglo-Catholic doctrine he had
imbibed as an undergraduate. After an attack
of influenza which had left him very weak in the
spring of 1891, he endangered his life by attending a meeting on behalf of the Colonial Bishoprics
Fund, for which he had spoken fifty years before.
His theological opinions tinged his views upon
political subjects. They filled him with dislike of
the legalisation of marriage with a deceased wife's
sister; they made him a vehement opponent of
the bill which established the English Divorce
Court in 1857, and a watchfully hostile critic of

all divorce legislation in America afterwards. Some of his friends traced to the same cause his less than adequate appreciation of German literature (though he admired Goethe and Schiller) and even his political coldness towards Prussia and afterwards towards the German Empire. He could not forget that Germany had been the fountain of rationalism, while German Evangelical Protestantism was more schismatic and further removed from the mediæval Catholic Church than it pleased him to deem the Church of England to be. He had an exceedingly high sense of the duty of purity of life and of the sanctity of domestic relations, and his rigid ideas of decorum inspired so much awe that it used to be said to a person who had told an anecdote with ever so slight a tinge of impropriety, " How many thousands of pounds would you take to tell that to Gladstone?"   When living in the country, it was his practice to attend daily morning service in the parish church, and on Sunday to read in church the lessons for the day; and he rarely, if ever, transgressed his rule against Sunday labour. Religious feeling, coupled with a system of firm dogmatic beliefs, was the mainspring of his life, a guiding light in perplexities, a source of strength in adverse fortune, a consolation in sorrow, a beacon of hope beyond the failures and disappointments of this present world. He did not make what is commonly called a profession of

religion, and talked little about it in general
society, although always ready to plunge into a
magazine controversy when Christianity was assailed. But those who knew him best knew that
he was always referring current questions to,
and trying his own conduct by, a religious
standard. He believed in the efficacy of prayer,
and sought through prayer for strength and for
direction in the affairs of state. He was a remarkable example of the coexistence together
with a Christian virtue of a quality which
Catholic theologians treat as a mortal sin. He
was an exceedingly proud man, yet an exceedingly humble Christian. With a high regard for
his own dignity and a sensitiveness to any impu-
tation on his honour, he was deeply conscious of
his imperfections in the eye of God, realising the
weakness and sinfulness of human nature with
a mediæval intensity. The language of self-
depreciation he was wont to use, sometimes
deemed unreal, expressed his genuine sense of
the contrast between the religious ideal he set
up and his own attainment. And the tolerance
which he extended to those who attacked him
or who had (as he thought) behaved ill in public
life was largely due to this pervading sense of the
frailty of human character, and of the inextricable
mixture in conduct of good and bad motives.
" It is always best to take the charitable view,"
he once observed when I had quoted to him the

saying of Dean Church that Mark Pattison had painted himself too black in his autobiography — "always best," adding, with grim emphasis, "especially in politics."

In this indulgent view, more evident in his later years, and the more remarkable because his expressions were often too vehement, there was nothing of the cynical "man of the world" acceptance of a low standard as the only possible standard, for his moral earnestness was as fervent at eighty-eight as it had been at thirty, and he retained a simplicity and an unwillingness to suspect sinister motives, singular in one who had seen so much.   Although accessible and frank in the ordinary converse of society, he was in reality a reserved man ; not shy, stiff, and externally cold, like Peel, nor always standing on a pedestal of dignity, like the younger Pitt, but revealing his deepest thoughts only to a few intimate friends, and treating others with a courteous kindliness which, though it put them at their ease, did not encourage them to approach nearer. Thus, while he was admired by the mass of his followers, and beloved by the small inner group of family friends, the majority of his colleagues, official subordinates, and political or ecclesiastical associates, would have hesitated to give him any of friendship's confidences.   Though quick to mark and acknowledge good service, or to offer to a junior an opportunity of distinction, many deemed him

too much occupied with his own thoughts to
show interest in his disciples, or to bestow those
counsels which a young man prizes from his
chief. But for the warmth of his devotion to a
few early friends and the reverence he paid to
their memory, a reverence touchingly shown in
the article on Arthur Hallam which he published
near the end of his own life, sixty-five years after
Hallam's death, there might have seemed to be
a measure of truth in the judgment that he cared
less for men than for ideas and causes. Those,
however, who marked the pang which the departure to the Roman Church of his friend Hope
Scott caused him, those who in later days noted
the enthusiasm with which he would speak of
Lord Althorp, his opponent, and of Lord Aberdeen, his chief, dwelling upon the truthfulness and
uprightness of the former and the amiability of
the latter, knew that the impression of detachment he gave wronged the sensibility of his own
heart. Of how few who have lived for more than
sixty years in the full sight of their countrymen,
and have been as party leaders exposed to angry
and sometimes spiteful criticism, can it be said
that there stands on record against them no
malignant word and no vindictive act! This
was due not perhaps entirely to natural sweetness of disposition, but rather to self-control
and to a certain largeness of soul which would
not condescend to anything mean or petty.

Pride, though it may be a sin, is to most of us a useful, to some an indispensable, buttress of virtue. Nor should it be forgotten that the perfectly happy life which he led at home, cared for in everything by a devoted wife, kept far from him those domestic troubles which have soured the temper and embittered the judgments of not a few famous men. Reviewing his whole career, and summing up the concurrent impressions and recollections of those who knew him best, this dignity is the feature which dwells most in the mind, as the outline of some majestic Alp thrills one from afar when all the lesser beauties of glen and wood, of crag and glacier, have faded in the distance. As elevation was the note of his oratory, so was magnanimity the note of his character.

The Greek maxim that no one can be called happy till his life is closed must, in the case of statesmen, be extended to warn us from the attempt to fix a man's place in history till a generation has arisen to whom he is a mere name, not a familiar figure to be loved or hated. Few reputations made in politics so far retain their lustre that curiosity continues to play round the person when those who can remember him living have departed. Dante has in immortal stanzas contrasted the fame of Provenzano Salvani that sounded through all Tuscany while he lived with the faint whispers of his name heard in his own Siena forty years after his death.[1] So out of all the men who have held a foremost place in English public life in the nineteenth century there are but six or seven — Pitt, Fox, Wellington, Peel, Disraeli, possibly Canning or O'Connell or Melbourne — whose names are to-day upon our lips. The great poet or the great artist lives as long as his books or his pictures; the statesman, like the singer or the actor, begins to be forgotten so soon as his voice is still, unless he has so dominated the men of his own time, and made himself a part of his country's history, that his personal character is indissolubly linked to the events the course of which he helped to determine. Tried by this test, Mr. Gladstone's fame seems destined to endure. His eloquence will soon become merely a tradition, for his printed speeches do not preserve its charm. If some of his books continue to be read, it will be rather because they are his than in respect of any permanent contribution they have made to knowledge. The wisdom of his policy, foreign and domestic, will have to be judged, not only by the consequences we see, but also by other consequences still hidden in the future. Yet among his acts there are some with which history cannot fail to concern herself, and which will keep fresh the memory of their author's energy and courage. Whoever follows the an-

[1] *Purgat.*, xi. 100-126.

nals of England during the memorable years
from 1843 to 1894 will meet his name on almost
every page, will feel how great must have been
the force of an intellect that could so interpene-
trate the story of its time, and will seek to
know something of the dauntless figure that
rose always conspicuous above the struggling
throng.

There is a passage in the *Odyssey* where the
seer Theoclymenus says, in describing a vision
of death: " The sun has perished out of heaven."
To Englishmen, Mr. Gladstone had been like
a sun which, sinking slowly, had grown larger
as he sank, and filled the sky with radiance
even while he trembled on the verge of the
horizon.   There were men of ability and men of
renown, but there was no one comparable to him
in fame and power and honour.   When he departed the light seemed to have died out of
the sky.

INDEX

Index 483